The Law
and the
Individual

MACMILLAN TEXTS FOR BUSINESS STUDIES

Published

The Law and the Individual

James Dunbar-Brunton
M.A. (Cantab.)

Barrister-at-Law of Gray's Inn

*Head of Department of Business and
Secretarial Studies, South Warwickshire
College of Further Education
Stratford-upon-Avon*

REVISED EDITION

First edition 1973
Reprinted 1975, 1977
Revised edition 1979
Reprinted 1983

Published by
THE MACMILLAN PRESS LTD
London and Basingstoke
Associated companies in Delhi Dublin
Hong Kong Johannesburg Lagos Melbourne
New York Singapore and Tokyo

Printed in Hong Kong

British Library Cataloguing in Publication Data

Dunbar-Brunton, James
    The law and the individual. — Revised ed. —
(Macmillan texts for business studies).
    1. Law — England
    I. Title
    340'.0942   KD660

    ISBN 0—333—26176—3

To the memory of my father

Contents

Preface to the Revised Edition

Since the first edition the Business Education Council (B.E.C.) has created new-style courses with new-style subject areas. Apart from updating the law since the first edition, this book is now designed to assist students through the option modules Law and the Individual, Consumer Legislation and Health and Safety in the General Level B.E.C. courses.

However, Law remains Law wherever and however it may be applied and whatever the syllabus; so this book will continue to assist the many students who are looking for a general introduction to legal studies.

My thanks are due to Irene Spicer for her help.

Stratford   J.D.-B.
October 1978

Preface to the First Edition

English law is complex, the offspring of many mixed marriages. Originating in custom and tradition, based upon reason, fixed by precedent, defined and re-defined by the courts and parliament, it has developed a lusty independence and need answer to no one but itself. In this sense, law is absolute. As the inscrutable judge says by way of explanation in a poem by W. H. Auden, 'Law', quite simply, 'is the Law'.

Yet paradoxically, as Auden says in the same poem,

> Law is only crimes
> Punished by places and by times.

So that, although the law itself may be absolute at a particular time, the moral system which it exists to protect need not necessarily be so. Made by man, the law can be changed by man, and is thus fashioned to reflect the values of the society in which he lives.

In writing about law, one is bound to deal with both these aspects, the absolute and the temporal, the permanent and the changing. I have tried to do this in a way that is simple and factual, and at the same time supported throughout by explanation.

Although this book is intended primarily as an aid to students of the C.O.S. examination 'Law and the Individual', I hope that many others will find it both interesting and useful.

J. D.-B.

Sussex
July 1972

PART ONE

PART ONE

1. The Nature of Law

The Need for Law and Order
The rule that a ripe apple must fall to the ground and the command that 'thou shalt not kill' are both described as 'laws'. Yet, in each sense the word 'law' has a different meaning. In the first sense the 'law', in the laws of gravity, is used to describe a rule of nature. In the second sense 'law' refers to a rule that has been made in order to regulate the conduct of one individual towards another.

In whatever sense 'law' is used it applies to orderly and regulated behaviour. Both the discovering of scientific laws and the creating of man-made rules form part of the same need in man: his search for a regularity and certainty in his life and the need to live in an ordered rather than an unknown and chaotic world.

Laws of Science
The laws of science demonstrate that some form of order prevails over chaos in the natural world. The earth follows a fixed orbit around the sun, there is a regularity in the seasons of the year, and the basic elements of the physical universe, such as fire and water, have certain unvarying qualities which man can rely on.

As long as man is able to find some law and order to nature, he will be able to predict the future with a certainty that is sufficient for him to plan his life. Thus he relies on such obvious laws as that the sun will rise tomorrow morning and that apples will continue to fall rather than float.

Laws of Man
As well as seeking an order in the universe and natural environment, man needs some form of order in his own behaviour and the behaviour of others about him.

Man in his everyday life is a creature of routine rather than irregularity. He will set aside times for sleeping, eating and working, and times for his leisure. Furthermore, man is a creature of association and, as such, as well as regulating his own affairs, he will have to take into account the presence of others with whom he is likely to come into contact. With these other individuals he will establish set rules of behaviour and expect the same in return. For example, man does not live as an individual but as a member of a family, and within every family there will be rules for carrying out the household chores and rules for the standard of behaviour among its members. Also, in his leisure hours man will associate with others who have the same interests

3

and pastimes and within such groups will have rules for conducting their behaviour, such as rules of etiquette, rules for joining or leaving the club and rules for playing the game.

From a very early time the family unit has been part of a larger social and political State. The need for some order and regularity of conduct within the State is even greater than for the family or friendly group, for a State consists of individuals who are not necessarily kept together by family ties or mutual interests. No State can exist without some form of social order, and it has been found that there is a need for such order not only in the relationship of one individual to another within the State, but also in the relationship of the individual to the State itself. It is for these reasons that there are laws, and law is only one form of social control. In the beginnings of society law was indistinguishable from other forms of social control, such as morals and religion.

Without some form of law and social order within the State, life would be unliveable. If each individual were able to behave exactly as he liked, without regard for the security of the State as a whole or unconcerned for his fellow-men, progress towards a more peaceful existence within society would be impossible. A State without laws or some form of social control over individuals would be as disordered as a world without the certainty of gravity or with an unpredictable sun. It is these man-made laws which lay down the position of the individual within the State and regulate the conduct of individuals between each other that we are concerned with in this book.

Law as Social Control
It has been mentioned that law is a form of social control, but it is not the only way of producing order within the State. In understanding the position and nature of law within a society, it is interesting to look at two types of society where order is maintained without any reliance on a true system of law.

Despotism
A State where one individual holds an unlimited, tyrannical power over all the community and where he exercises his power in a completely arbitrary and capricious way is called a despotic State.

To be an absolute despot the individual ruler must issue his commands in accordance with his free and unrestricted will and in response to his casual whims and fancies. For instance, he may order that all children under the age of two should be put to death; on one day he may sentence a man to death because he has painted his white roses red, and on another day the favourite courtier may suddenly find himself incarcerated for not letting the despot win at croquet.

The commands of a despot cannot be described as laws, for although he may profess to keep order within the State and settle disputes between his subjects, he can hardly be said to administer justice, and as his rules are unpredictable they cannot really be said to follow any order. Individuals would not be assured of any certain rights within the State and could only rely upon the rules that might be repealed as easily and suddenly as they were made. Individuals would not seek justice from the State for fear of what the decision might be.

One of the main functions of the law is to set up fundamental rules between the State and the individual so that the individual may conduct his life with the certainty that he will not be interfered with by the State or ruler unless he has broken one of these rules. It is also essential that the rules he will have to obey should be reasonable ones. At least one example is to be found in fiction of a ruler who professed to be both reasonable and a despot at the same time. This is the king in *The Little Prince* by Antoine de Saint-Exupéry:

> ... what the king fundamentally insisted upon was that his authority should be respected. He tolerated no disobedience. He was an absolute monarch. But, because he was a very good man, he made his orders reasonable ...
>
> 'If I order a general to fly from one flower to another like a butterfly, or to write a tragic drama, or to change himself into a sea bird, and if the general did not carry out the order that he had received, which one of us would be in the wrong?' the king demanded: 'The general, or myself?'
>
> 'You,' said the prince firmly.
>
> 'Exactly. One must require from each one the duty which each one can perform,' the king went on. 'Accepted authority rests first of all on reason. If you ordered your people to go and throw themselves into the sea, they would rise up in revolution. I have the right to require obedience because my orders are reasonable.'

But whether we could find such a combination in reality is doubtful.

Anarchy

The extreme opposite to despotism is anarchy. Anarchy means that all individuals within the community have unlimited freedom. In a totally anarchic society an individual neither submits himself to the law nor can he claim benefit from it: he has no legal obligations and correspondingly he has no legal rights. Every person is free to follow his own impulses unrestrained by restrictions laid down by the State or the commands of a despot.

We do not know of any society which has survived for very long on a purely anarchic basis. Therefore there is no reliable evidence as to how men would actually cope if States and their laws were abolished and a 'lawless constitution' was created. Leo Tolstoy, the Russian novelist, believed it possible to have a 'non-coercive' society, in other words a society where all individuals conducted their lives on the basis of mutual affection, rather than by the commands of the law. Of course, for this theory to have any foundation one would have to believe that individuals are essentially (or potentially) good.

This theory of a society without laws may be possible, but it is not very probable that the complete elimination of the State and its legal system would bring about a 'utopian' society of the kind described by many philosophers. Although the majority of men may be good most of the time, we can be sure that not all men will be good all the time. It is the unsociable minority that makes law necessary. Men are by their nature aggressive and liable to outbursts which are bound to manifest themselves in ways that the majority will not tolerate.

Law as Social Control
Law is a form of social order that is opposed to the extremes of despotism and anarchy. Its basic function is to resolve the possible tension between the interests of the individual and the authority of the State. This it sets out to do, on the one hand, in limiting the absolute freedom of individuals by introducing order into their conduct only insofar as it is necessary for the protection of the interests of other individuals and for the security of the State. On the other hand, it attempts to avoid the tyranny of an arbitrary government by placing certain restraints on the power of the State and its officials. Thus, the position of law as a form of social control within the State is, ideally, midway between despotism and anarchy.

It will be seen later that the law within the British constitution attempts to achieve this equidistant position by holding a constitutional position within the State that is independent of the direct commands and influences of government authorities and is also aloof and sufficiently rigid to withstand the quickly changing fancies of its subjects.

Obedience to the Law
It has been shown that law is a set of rules whose function is to regulate the conduct of the State and of its individuals. In order to achieve this the law must be recognised as being binding, for rules that do not require obedience cannot be effective, and are not rules of law. In this sense laws must be absolute and their authority unquestionable. What is the basis of this authority?

Law as Command

One theory is based on the proposition that law is the command of the 'sovereign', and a 'sovereign' is any person or body of persons who within the State has the power to exact obedience from all others. In this sense, law is said to be that which the will of the State commands.

For some purposes, especially in the criminal law, it is essential that the State should be capable of commanding obedience, for it has the responsibility of keeping the peace. The civilised State, on the whole, manages effectively to compel its individuals to obey the law. If some individual transgresses the law, the State will effectively restrain him by whatever means is fitting for the occasion. If a State is unable to do this, society is in a state of anarchy. The power to command obedience is essential to many branches of the law, and to think of such laws without the element of command is a contradiction in terms.

Law as Consent

It is unfortunate that in modern States law tends to become identified with the will of the State as expressed by parliament in statutes. To regard law merely as that which the State commands would not be doing justice to many of its rules.

A theory in direct contrast to the idea of a 'sovereign' power is that law is obeyed because individuals consent to be subject to rules which they realise are in the interests of a peaceful society. Naturally, to believe that this is the sole reason why laws are obeyed would be as one-sided as the imperative theory of obedience to law.

It will be seen, however, in the second part of this book, that in many branches of the civil law, such as the making of contracts, or in being a neighbour, or in taking employment, there is an element of reason and consent, rather than coercion, in the obedience to law.

Law in a Democratic Society

Observance of the law, as we have seen in the description of despotism, cannot justly be attained only by command or force. On the other hand, if a State is to be permanent it needs laws which are something more than social order by consent. In practice, law must be a mixture of command and consent. Law needs the element of command to require obedience from the minority, yet it should also, if it is to work effectively, reflect the needs and wishes of the majority of the people. Within the British constitution this is achieved by parliament being the sovereign law-making authority which has the power to make or repeal any law and to command obedience. Yet as this is a democratic society, parliament consists of an elected body of persons who represent the people, and the primary obligation of the elected body is to carry out as best it can the interests of the people under the fear that if it fails it will be voted out of power.

The Classification of Law

It has been seen that rules of law in a legal system do not exist for the exclusive benefit of either the State or the individual. However, there are some legal rules primarily concerned with the protection and interests of the State, known as public law; just as there are other kinds of law more concerned with the behaviour of individuals among themselves, and these are known as private law. Under each of these main divisions of the law there are numerous subdivisions.

Public Law

Public law includes all those legal rules that directly concern or affect the State. The two main subdivisions are constitutional law and criminal law.

(1) Constitutional law. Constitutional law presupposes the existence of a constitution, which will be discussed in detail in the next chapter. At present it is enough to say that in most States the constitution refers to a special document that is the legal foundation of the State itself and which prescribes the composition and powers of the legislature, the nature and functions of the executive and the position of the judiciary. The rules that formulate the structure of the State and regulate the functioning of its powers are known as constitutional law.

As the British constitution has no 'written' constitution contained in a document, but is based on conventions and the ordinary laws of the land, the constitutional law of England is derived from the same sources of law as any other rule of law. It will be seen later that in the English legal system all laws are basically of the same strength, whether the matter is considered of constitutional importance or is only of private concern.

(2) Criminal law. Criminal law deals with crimes. Crimes are the type of wrongful behaviour of an individual which the State is concerned to prevent and, failing that, to punish. Crimes may be classified according to the degree of importance placed upon them by the State. Thus, serious crimes are known as indictable offences which, in the main, are heard in the Crown Court before a judge and jury. The minor crimes are called summary offences which are usually heard in a Magistrates' Court without a jury. For other purposes crimes may be classified according to the type of conduct which constitutes the crime. This classification is as follows:

Offences against the person:
These include murder, manslaughter, rape, grievous bodily harm and

numerous other offences against the individual himself rather than his property.

Offences against property:

These include arson, forgery, malicious damage, housebreaking, robbery and a whole range of offences involving theft and dishonesty.

Offences against the State:

These include treason, sedition, unlawful assembly, riot, rout and affray, many of which are mentioned in detail later.

Offences against public morality:

These include bigamy, indecency and obscenity.

The main purpose of the criminal law is to impose the punishment on the offender that he deserves. This explains why there are varying punishments for crimes, depending on their seriousness. Punishment is usually by imprisonment or fine. The death penalty has now virtually disappeared and flogging, branding and deportation no longer exist. In some cases, however, the court may make a probation order which allows the convicted person to continue his life in the community, but under the continual supervision of a probation officer and subject to special conditions concerning his behaviour.

Private Law

Private law consists of the branches of law which are concerned with formulating the rights and duties between private individuals.

The types of behaviour and relationships that can take place between individuals are infinitely varied. The law, for practical reasons, has divided private law into different branches according to the relationship one individual has with another. To mention only a few examples, the law of contract deals with commercial agreements between individuals; the law of tort deals with wrongful behaviour by one individual towards another where there is no agreement. Even these branches of law can be subdivided: contract into the law of agency and sale of goods; tort into trespass, nuisance and defamation. All these branches of private law will be explained later in this book.

The Distinction between Criminal and Civil Law

Private law is more commonly known as civil law to distinguish it specifically from criminal law which, although it involves individuals, has the distinction that it is enforced by the State.

The main distinction between criminal wrongs and civil wrongs is that in the former the behaviour is considered to be of sufficient public concern to justify the intervention of the State. Thus, in criminal cases it is the State which prosecutes the offender. It is for this reason that criminal cases are described as 'The Queen versus the Accused', the abbreviation being '*R*. (standing for *Regina*) v. *John Doe*' (the name of the accused).

In civil wrongs the State considers that it can be left to the individual who has been wronged to bring the wrongdoer before the court. For example, if one person owes another a sum of money, or has told unpleasant lies about another, it is the responsibility of the party who has suffered to claim his legal rights. This is why in civil cases it is the 'Plaintiff v. Defendant': for example, *Carlill* v. *Carbolic Smoke Ball Co.*

A second distinction between criminal and civil law is in their purpose. The main purpose for prosecuting the criminal is to punish him. Under the civil law the purpose of bringing an action in court against the wrongdoer (the defendant) is to seek a remedy for the wrong that has been suffered. For example, under contract and tort the remedy the plaintiff usually claims is damages. This generally consists of financial compensation for the loss that has been suffered.

There are numerous branches of the civil law and their remedies can differ. For example, under family law the individual might seek to have her marriage ended, or claim maintenance for herself or custody of her child. An explanation of certain remedies that are available under the civil law will be mentioned with the particular branch of law discussed.

One further important difference between criminal and civil law is the courts in which the disputes are heard and the different procedures that are involved. More is said on this in Chapter 3, on the administration of justice.

1. What do you understand by the word 'law'?
2. 'Give me a State under the absolute control of a dictator. . . ' (Plato). Do you agree?
3. What distinguishes the rules of everyday social conduct from rules of law?
4. What are the differences between the civil and criminal branches of law?
5. Distinguish between public and private law.
6. What is the meaning of (a) anarchism (b) despotism and (c) democracy?
7. Give your opinion on the following:
   (1) Do you think that you obey laws —
       (a) because you feel obliged to do so, whatever the laws may be, or
       (b) because you believe the laws to be reasonable ones, or

      (c) because you fear the consequences of breaking the law, or

      (d) if you obey the law for some other reason, not already mentioned, what is this reason?

  (2) Do you consider it possible to have a civilized community without laws?

  (3) What are the main reasons, in your opinion, for persons breaking the law—is it because:

      (a) they thought that they would not be found out, or

      (b) they did not know that they were breaking the law, or

      (c) they consider that particular law to be an unjust one, or

      (d) for some other reason? If so, what?

8. Most needs which society considers to be fundamental to human existence within a civilised society are recognised by the law, e.g. housing, health, education and protection of property. Discuss in general terms:

  (1) whether you think there are any fundamental needs that are not, yet should be, given legal recognition, and

  (2) whether you consider that legal recognition of such needs as housing, health and education is in fact necessary — what if the law did not cover them?

9. Find your own examples, either from history, the present day or fiction, of the following:

  (1) law made as a means of controlling social order within a particular section of a society,

  (2) law made because of a change in the moral outlook of society,

  (3) a law which seems to have no bearing on moral behaviour whatsoever.

10. With the help of newspapers, textbooks, etc., explain the following means of punishment under the criminal law, and discuss their aims:

  (1) community service

  (2) imprisonment

  (3) fines

  (4) probation

2. The British Constitution

A. THE NATURE OF THE CONSTITUTION

Introduction

It has already been mentioned that individuals associate with each other because they share the same interests at work or enjoy the same pastimes, and that on a larger scale the individual considers himself part of a community. In small associations and likewise in large communities it has been found necessary to regulate the members and, furthermore, there usually has to be some person or group of persons with the power to make rules and decisions on behalf of everyone else. In most States this power exists in a body called the government.

A State

When there is an organised system of government over a defined territory and the government has the 'sovereign' power over the home and foreign affairs of the inhabitants of that territory, there is said to be a State. For example, the United Kingdom of Great Britain and Northern Ireland is one State, with the sovereign power vested in the parliament at Westminster and with the defined territory of England, Wales, Scotland and Northern Ireland.

A Constitution

In brief, a constitution sets out the structure of the State. The world is divided into States and within each there is usually a variety of separate organs of government: a legislature to make laws, a judiciary to enforce the law and to resolve disputes between those who are subject to the law, and an executive which consists of departments to implement government policies and decisions. These organs have been established by the concern for a well-organised administration of the State to cater for the needs of its subjects. The more complex a society becomes, the more numerous and varied become the departments of the State. All these organs and departments of the government within the State and the rules for their orderly administration and operation are described collectively as the 'constitution' of the State.

Written and Unwritten Constitutions

Most States today have as their foundation a written constitution. This consists of a constitutional document which has usually been enacted by a special process of the legislature of that State. The document sets out all the more important organs and departments of the State, their authority, and the laws which govern the way they are to operate. For example, the constitution of the United States of America is based on a written constitutional document which sets up the framework of the government, prescribes its powers and, as will be seen later, defines the liberties of its citizens.

The United Kingdom has an 'unwritten' constitution. This means there is no constitutional document. Instead, the structure of the organs of the State and government are based on the ordinary laws of the land that have been built up by the ordinary process of legislation and decisions in courts of law.

It is considered that one of the advantages of having a constitution which is unwritten is that it is less rigid and has a greater capacity to develop according to the contemporary needs of the State and its citizens. In a written constitution, if any alteration is considered necessary there is usually a long and elaborate procedure to be followed before the modification or addition can be incorporated in the constitutional document. Any alteration in the British constitution is effected by an ordinary Act of Parliament with a procedure that is no different from the passing of any other law, or the alteration may even take place by a decision of a court of law in a dispute that may have been brought by an individual against some government department.

Sources of the Constitution
In the case of written constitutions it is principally the document that is the source of all rules for the structure and working of the State. However, in the British constitution there are the following main sources:

Rules of Law
The legal authority for the working of the constitution originates from the ordinary rules of law which are made either by statutes passed by the ordinary legislative process of parliament or by decisions of judges in the courts of law. Laws from both sources are enforced by the ordinary courts of law. (For the doctrine of the Rule of Law, see Chapter 7 on the freedoms of the individual.)

(1) Legislation. A large part of the laws of the constitution originates from statutes. Although these statutes do not have the special legal sanctity that is given to a written constitutional document, there are certain Acts that are considered to be of constitutional importance and as such are 'regarded with peculiar veneration': for example, Magna Carta, 1215; the Bill of Rights, 1688; the Act of Settlement, 1700; the Act of Union with Scotland, 1706; and the Statute of Westminster, 1931, to list only a few.

(2) Judge-made law. This is case law or law that has been declared by the judges in the courts of law when deciding upon disputes that have been brought before them.

Conventions

Parliament and the courts are not the sole source of constitutional rules. There are some rules that are essentially rules of governmental practice which are for the guidance of persons concerned with the working of the government. These conventions, as they are called, are not laws and therefore are not legally binding, and any breach cannot be heard by the courts. Conventions are obeyed because it is accepted that they are for the benefit of a smooth-running State and because a failure to comply with them may involve a Minister or other official in loss of reputation or even of office. On some occasions conventions have been made laws, usually when they have been frequently or blatantly ignored.

Conventions may be formed in numerous ways, but normally they are said to exist because of long usage, general acceptance, and through a need for rules to supplement the legal framework of the constitution. They have the advantage over rules of law in that they are more flexible and can be adapted or modified to suit the changing needs and functions of the government. Some examples of conventions are:

(1) The Prime Minister. It is a convention that the Sovereign will accept the leader of the party having the majority of seats in the House of Commons to be Prime Minister and request him to form a government.

(2) The Cabinet. The existence and functioning of the Cabinet depend almost entirely upon conventions, which will be mentioned later.

(3) Dissolution of parliament. It is the prerogative of the Monarch to dissolve parliament, and by convention this is usually granted at the request or on the advice of the Prime Minister.

B. THE ORGANS OF GOVERNMENT

The Separation of Powers

There are three essential powers that are required by a government in its proper running of the State: the power to make laws, the power to put the laws into effect, and the power to enforce the laws. These are called the legislative, the executive and the judicial power, respectively.

In a democratic State it has for a long time been the theory that each of these powers should be in the hands of a separate organ within the State. This theory is known as the doctrine of the Separation of Powers, and its main principles are:

1. The powers should be exercised by different organs of government.
2. The same officials should not be connected to more than one organ of government.
3. One organ of government is not allowed to interfere with or carry out the work of either of the others.

The idea behind this doctrine is that if one person or body had control of two or more of these powers, their abuse would result in oppressive laws, the arbitrary enforcement of these laws and, consequently, tyranny within the State. This is because one person would be able to make what laws he wished, have the power to put them into effect and also enforce them. It is thought that by keeping the three powers separate, each under the control of a separate organ of the government, each organ will act as a check or a balance against the other organs using their powers wrongfully.

In practice the doctrine has found greater recognition in the United States of America than it has in the British constitution. This can be seen from the American constitutional document of 1787:

Article I.	'All legislative powers herein granted shall be vested in a Congress of the United States . . . '
Article II.	'The executive powers shall be vested in a President of the United States . . . '
Article III.	'The judicial power shall be vested in one Supreme Court . . . '

The British constitution does not adhere to a rigid separation of the powers of government, although the organs of the government are easily distinguishable as:

1. The legislature, which consists of the Queen, the House of Lords and the House of Commons.
2. The executive, which consists of the Cabinet, the Ministers of the Crown, the government departments and the civil service.
3. The judiciary, which consists of the courts of law and the judges who sit in them.

The only evidence of a true separation of these powers in England is in the virtual independence of the judiciary, which is a topic that will be dealt with in the following chapter. Apart from the judiciary, the legislature and the executive function more by co-operation than separation. They overlap and rely on each other in many areas. An important example of this can be seen from the convention that the Prime Minister and Ministers, who are part of the executive, must hold a seat in either House of Parliament, which are sections of the legislature.

Further examples of connections between the three organs of government which offend the doctrine of the Separation of Powers are:

1. The Monarch is the nominal head of all three organs of government. The legislature consists of the Queen in Parliament; the executive is known as Her Majesty's Government, or the Crown; and the judiciary consists of the Queen's Courts and Judges.
2. The office of the Lord Chancellor spans all three organs. He presides over the House of Lords in its legislative work. He occasionally sits with the Law Lords in the judicial function of the House of Lords and is the actual head of the judiciary. Furthermore, he is a member of the executive and holds a position in the Cabinet.
3. Parliament frequently delegates its legislative powers to the executive. This will be mentioned in greater detail in Chapter 5, on sources of law.
4. Parliament often confers judicial powers on the executive by giving Ministers or tribunals powers to hear disputes between the individual and the State. This is explained more fully in the following chapter.

Now that the position of the principal powers of government within the State has been explained, it is necessary to look at each of these organs in greater detail. In this chapter the legislature, the executive and local government will be considered; in the following chapter, the judiciary.

I. The Legislature

The Supremacy of Parliament

The legislative organ in the British constitution is the Queen in Parliament. Although this organ consists of three separate bodies, the Queen, the House of Lords and the House of Commons, it acts as a unit when carrying out its legislative or law-making powers. No law can be passed without the consent of all three bodies.

An important characteristic of the constitution is the legislative supremacy of parliament or, as it is often called, the sovereignty of parliament. This principle means that, firstly, parliament has the right to make or repeal any law whatsoever, and secondly, that there is no other power within the State which is recognised by law as having the right to overrule or set aside the laws made by Parliament. Examples of this legislative sovereignty are:

1. Parliament can alter the succession to the throne. On the abdication of Edward VIII, His Majesty's Declaration of Abdica-

tion Act, 1936, altered the succession as laid down in the Act of Settlement, 1700, by providing that King George VI, the then next in line for succession, should succeed Edward VIII, whose descendants should not have any right or title to succession.

2. Parliament, by Act of Parliament, has, on occasions altered the duration of its own life. For instance, during the world wars it extended its statutory five-year term of office by the Duration of Parliament Acts.

3. Parliament can legalise anything that was in the past illegal and can, but rarely does, make any past legal act illegal. This is known as retrospective legislation.

4. Parliament can override or repeal any law that has been laid down by the courts. The courts must enforce the laws passed by Parliament. They cannot question the validity of, or disregard, such laws, but may only interpret them. Thus case law is subordinate to statute law. For example, if Parliament made it illegal to smoke a pipe the courts would have to enforce this law (but such unreasonable laws are not enacted for fear of a disapproving electorate).

The only real legal limitation on the legislative power of Parliament is that it cannot effectively bind a future Parliament. In other words, Parliament cannot make a law today which some succeeding Parliament cannot unmake if it wishes to do so.

Although in theory Parliament is legally supreme, there are certain political limitations as to what Parliament should in fact do. Firstly, no Parliament is likely to pass an Act which it knows has not the approval of the electorate or is contrary to the Rule of Law. Secondly, in the case of complex or technical legislative matters, or matters which are likely to affect a particular section of the community, Parliament will usually ask the advice, or consult the interests, of bodies outside Parliament.

It has been mentioned that Parliament, when making laws, consists of three bodies acting collectively. However, because the Queen, the House of Lords and the House of Commons are very different in composition and function, it is necessary to consider each of these bodies in turn and in greater detail.

1. The Queen

The assent of the Monarch is required before any legislation can take effect. After a Bill has passed through all its stages in both Houses of Parliament, it is sent to the Queen for Royal Assent. It has become a convention that the Monarch should not withhold assent, and the refusal to give approval to legislation has not happened for over two centuries.

A more detailed study of the Queen's position both as Monarch and as Crown is dealt with under 'The Executive' (pp. 21-3 below).

2. The House of Lords

Composition

The House of Lords consists of the Lords Temporal and the Lords Spiritual. The Lords Temporal consist of (*a*) all hereditary peers and peeresses, (*b*) all life peers and peeresses created under the Life Peerages Act, 1958, and (*c*) Lords of Appeal in Ordinary who are appointed to assist the House in its functions as a court of law. Both hereditary and life peerages are conferred by the Monarch on the advice of the Prime Minister.

The Lords Spiritual are the Archbishops of Canterbury and York, the Bishops of London, Durham and Winchester, and twenty-one other bishops of the Church of England.

The House is presided over by the Lord Chancellor and there are a number of permanent officers of the House. These officers include the Clerk of the Parliaments who is responsible for keeping the records of proceedings, and the Gentleman Usher of the Black Rod, who enforces the orders of the House.

Functions of the Lords

Apart from its judicial functions, which will be mentioned in the next chapter, the main work of the House of Lords is as follows.

Firstly, this House is important in the process of law-making. However, the Parliament Act, 1911, considerably curtailed the functions of the Lords in the part it plays in the legislative process. The Act removed from the House of Lords all power over Money Bills, which have been certified as such by the Speaker of the House of Commons, and it also imposed a time limit of two years on the power of the Lords to delay a Bill that had been passed by the Commons. The Parliament Act, 1949, has further reduced this delaying power to one year. It is a power that has in the past been very useful, especially when the Bill to be made law was controversial and the extra time enabled public opinion to be fully expressed. Although in practice the majority of important Bills, and all Money Bills, are introduced in the Commons, a Bill may be presented in the Lords first. Furthermore, the power of the Lords to amend or revise a Bill can be of great assistance to the Commons who often have not sufficient time to spend on such matters.

Secondly, the House of Lords functions as a chamber for discussion and deliberation on matters of national importance. Its composition makes it well suited for this, as the atmosphere is comparatively free of political rivalry.

Reform of the House
Criticisms of its effectiveness and composition, together with proposals for its reform, frequently threaten the existence of the House of Lords in its present structure. The arguments have been, among others, that it is predominantly hereditary in composition, conservative in outlook and non-representative of the people. Some answers to these criticisms have been made: firstly, a conservative outlook is not entirely restricted to that House; secondly, the fact that its members are not elected makes it relatively free from party-political aggression, and if the House of Lords were an elected chamber it would soon lose its stability and become no more than another House of Commons.

3. The House of Commons

Composition
The House of Commons is an elected chamber representing the community as a whole. The elected members are known as Members of Parliament and usually hold office from the time they are elected or re-elected at a general election, or by-election, until Parliament is dissolved.

The chief officer of the House is the Speaker, who is elected by the Commons, from any political party, to preside over the usual business of the House. He is responsible for the procedure of the House, supervising debates, and is impartial in his office. Other parliamentary officers of the House are the Chairman of Ways and Means and the Deputy Chairman. Both officers are elected by the House on the nomination of the Government and, like the Speaker, neither takes part in debates nor votes other than by way of their office.

There are some permanent members of the House of Commons who are not M.P.s. These include the Clerk of the House of Commons who keeps the record of business of the House.

Functions of the House
It is not the responsibility of the House of Commons to govern: this is the duty of the political party in power. Its main functions are as follows.

Firstly, the Commons has sole responsibility for the control of national finance.

Secondly, the Commons is part of the legislative process, the procedure for which will be described in Chapter 5.

Thirdly, the Commons is a chamber for debating all matters of

importance concerning home and foreign affairs. It also discusses the
policies that the government contemplates putting into practice.

Election to the House of Commons.
For the purpose of the community being represented in parliament the
United Kingdom is divided into constituencies, each one represented by
a seat in the House of Commons and returning an elected member to
Westminster.

In order to stand as a candidate for a parliamentary constituency,
the individual must be a British subject and must not be disqualified by
reason of being a member of the House of Lords, a clergyman of the
Church of England or the Church of Scotland or a priest of the Roman
Catholic Church, a person holding high office in the civil service, a
judge, an ambassador, a member of the armed forces or an undischarged
bankrupt.

The law relating to parliamentary elections is set out in the
Representation of the People Act, 1949, which was amended in 1969.
These Acts state that all persons over the age of eighteen years are
entitled to vote by secret ballot. They also set out the rules concerning
the conduct of persons at elections and the procedure to be followed if
there should be any allegation of corruption.

The Party System
The system of organised political parties has developed over the past
hundred years into an important consideration in the working of the
constitution. Whenever there is a general election, or a seat falls vacant
during the life of parliament and there is a by-election, the major
political parties put up candidates in each constituency among other
independent candidates who wish to be elected to the Commons. At
the present time the practice of the electorate voting for a political
party or a leader, rather than for a local individual representative, is
very strong. The major political parties have opposing policies, usually
contained in their election manifestos, which are designed to gain the
support of the voting public.

The political party which attains the majority of constituency seats,
therefore having the majority vote in the Commons, usually forms the
government. The Prime Minister will form a Ministry, almost inevitably
from party members who hold a constituency seat and who have been
appointed as heads of the various government departments. The
Ministers heading the principal departments will usually form the
Cabinet.

The political party with the largest minority of seats in the
Commons will form the opposition and will have its own party leader
and a Shadow Cabinet.

The functioning of the Commons according to the party system depends on the balance that can be achieved between the governing party and the opposition. This is effected, to a considerable extent, by agreement. The opposition agrees that the majority party has the responsibility of governing, and the government understands that the opposition will criticise government activities and policies in the interests of the public.

II. The Executive

The executive is the organ responsible for putting the will of the legislature into effect and performing the routine administration of the State. In law the executive is referred to as the Crown, which covers all functions of the government. The principal components of the executive are as follows.

1. The Monarch

The United Kingdom is a constitutional monarchy, at the head of which is the Queen.

The present Monarch has inherited the throne from the Protestant Hanoverian line which was established by the Act of Settlement, 1700. By this Act no Roman Catholic or anyone married to a Roman Catholic can succeed to the throne. The Regency Acts, 1937–1953, state that in the case of the infancy or incapacity of the Monarch there shall be a Regent. The appointment of a Regent is automatic on the succession of a minor to the throne, but in other cases the appointment and termination will be by declaration of the Privy Council. A Regent is able to exercise all the Royal duties except for assenting to a law to change the line of succession. During the temporary absence or illness of the Monarch, Counsellors of State may be appointed by the Monarch to perform her duties in the meantime. The Counsellors are the Consort of the Monarch, the four persons next in line of succession, if of full age, and the Queen Mother.

Position of the Monarch

A constitutional Monarch means that the Monarch carries out her duties on the advice and guidance of her Ministers. The position of the Monarch within the constitution is complex. She is the personification of the State and acts as its non-political and permanent head. Furthermore, the Monarch is the constitutional and personal link between the Commonwealth of independent nations from whom she is owed allegiance. She is head of the Church of England and the armed forces.

The expenses of the Royal Household and the allowances to the

Queen and the Royal Family are paid out of the Consolidated Fund by means of a Civil List Act. Although the Monarch does own property in her personal capacity, 'Crown property' is not owned by the Monarch personally but by the Crown in its executive capacity.

The Royal Prerogative

Professor A. V. Dicey said that the Royal Prerogative consisted of 'The residue of arbitrary power which at any given time is legally left in the hands of the Crown'. Today it means the powers that are recognised by the common law as belonging to the Monarch. It does not include powers granted to her by statute. For example, the granting of Royal Charters to boroughs was once a prerogative of the Crown but is now exercised under a statutory power.

The wide prerogative powers that once belonged to the Monarch are now, on the whole, exercised by parliament, and of the few powers that still remain with the Monarch, the majority are exercised only on the advice of the government. If there is any dispute as to whether or not a prerogative power resides with the Monarch, it is for the courts of law to decide.

Examples of prerogative powers that still remain with the Monarch are:

1. In the Monarch's capacity as head of State there are numerous powers in relation to the State's dealings with other States, for instance the declaring of war or the making of peace. Acts done under this branch of the prerogative are known as acts of State.
2. The Monarch exercises the prerogative to summon and dissolve parliament.
3. The Monarch by the prerogative has the sole power to confer honours and decorations.
4. By Orders in Council the Monarch may exercise the prerogative to legislate for certain colonies.

Proceedings Involving the Crown

The Monarch in her personal capacity cannot be sued or prosecuted. This rule is derived from the old maxims that 'The King can do no wrong' and 'The King cannot be sued in his own courts'.

However, the Crown Proceedings Act, 1947, states that the Crown, meaning the executive and departments of the government, can be sued through the normal procedure in the ordinary courts of law, the same as any individual. This is possible in the following cases:

(1) In tort.

(a)   For torts committed by the servants or agents of the Crown. Thus the Crown is liable in the same way as any other employer for the wrongs of its employees (see 'Vicarious

Liability', p. 222 below).

(*b*)   For breach of a statutory duty where the Crown is specifically bound by an Act of Parliament.

(*c*)   For breach of common law duties which the Crown owes to its servants or agents.

(*d*)   For breaches of a common law duty attaching to the ownership, occupation, possession or control of property.

(2) In contract. In certain limited situations the Crown will be liable for the contracts that are made by its agents. However, the Crown cannot be held liable for a breach of contract of service (employment). For instance, civil servants or members of the armed forces cannot bring an action against the Crown for breach of their service contracts.

Such actions, by or against the Crown, are brought in the name either of the government department concerned or in the name of the Attorney-General. Furthermore, the remedies of specific performance and injunction cannot be ordered against the Crown.

2. The Privy Council
Composition
The Privy Council is composed only of British subjects and they are appointed by Letters Patent. These include the Lord President of the Council who is a Cabinet Minister, persons who hold or have held high judicial or political office, the Archbishops of Canterbury and York, leading Commonwealth statesmen and British ambassadors.

Functions
Owing to the development of the Cabinet, the Privy Council has lost most of its advisory and administrative duties. Today it does little more than give formal approval to certain acts of the Monarch done under the prerogative. For example, Orders in Council are issued at a meeting between four or five members of the Privy Council and approved by the Monarch. Orders in Council are dealt with in greater detail under 'Delegated Legislation' (p. 64 below).

There are various committees of the Privy Council which usually act in an advisory capacity to the Crown, in such matters as the grant of Royal Charters to new boroughs. One such committee is the Committee for the Channel Islands and another is the Judicial Committee of the Privy Council.

The Judicial Committee of the Privy Council
This is a court of law for the hearing of appeals from the courts of the Channel Islands, British colonies and some Commonwealth countries. It also hears appeals in ecclesiastical cases and from some domestic

tribunals, such as the General Medical Council.

The bench consists of the existing and former Lords President of the Council, Privy Councillors who hold or have held high judicial office, Lords of Appeal in Ordinary, Lord Justices of Appeal and former Lord Chancellors. In practice the bench will be similar to that of the House of Lords, that is, consisting of between three and five Lords of Appeal in Ordinary.

Like other committees of the Privy Council, the Judicial Committee gives its decision by way of advice to the Monarch who, by convention, accepts it.

Although its decisions are not binding on the English courts, they have a great persuasive authority.

3. The Cabinet
Composition
The political party that has the responsibility of governing forms a Ministry which consists of Ministers of State, each one usually being the head of a government department. Within the Ministry there is a need for a smaller group of Ministers to formulate and co-ordinate policy between the departments. This smaller, inner group is known as the Cabinet.

The members of the Cabinet are chosen by the Prime Minister and usually consist of the principal Ministers of State, especially the Chancellor of the Exchequer, the Home Secretary, the Foreign Secretary, the Lord Chancellor, the Defence Secretary and the Secretaries for Scotland and Wales. The size of the Cabinet is at the discretion of the Prime Minister.

Functions
The Haldane Report on the Machinery of Government said that the main functions of the Cabinet were as follows:
1. The final determination of the policy to be submitted to parliament.
2. The supreme control of the national executive in accordance with the policy prescribed by parliament.
3. The continuous co-ordination of the activities of the departments of State.

Conventions
Although the Cabinet supervises the administration of the government and its departments, initiates all important legislation and determines all major matters of national finance and foreign policy, it is a body that is not recognised by the law. There are no statutes or rules of common law to regulate its functions or lay down its powers. Its

existence is based largely upon conventions. For example:

1. The leader of the majority party is asked by the Queen to form a Ministry.
2. The Queen acts on the advice of her Cabinet Ministers.
3. The Cabinet must command a majority of votes in the Commons. If it loses that support, it must resign.
4. Members of the Cabinet should be members of one or other House of Parliament. In practice the Prime Minister is a member of the Commons.
5. Cabinet Ministers are collectively responsible to parliament for its acts and decisions. In other words, the Cabinet Ministers share the responsibility and stand or fall together. The Cabinet acts as a unit and gives a unanimous decision to parliament, and a Minister will resign from the Cabinet if he does not agree with its decision. (All Ministers, including those outside the Cabinet, are individually responsible to parliament for the work of their particular department.)

4. Central Government Departments
Composition
Each department is usually headed by a Minister or a Secretary of State. This is a political appointment which will change with the government. Within the department there may be a Parliamentary Secretary or junior Minister, which are also political appointments. There will also be a Permanent Secretary or Under-Secretary with a staff of civil servants, all of whom continue to work for the department whatever changes might take place in governments or whichever Ministers are reshuffled.

Ministerial Responsibility
Each Minister is individually responsible, both legally and by convention, in his official capacity for the work carried out by himself or by any of his civil servants within his department. By law the Minister is accountable to the Sovereign, for he is a Minister of the Crown and will be liable in criminal or civil proceedings for illegal acts done by the Crown. By convention he is answerable to parliament, and he must reply to questions in parliament concerning the policies or actions of his department. A Minister who is not a member of the Cabinet has not the collective responsibility that Cabinet Ministers owe by convention to the Sovereign and parliament.

Functions
The functions of a government department are principally executive. It is their responsibility to administer the State services, to put into effect

any legislation concerning their department that has been passed by parliament, and to carry out the policy of the present government.

It will be seen later, in Chapter 5, that Ministers or government departments sometimes have delegated to them by parliament the power to make rules, orders and regulations concerning matters which are the responsibility of their particular department. Furthermore, certain Ministers have been given judicial powers by parliament to settle disputes which may arise as a result of that department's work.

The Main Government Departments

This book is not the place for a list or an examination of the functions of the various departments of State, for they are numerous. The departments vary considerably in size, each concerned with a particular field of State activity. This can be appreciated by taking the functions of the Home Office as an example. The Minister responsible for the Home Office is the Home Secretary, who is responsible for maintaining law and order within the State; the police and prison services; the probation and after-care services; the fire service; Civil Defence; the organisation of Magistrates' Courts; immigration control of Commonwealth citizens and aliens and the naturalisation and deportation of aliens.

The Law Officers' Department

The Law Officers are the Attorney-General and the Solicitor-General. They are appointed from the ranks of leading barristers and are also members of the House of Commons. They are responsible for giving legal advice to the Crown and to the Government.

The Attorney-General is the senior law officer and he is assisted by the Solicitor-General. The former is the representative of the Crown in civil proceedings; his consent is required for the prosecution of certain offences, and he supervises the work of the Director of Public Prosecutions.

The Civil Service

Each central government department has a permanent staff of civil servants. Within each department the structure of the civil servants is divided into various groups, such as the Administrative Group, Departmental Executive Classes and the Science and Specialist Groups.

There is no specific legal definition of a civil servant, but the term is applied in a general sense to an individual who is employed by the Crown, paid by the Crown from moneys voted and set aside by parliament, and usually working for a central government department. The term does not include individuals holding a political office, working for public corporations or employed by a local authority.

Civil servants hold office during the pleasure of the Crown and may, in theory, be dismissed at any time without any redress in a court of law. In practice, however, they enjoy a greater security of employment than many other employees.

A civil servant is not personally liable for a contract that he has made on behalf of the Crown. Furthermore, since the Crown Proceedings Act, 1947, the Crown is vicariously liable for the torts committed by civil servants in the course of their work, in the same way as an employer is liable for the torts of his employees. However, the civil servant will still, himself, be liable for the wrong he has committed.

No civil servant can continue working for the Crown and be a Member of Parliament. Apart from this major limitation, there are various other restrictions imposed upon their political activities. The senior grades cannot take any part in national politics, and other grades can do so only in certain circumstances. However, all grades have the right to vote at parliamentary elections and to take part in local government activities.

C. THE EUROPEAN COMMUNITY

On 1 January 1973 the United Kingdom became a member of the European Community. This took place by an agreement called the Accession Treaty. The treaty involved the United Kingdom becoming a party to three more major treaties, whose other members were France, West Germany, Italy, Belgium, Holland, Luxembourg, Denmark and Ireland. These treaties were:

(a) the European Coal and Steel Community
(b) the Euratom treaty
(c) the European Economic Community (E.E.C.)

By joining these communities the U.K. Parliament has surrendered an element of its sovereignty. For instance, if there should be any conflict between laws of a member state and Community laws, then the latter has supremacy and must be followed.

Community Institutions
The functions of the Community are carried out by four main institutions:

(i) *The Commission.* This is the executive body and consists of thirteen Commissioners appointed with agreement of member governments. The United Kingdom, France, West Germany and Italy have two each, other members have one. The Commission is responsible for community policy throughout the three communities. It has some legislative powers, for instance the drafting of most community legislation, and some executive powers in that it can ensure enforcement of the Council's decisions. Its judicial powers are slight.

(ii) *The Council of Ministers*. This is the legislative body for the communities. It normally consists of the Foreign Minister of each member State. In practice the Council only acts on the draft proposals forwarded from the Commission.

(iii) *The Court of Justice of the European Community*. This is the judiciary for the communities. Its decisions are binding on the national courts and there is no right of appeal from the court. Its bench is composed of a judge from each member State and they elect their President of the Court. The Court's jurisdiction is based on treaties signed by the members of the communities. It includes actions involving breach of duties under the treaties; actions between the institutions of the Community; disputes involving employment of individuals within the Community; giving advice to any national court or institution on the wording and meaning of the treaties; and so forth.

(iv) *The Assembly*. This consists of 198 representatives from member States. Although it is usually referred to as the European Parliament, its powers are more advisory and consultative than legislative. It has power to put questions to the Council and the Commission and also has power to remove the Commission by a two-thirds majority on a vote of censure.

1. What is the difference between a written and an unwritten constitution? What do you consider to be the advantages and disadvantages of each?
2. Explain the position of the following as sources of the British constitution— (a) Acts of Parliament (b) Case law (c) Conventions of Parliament.
3. If you had to draft a written constitution, what are the most important topics that you would include?
4. Explain what is meant by a Convention of the constitution. Illustrate your answer by the use of examples.
5. What is meant by the 'sovereignty of Parliament'?
6. Explain the meaning of (a) legislative power (b) executive power and (c) the judiciary. To what extent do these powers function separately in this country?
7. What is the position of the Monarch within the British constitution?
8. Explain the functions of the House of Commons and the House of

Lords. Do you think the House of Lords does anything that could not be done by the House of Commons?

9. You should research into a topic of recent local interest that has led to a changing of the by-laws. State the problems existing before the change and how the by-law has solved them.

10. Draw a chart which shows the main committees of your local authority and the work they carry out.

Give short answers to the following:
(1) What is a constitution?
(2) Distinguish constitutional law from other branches of law.
(3) In what ways is the supremacy of parliament restricted?
(4) In what ways can it be said that parliament controls the Executive, and vice versa?
(5) What is the function of local government?
(6) What is meant by Royal Prerogative?
(7) From which sources do local authorities receive their finance?
(8) What is meant by ministerial responsibility?
(9) Explain the position of the Civil Service within the constitution.

Distinguish between:
(a) Cabinet Ministers and other Ministers
(b) the executive and the legislature
(c) the composition of the Houses of Parliament
(d) parliamentary and local government elections
(e) H.M. Government and the opposition
(f) legal rules and constitutional conventions
(g) the Privy Council and the Cabinet.
(h) Government and Parliament
(i) Cabinet and Shadow Cabinet
(j) local M.P. and local councillor.

3. The Administration of Justice

Introduction

Individuals will always have conflicting interests and it is the function of the law to settle any dispute in a just way. For the effective dispensation of justice, the law must also be efficiently administered. Left to their own devices, and prompted by natural passions, men will often carry out their own private 'justice', as for example in the idea of vendetta, or will use violent means to achieve personal ends. Men may do this even despite the law, for as Portia, in *The Merchant of Venice*, says: 'The brain may devise laws for the blood, but a hot temper leaps o'er a cold decree.' However, to prevent this from being a common occurrence there is a real need, not only for law, but also for a strong system of courts. These courts must be capable of administering the law so that the individual, rather than using his own weapons and devices, will rely on the sword and scales of justice administered through the courts of law.

It may be possible for the State, by force or intimidation, to compel its subjects to settle their disputes in the courts. However, it is far better that individuals should resort to the law courts because they have confidence not only in the justice that is dispensed but also in the freedom of the courts from government interference or from an unjust bias to either party.

Therefore, it is not only important to have a structure of courts, but also that their administration should not be corrupt. In the British constitution this has been attained by completely separating the functions of the judiciary from the other powers within the State.

A. THE COURTS OF LAW

Their Authority

The courts of law are a separate and independent institution of the State which nevertheless derive their authority from the constitution of the State. Originally their position and authority within the constitution were based on custom and long-established tradition, but over the past hundred and fifty years all the courts have received statutory recognition. As an example, the Judicature Acts, 1873 and 1875, established the Supreme Court of Judicature, and the Courts Act, 1971, apart from establishing the Crown Courts, abolished many local and customary courts such as the Tolzey and Pie Poudre Courts of Bristol, the Hundred of Salford and the Liverpool Court of Passage.

Their Jurisdiction
The word 'jurisdiction' is used in two senses. It may refer to the type of legal disputes a court is authorised to settle, or it may mean the territorial area over which the court exercises its powers.

With regard to a court's 'legal' jurisdiction, no single court, apart from the House of Lords, has been given a jurisdiction that embraces all branches of the law. As the main classification of law is into civil and criminal law, the system of the courts can be classified basically according to whether they have civil or criminal jurisdiction. Furthermore, it will be seen later, when dealing with each court, that within this main division of the courts the individual courts have been allotted specific branches of the civil or criminal law as their field of jurisdiction. For example, the County Court has an entirely civil jurisdiction and this is limited to minor civil claims, such as small debts.

When referring to a court's 'territorial' jurisdiction, it means the operation of the court may be limited to disputes arising within a certain geographical area. Some courts have a wide territorial jurisdiction; the House of Lords is able to hear cases from England, Wales, Scotland and Northern Ireland and the High Court is able to hear cases from England and Wales. Other courts have a far more limited territorial jurisdiction; the Magistrates' Courts are confined to their particular Petty Sessional Division and the County Court is confined to disputes within the County Court District.

Their Procedure
Each court is bound by and operates according to rules of procedure. These regulate the preparation of legal disputes for a court hearing, the actual conduct of the court trial and the enforcement of the court's decision.

The rules of procedure differ greatly according to whether the dispute is a civil or a criminal matter. For example, the rules of procedure for a criminal case in a Magistrates' Court differ from the bringing of a civil action in a County Court. The rules will also vary in some degree according to the level of the court in which the dispute is to be heard; for example, the civil procedure for a County Court differs from the rules of civil procedure in High Court cases.

It is essential that each court of law should be subject to procedural rules which enable each party to have a fair chance of stating his case and answering the allegations that are made against him. A general rule of procedure in both civil and criminal cases is that the individual claiming will have to prove his case against the defendant in the presentation of his evidence. If the evidence he brings against the defendant is not sufficient to prove his allegation, the case will be dismissed. Otherwise, if the plaintiff makes out a case against the defendant, the latter will have to present his evidence to answer and disprove the allegations. Then, after hearing both parties, the court will come to its decision.

To have a court without rules of procedure would prejudice an individual's chances of a fair trial; the order of evidence could possibly be at the whim of the presiding judge, and this, as we can see from the following, could have grave consequences. In *Alice in Wonderland* the White Rabbit read the charge against the Knave, who stood in custody before the King, as follows:

'The Queen of Hearts she made some tarts
All on a summer day:
The Knave of Hearts he stole those tarts,
And took them quite away!'
   'Now for the evidence,' said the King, 'and then the sentence.'
   'No!' cried the Queen, 'first the sentence, and then the evidence!'
   'Nonsense!' cried Alice, so loudly that everybody jumped, 'the idea of having the sentence first.'

Appeals

It would not be just if an individual who had been the subject of an error during the hearing of his court case could not have the mistake corrected. For this reason, in the administration of justice, there is a hierarchy of courts and a system of appeal to higher courts.

A system of endless appeals cannot be allowed merely because the losing party is dissatisfied. This would be costly and time-consuming, and a mere quantity of appeals does not necessarily define the quality of justice. Furthermore, the more appeals, the greater the divergence in decisions and the less confidence in the law.

The procedure in an appeal varies from a complete rehearing of the case before another court to a review of the previous court proceedings from the written evidence that was taken at the trial. The actual appeal structure for each court will be mentioned when dealing with the court in question.

Superior and Inferior Courts

An important characteristic of English courts is the way in which they are divided into superior and inferior courts. The jurisdiction of superior courts is not limited by the value of the subject-matter in dispute, nor are they restricted geographically. The jurisdiction of inferior courts is limited both in territory and in value of subject-matter. Furthermore, superior courts have a wider power to punish for contempt of court than inferior courts. Contempt of court is where a person has in some way shown disrespect for the court, for example by failing to carry out an order of the court or by behaving improperly in court.

The main superior courts are the House of Lords, the Court of Appeal, the High Court and the Crown Court. The County Court and the Magistrates' Court are inferior courts.

B. THE SUPERIOR COURTS

I. The House of Lords

Jurisdiction

The House of Lords is the highest court in the country and all cases that come before it are on appeal from a lower court. It has virtually no original jurisdiction; in other words, it will not be the first court to which a dispute is taken.

In civil cases the court hears appeals from the Court of Appeal (Civil Division), provided leave to appeal has been granted, either by the Court of Appeal or by the Appeals Committee of the House of Lords. Similarly, the court hears appeals from the equivalent civil courts of Scotland and Northern Ireland.

In criminal cases the court hears appeals from the Court of Appeal (Criminal Division) if the lower court certifies that a point of law of general public importance is involved in the decision *and* either the Court of Appeal or the House of Lords grants leave to appeal. There is also a limited right of appeal on the point of law from the Divisional Court of the Queen's Bench Division in summary cases that were originally heard in a Magistrates' Court.

The Bench

The bench of the court, which must consist of at least three members, is chosen from the Lord Chancellor, any Lord of Appeal in Ordinary or any other peer who holds or has held a high judicial office. The Lords of Appeal in Ordinary ('Law Lords') are the senior members of the judiciary and are generally appointed from judges of the Court of Appeal.

II. The Supreme Court of Judicature

The Judicature Acts, 1873 and 1875, created the Supreme Court of Judicature into which was merged the administration of all the superior courts. The 1875 Act established a uniform set of procedural rules to operate throughout the superior courts. These are called the Rules of the Supreme Court. The Supreme Court today is divided into two main parts, the Court of Appeal (Civil and Criminal Divisions) and the High Court of Justice. The Courts Act, 1971, states that the Crown Court is also part of the Supreme Court of Judicature.

III. The Court of Appeal

Jurisdiction

(a) Civil Division

Its jurisdiction is entirely civil and appellate. It hears appeals from the High Court, County Courts, the Restrictive Practices Court, the National Industrial Relations Court and various tribunals.

The appeal is by way of a rehearing of the case based on the transcript of the proceedings of the lower court. However, the court is able to hear fresh evidence, either written or oral, that was not available at the previous hearing, even though it is reluctant to admit such evidence.

The court has power, on the hearing of any appeal, to order a new trial, set aside the verdict or judgment of the lower court or, in certain circumstances, substitute a proper sum as damages where the damages were excessive or inadequate.

(b) Criminal Division

Its jurisdiction is entirely criminal and appellate. This division of the Court of Appeal may hear appeals against the conviction on indictment of the accused, or against the sentence imposed on conviction, by a Crown Court. Permission is required from the trial judge or the Criminal Division itself before an appeal can be brought.

The hearing of the appeal is usually on the transcript of evidence given in the trial court, yet like the Civil Division it will only reluctantly hear fresh evidence. This will usually be where it appears to the court that the evidence is likely to be credible and would have been admissible in the trial court and there is also a reasonable explanation why the evidence was not originally heard in the lower court. The court has numerous powers, such as being able to order a new trial or quash the original conviction or sentence.

The Bench

The senior judge of the Civil Division is the Master of the Rolls. The Lord Chief Justice of England is head of the Criminal Division.

Both divisions are staffed by Lord Justices of Appeal. A minimum of three judges is needed to constitute the bench.

IV. The High Court of Justice

This superior court is the lower part of the Supreme Court of Judicature. For convenience, the High Court is divided into divisions: the Queen's Bench, the Chancery and the Family Division. Legally, any division is competent to try any case within the whole of the High Court jurisdiction, but for the practical reason of specialisation the work of the divisions is kept separate. The Courts Act, 1971, states that sittings of the High Court need not be confined to London but that any of its business can be conducted at any first-tier centre of the Crown Court.

The judges of each division consist of a head and High Court judges. The head of the Queen's Bench Division is the Lord Chief Justice, the Lord Chancellor is nominal head of the Chancery Division, and there is a President in charge of the Family Division. High Court judges (often known as 'puisne' judges) must be barristers of not less than ten years' standing, and they are appointed by the Monarch usually to the particular division that deals with the type of cases in which they had previously specialised.

1. Queen's Bench Division

The jurisdiction of this division of the High Court is wider in scope than either of the other two divisions. It hears both civil and criminal and both original and appellate cases. In addition to this it exercises a supervisory jurisdiction.

Original Civil Jurisdiction

The majority of the work of the Queen's Bench consists of its first-instance jurisdiction over civil disputes, mainly contract and tort. Jurisdiction over commercial matters is exercised in the Commercial Court and Admiralty business will be heard by the Admiralty Court. Both these courts are constituted as part of the Queen's Bench Division.

Appellate Criminal Jurisdiction

Appeals in criminal cases are dealt with by the Divisional Court of the Queen's Bench Division. The Divisional Court must not be confused with an ordinary court of the Queen's Bench Division. The former usually consists of two or three puisne judges constituted for the purpose of hearing appeals. The latter is a court of the division hearing a case at first instance and consists of a single puisne judge. The appellate criminal jurisdiction consists of appeals by way of 'case stated' from Magistrates' Courts and the Crown Court. This form of appeal means that the magistrates or Crown Court state a case for the opinion of the Divisional Court, usually on the grounds that there is an error in the law. From the Divisional Court, appeal by way of 'case stated' is to the House of Lords.

Supervisory Jurisdiction
The Divisional Court of the Q.B.D. has power to supervise the conduct of inferior courts and tribunals. This supervisory power is exercised by means of the prerogative orders of mandamus, prohibition and certiorari (which are described later in this chapter). For instance, if a Magistrates' Court refuses to 'state a case' for the opinion of the Divisional Court when it should have granted the appeal, the magistrates may be compelled by the order of mandamus to do so. Similarly, if there has not been a proper trial, the magistrates may be restrained by the order of prohibition from imposing any sentence. Finally, if a Magistrates' Court exceeds its jurisdiction or offends any of the rules of natural justice, the whole proceedings may be removed by the order of certiorari to the High Court for consideration.

2. Chancery Division
This division has a predominantly original jurisdiction. The most important matters dealt with are the administration of estates of deceased persons and probate, trusts, mortgages, partnership actions, landlord and tenant disputes and revenue matters.

The Companies Court, Bankruptcy Court and Court of Protection all come within the jurisdiction of the Chancery Division. The Court of Protection deals with matters concerning the protection and management of property of persons suffering from mental disability.

3. Family Division
This division was established by the Administration of Justice Act, 1970. Before this date the division was known as the Probate, Divorce and Admiralty Division. Now most of the probate work has been allocated to the Chancery Division and the Admiralty work is carried out as part of the Queen's Bench Division.

The original jurisdiction of the division is concerned with such proceedings as the dissolution of marriages, validity of marriages, legitimacy, adoption and wardship of minors. There is also an appellate jurisdiction, for instance from Magistrates' Courts in matrimonial cases.

V. Other Courts of High Court Status

In addition to the High Court proper, there are a number of other courts associated with it and given High Court status. Two in particular deserve mention.

1. Restrictive Practices Court

This court was created by the Restrictive Trade Practices Act, 1956. The court consists of three High Court judges, one Scottish judge, one Northern Irish judge, together with up to ten lay members appointed because of their special knowledge of, or experience in, industry and commerce. The bench must consist of one judge and two other members. Appeal lies to the Court of Appeal (Civil Division).

The court has jurisdiction over cases arising from the Restrictive Trade Practices Act, 1956, and the Resale Prices Act, 1964, both of which are dealt with later.

2. The Commercial Court

The Commercial Court was created by the Administration of Justice Act, 1970.

The Bench

The court consists of High Court Judges nominated by the Lord Chancellor to take commercial cases as well as their normal High Court quota. The cases in this court may be tried by a judge alone or by judge and jury. No longer may the jury consist of persons with specialist commercial knowledge; rather, they are to be laymen.

The Procedure

In some cases this court is allowed to depart from the usual High Court rules of procedure. The court may sit in private and listen to evidence which may not be admissible in an ordinary court. This may be so where the parties consent, or where the interests of justice demand it, or where it is necessary to carry out the court's business.

Jurisdiction

As well as sitting as an ordinary court the judge may in certain circumstances sit as an arbitrator, in private or in any place convenient to the parties. Arbitration forms a large part of the court's work and is very often requested by the parties as not only is the hearing in private but the outcome is not published in the same way as an ordinary court judgement.

VI. The Crown Court

Section 1 of the Courts Act, 1971, states: 'The Supreme Court shall consist of the Court of Appeal and the High Court, together with the Crown Court established by this Act.'

This Act abolished all courts of Assize and Quarter Sessions and created in their place the Crown Court as a superior court to hear all criminal cases that are tried on indictment.

Its Structure
For the purposes of its geographical jurisdiction England and Wales is divided into six circuits. Each of these circuits is divided into three tiers. For example, there is a South Eastern Circuit. Within this circuit the first-tier centres are Greater London (the Central Criminal Court) and Norwich. The second-tier centres are Chelmsford, Ipswich, Lewes, Maidstone, Reading and St Albans. The third-tier centres are Aylesbury, Bedford, Brighton, Bury St Edmunds, Cambridge, Canterbury, Chichester, Guildford, King's Lynn and Southend.

The first-tier centres of the Crown Court have a bench of a High Court judge or a Circuit judge. The towns listed as first-tier centres, where the High Court judges and Circuit judges deal with criminal cases, may be used as branches of the High Court where the High Court judge will be available to hear civil cases.

The second-tier centres deal only with criminal matters and are served by both High Court and Circuit judges.

The third-tier centres, dealing with criminal cases only, are served by Circuit judges.

Full-time Judges
Two classes of full-time judges serve the Crown Court: firstly, the High Court judges, and secondly, the Circuit judges.

The High Court judges are usually the puisne judges of the Queen's Bench Division. From time to time, they visit first-tier centres and sit in the Crown Court for the trial of the more serious crimes. As already mentioned, these judges also exercise the civil jurisdiction of the High Court within that circuit.

The Circuit judges are a new category of judge created by the Courts Act, 1971. They are either barristers of at least ten years' standing or Recorders of at least five years' standing. They are appointed by the Crown on the recommendation of the Lord Chancellor. A number of County Court judges also act as Circuit judges, which means they deal with civil cases in the County Court as well as criminal cases in the Crown Court.

Part-time Judges
The full-time judges are assisted by Recorders and Justices of the Peace.

Recorders are a new type of judge created by the 1971 Act. The previous office of Recorder has been abolished. They are appointed by the Crown on the recommendation of the Lord Chancellor. They are barristers or solicitors of ten years' standing. Although they are only part-time, they have the same powers as a Circuit judge.

The Courts Act, 1971, provides for the Crown Court to consist of a qualified judge, either a High Court judge, Circuit judge or Recorder, sitting with two to four lay Justices of the Peace. This will usually be in such cases as appeals and committals for sentence from Magistrates' Courts.

Its Jurisdiction
The Crown Court has jurisdiction throughout England and Wales in criminal matters. All trials on indictment, in other words trials with a jury, must be brought before it. The court has taken over the jurisdiction of Assizes and Quarter Sessions. It has also inherited from Quarter Sessions their appellate jurisdiction which includes a variety of civil and administrative matters, appeals from Magistrates' Courts in criminal cases and committals from Magistrates' Courts.

The types of criminal cases that are tried in the Crown Court are divided into four classes:

Class I   Cases to be tried by a High Court judge. These include serious offences such as murder and treason.

Class II   Cases normally to be tried by a High Court judge unless released for hearing by a Circuit judge. These cases include manslaughter, rape and sedition.

Class III Cases to be tried by a High Court judge but which may be released for hearing by a Circuit judge or Recorder. These include all the offences that are not within the other three classes.

Class IV   Cases normally tried by Circuit judges or Recorders but which may be tried by a High Court judge. These cases make up the bulk of Crown Court work and include such offences as theft, wounding and indictable road traffic offences.

Appeals
There may be an appeal to the Court of Appeal (Criminal Division) against conviction or sentence of the accused. Also, there may be an appeal by way of 'case stated' to the Divisional Court of the Queen's Bench Division.

C. THE INFERIOR COURTS

The County Court
The County Courts were created by the County Courts Act, 1846, for the purpose of establishing an inferior court to deal with minor civil cases at a local level.

England and Wales are divided into County Court circuits with each circuit consisting of County Court districts. The geographical and legal jurisdiction of each court is confined to its district.

The cases are heard by a County Court judge sitting alone. One judge may cover more than one district. County Court judges must be barristers of at least seven years' standing and are appointed by the Crown on the recommendation of the Lord Chancellor.

The jurisdiction of the court is in civil cases at first instance. The disputes will involve relatively small sums of money. The cases they hear include contract, tort, disputes concerning land, partnerships and a small bankruptcy jurisdiction. They also hear certain matrimonial cases such as undefended divorces. If a case involves a sum of money which exceeds the authorised jurisdiction of a County Court, it will be heard by the appropriate section of the High Court.

Appeals from the County Court are to the Court of Appeal (Civil Division), except bankruptcy matters which go to the Divisional Court of the Chancery Division.

The Magistrates' Court
Magistrates

A Magistrates' Court consists of Justices of the Peace who have been appointed by a document known as the Commission of the Peace. Every county and many boroughs have a separate Commission of the Peace for appointing the J.P.s to serve in their area. Justices of the Peace need no legal qualifications as they are appointed for their qualities of integrity and understanding and are persons who are broadly representative of the community which they serve. On appointment they undertake a period of basic training in order to obtain sufficient knowledge of the law, procedure and sentencing. They are unpaid.

Some boroughs have full-time, paid magistrates who are lawyers. These are known as Stipendiary Magistrates. In London they are known as Metropolitan Stipendiary Magistrates.

As well as sitting in Magistrates' Courts, the Courts Act, 1971, states that Justices of the Peace, in certain cases, may sit in the Crown Court with either a High Court judge, Circuit judge or Recorder.

Criminal Jurisdiction

(1) Summary offences. The main criminal jurisdiction of magistrates concerns summary offences. These are offences that have been created by statutes and the statutes have said that the offenders are to be tried without a jury. These offences are of a minor character, such as breaches of the Road Traffic Acts, vagrancy and drunkenness. The

court will also try certain minor indictable offences, usually when the accused has elected for a summary trial rather than a trial by jury. In most cases that are heard before magistrates there is a right of appeal against conviction or sentence which will be heard in the Crown Court. Furthermore, the magistrates may wish to commit the accused to the Crown Court for sentencing if they feel he is deserving of a greater punishment than they are able to impose. For the trial of a case in a Magistrates' Court there must usually be two or more Justices of the Peace, or one Stipendiary Magistrate.

(2) Committal Proceedings. The Magistrates' Court also acts as a court of preliminary investigation for indictable offences. When the court acts in this capacity, only one magistrate need be present and the proceedings are called committal proceedings. The object of the investigation is for the court to discover whether the prosecution has a sufficient case against the accused to require him to be tried before a judge and jury in the Crown Court. The Magistrates' Court will listen to the prosecution evidence and if, on the face of it, it appears that the accused has a reasonable case to answer, the court will commit the accused to the Crown Court for trial.

(3) Juvenile Court. A Juvenile Court is a special sitting of the Magistrates' Court. It hears the majority of summary and indictable offences committed by children (persons under fourteen years) and young persons (persons between fourteen and seventeen years old). The court will usually consist of three magistrates (at least one must be a woman) drawn from a panel of Justices who are specially qualified to deal with juvenile cases. The procedure in court is more informal than the ordinary Magistrates' Court and the court is not open to the general public. The court has power to place the juvenile on probation, impose a fine, commit to an approved school or detention centre or place him in care of a 'fit person'. They have no power to send him to prison but may commit him to the Crown Court with a recommendation for borstal training.

Civil Jurisdiction
Although the majority of the work in a Magistrates' Court is concerned with the criminal law, the court does have a small and varied jurisdiction over civil cases. This concerns the recovery of certain debts such as income tax, national insurance contributions, electricity, gas and rates. The court also has a jurisdiction to hear domestic cases such as affiliation and adoption orders and an administrative jurisdiction in the granting of licences such as those for the sale of liquor or the showing of films.

D. TRIBUNALS

The courts of law must now be distinguished from tribunals. The latter consist of persons or bodies who, although they are outside the structure of the ordinary courts, exercise certain judicial functions such as the hearing of various disputes between private citizens and government officials.

Acts of Parliament have granted many discretionary powers to Ministers and public bodies. These powers include the discretion to issue licences, to award grants or pensions and to assess rents, rates or taxes. Furthermore, instead of granting the jurisdiction for hearing disputes on such matters to the ordinary courts of law, many tribunals have been established by Acts of Parliament to hear such cases.

These tribunals are a form of court, and the types of disputes they hear vary according to the purpose for which they were established. Unlike the ordinary courts of law, these tribunals have no real independence within the constitution, as they are usually closely connected with the executive. It has often been the case that the benches of tribunals have been appointed by a central government department or by a Minister and, furthermore, the tribunals are often required to base their decision on government policy rather than on rules of law.

Examples of Tribunals

Since the advent of the welfare State a variety of tribunals have been appointed by Acts of Parliament to hear disputes concerning national insurance, unemployment, industrial injuries and various aspects of the National Health Service.

The Furnished Houses (Rent Control) Act, 1946, established the Rent Tribunals to hear disputes between landlord and tenant concerning a reasonable rent for the letting of certain furnished premises. The bench usually consists of a lawyer as a chairman and two members appointed by the Secretary of State for the Environment.

The Transport Act, 1962, established the Transport Tribunal which, among other functions, deals with road and rail passenger fares in London. It consists of permanent members appointed by the Crown on the recommendation of the Lord Chancellor and the Secretary of State for the Environment.

Control by the Courts

Although administrative tribunals are now an accepted part of our constitution, the courts of law do exercise some degree of control over the work they carry out.

Appeals
The Acts of Parliament which establish these tribunals often provide for an appeal to the ordinary courts for a person aggrieved by a tribunal's decision. For instance, the Lands Tribunal was established by the Lands Tribunal Act, 1949, to assess, among other matters, the value of land and premises for compulsory acquisition and to hear any dispute concerning such valuation. Furthermore, it provided for an appeal against its decisions to the Court of Appeal (Civil Division). Also, in the case of Rent Tribunals an appeal lies to the Divisional Court of the Queen's Bench Division. In other cases, where no right of appeal is specifically provided for, the Tribunals and Inquiries Act, 1971, provides for an appeal, at least on a point of law even if not on the facts in dispute, from all the more important tribunals to the High Court.

Prerogative Orders
Apart from this right of appeal from the decisions of tribunals to a court of law, the courts exercise control over tribunals by using the prerogative orders of mandamus, prohibition and certiorari issued by the Queen's Bench Division. These orders were originally the process by which the High Court was able to control the working of inferior courts, but they now extend to the functions of tribunals.

The order of mandamus may be used to require tribunals to carry out their duties. The order will not force a tribunal to exercise its discretion in a particular way, for the policy is that if a tribunal has been granted a discretion, only the tribunal can exercise it.

Prohibition may be used to stop an administrative tribunal from proceeding any further with the case before it, for instance where the court is persuaded that the tribunal is acting *ultra vires* (beyond its powers) the authority it has been granted.

The order of certiorari is used by the Queen's Bench Division to review or examine the decisions of tribunals. These decisions may be set aside if it is found that the tribunals have been acting contrary to the rules of natural justice or have acted *ultra vires*.

Rules of Natural Justice
It is a fundamental rule of the constitution that any person or body which acts in any judicial capacity must comply with the rules of natural justice. Apart from applying to all the ordinary courts of law, these rules apply to all tribunals which exercise a judicial power. Compliance with these rules of natural justice is enforced by the ordinary courts of law, which may set aside any decision of a tribunal which has been reached contrary to the rules of natural justice. There are two important rules that must be noted.

(1) No man may be a judge of his own cause. All judges must be

free, and be seen to be free, from any form of bias or personal interest concerning the cases brought before them. Therefore a judge who has any pecuniary interest in a case or has any personal hostility or friendship towards one of the parties is considered not to be in a fit position to give a fair decision.

In *Cottle* v. *Cottle* the decision of a matrimonial dispute in a Magistrates' Court was set aside when it was discovered that the magistrate was a close friend of the mother of one of the parties. A case that concerned a domestic tribunal was *Cooper* v. *Wilson*. Here, the plaintiff was a police sergeant who was dismissed from the service by the Chief Constable for various disciplinary offences. The plaintiff appealed against the decision and his appeal was dismissed by the Watch Committee at which the Chief Constable was present. The Court of Appeal held that the presence of the Chief Constable on the board of the Watch Committee when they were deliberating the appeal was contrary to natural justice. Consequently, the decision of the Watch Committee was set aside.

The Donoughmore Committee on Ministers' Powers, 1932, when considering the judicial functions that had been granted to Ministers, said: 'Parliament should keep clearly in mind the maxim that no man is to be judge in a cause in which he has an interest', and that 'in any case in which the Minister's department would naturally approach the issue to be determined with a desire that the decision should go one way rather than the other, the Minister should be regarded as having an interest in the cause'.

In *Errington* v. *Minister of Health* the case concerned a slum-clearance scheme in Jarrow to which there were many objections at a public local inquiry. The Minister made inspections of the area, obtained information behind the backs of the objectors and then confirmed the clearance order. The Court of Appeal quashed the Minister's decision because, as the Minister had instigated a public inquiry, he was acting in a judicial capacity and it was contrary to the rules of natural justice to then hold a private inquiry to which the objecting party was not admitted. It was also felt that the Minister could not have been totally uninfluenced by all that he had heard at the private inquiry.

(2) Both sides of the dispute must be heard. 'Even God himself did not pass sentence upon Adam before he was called upon to make his defence' (*Dr Bentley's Case*, 1723) and likewise, in every case, each party to the dispute must be told the charges that have been made against him, given an opportunity of preparing a case to answer these charges, and must not be condemned without the opportunity of having his case heard.

In *Ridge* v. *Baldwin* the Brighton Watch Committee dismissed their Chief Constable without giving him an opportunity to appear before them to answer the charges that had been made against him. The House of Lords declared that his dismissal was invalid on the grounds that their decision had contravened this rule of natural justice. A further example is *Cooper* v. *Wandsworth Board of Works*, where a demolition order issued by the defendants was quashed by the court because the owner of the property had had no opportunity of having his side of the case heard.

The Ultra Vires *Rule*
The doctrine of *ultra vires* means that where parliament has granted certain powers to a person or body, the latter can do only those things which are lawfully within the authority given to them. If they exceed the powers given to them, the acts done are said to be *ultra vires* (beyond its powers) and they will be of no effect.

This doctrine applies to such public bodies as local authorities and public corporations as well as to administrative tribunals.

The Tribunals and Inquiries Act, 1958
The Report of the Committee on Administrative Tribunals and Inquiries (known as the Franks Report) published in 1957 the results of its investigations into administrative tribunals and inquiries. The main recommendations made in the report became law in the Tribunals and Inquiries Act, 1958.

Importance of Administrative Tribunals
The Franks Report stated that since the Second World War the importance of tribunals had grown substantially in accordance with the continuing extension of government interest in the general well-being of the community. They stated that although tribunals are not ordinary courts, they are not to be considered as mere appendages of government departments: they must be considered as a separate and independent part of the machinery of administration which supplements the ordinary courts of law. The report said that the advantage of administrative justice being carried out by tribunals rather than by the ordinary courts was that tribunals could develop an expertise in their own technical field and would be less expensive, more informal and quicker than a court of law.

Basic Characteristics of Tribunals
The Franks Report expressed the belief that administrative tribunals should possess three basic characteristics, 'openness, fairness and impartiality'.

(1) 'Openness'. 'In the field of tribunals', the report said, 'openness appears to us to require the publicity of proceedings and knowledge of the essential reasoning underlying the decisions.' The 1958 Act implemented these views by stating that in most cases the hearings of tribunals should be in public and that the tribunal was under a duty to give the reasons for its decisions if requested.

(2) 'Fairness'. The report stated that this characteristic meant 'fairness to require the adoption of a clear procedure which enables parties to know their rights, to present their case fully and to know the case which they have to meet'. The characteristic of 'fairness' coincides with the rules of natural justice which have also been made firm by the 1958 Act, which states that no administrative tribunal can be excluded from the control of the ordinary courts of law.

(3) 'Impartiality'. The Franks Report stated that this third basic characteristic meant 'impartiality to require the freedom of tribunals from the influence ... of departments concerned with the subject-matter of their decision'. This has been implemented by the 1958 Act, which requires that the chairman of an administrative tribunal must be a lawyer appointed from a panel of names to be kept by the Lord Chancellor, and the Council of Tribunals is to make general recommendations for the appointment of its other members.

The Council of Tribunals

On the recommendation of the Franks Report, the 1958 Act established the Council of Tribunals which is an advisory body with the duty of keeping under review the constitution and working of administrative tribunals. The Council is directly answerable to the Lord Chancellor for carrying out its duties and for the making of reports. The Council is not concerned with the workings of domestic tribunals.

Domestic Tribunals

In addition to administrative tribunals, there is another form of tribunal, known as a domestic tribunal, which is quite different in nature. These domestic tribunals are usually disciplinary bodies set up by a particular trade or profession to settle the rights of its members and to exercise disciplinary measures over their conduct.

These tribunals, such as the General Medical Council and the Disciplinary Committee of the Law Society, are not set up by statute but by the rules of the organisation concerned. The exercise of their internal jurisdiction is based on the agreement of each member, on joining the trade or profession, to obey its rules. Thus, domestic tribunals only have power to deal with members of the profession, and may punish by fine or expulsion. Such punishment may have an effect more serious than the punishment of a law court, for a domestic tribunal could deprive a man of his livelihood.

Although the Tribunals and Inquiries Act, 1958, and the Council of Tribunals do not refer to domestic tribunals, an individual who considers that he has received an unjust decision from a domestic tribunal may still resort to the courts of law where the decision was considered as contrary to natural justice.

1. Explain the system of appeals that are available to the defendant in a summary criminal case.
2. What courts form the High Court of Justice and what types of cases do they hear?
3. Explain the various functions of the Magistrates' Court.
4. What types of judges sit in the Crown Courts? How are these various judges appointed?
5. Explain the jurisdiction of the Crown Courts.
6. In what ways are the courts of law able to control the functions of tribunals?
7. Explain what is meant by the expression 'rules of natural justice'.
8. What do you consider to be the advantages of tribunals over the ordinary courts of law?
9. A very important means of obtaining 'simple, swift and inexpensive' justice is the Small Claims Court. Find out all that you can about this court. For instance:
   (a) What is the maximum financial limit of a claim?
   (b) How informal/formal is it?
   (c) Is legal representation necessary?
   (d) What is the procedure for bringing a case to this court?
   (e) Is the court less expensive than others in the legal system?
10. Watch the proceedings in first the Crown Court and then the County Court. Then explain the following:
    (a) In which court was there a jury? Do you think it was an essential element in the course of justice?
    (b) Did the order of the hearing of the case vary between the two?
    (c) Give a brief report of each court hearing:
       (i) as if you were a reporter for the local newspaper, and
       (ii) as if you were going to include it in a law textbook.

What is meant by:
(1) the jurisdiction of a court
(2) superior and inferior courts
(3) the Supreme Court of Judicature

(4) committal proceedings
(5) prerogative orders
(6) domestic tribunals
(7) a Juvenile Court.

In which courts do the following judges sit:
(a) the Lord Chancellor
(b) a puisne judge
(c) the Master of the Rolls
(d) a Justice of the Peace
(e) a Recorder
(f) a Lord of Appeal in Ordinary.

Draw a plan of the criminal court system in England.

4. The Personnel of the Law

A. THE LEGAL PROFESSION

The structure of the legal profession has for a very long time been characterised by a broad division between barristers and solicitors. This is the most significant difference between the legal profession in England and other European countries, and the reason for the division is historical. The function of the barrister is primarily as advocate, and he specialises in disputes which are likely to be the subject of court proceedings. The solicitor deals with legal matters which do not involve court proceedings, as well as preparing cases that will have to be decided in court.

Solicitors

A person wishing to be a solicitor must be considered suitable by the Law Society, which is the professional body for solicitors. He must enter into articles of clerkship with a practising solicitor of not less than five years' experience. This term of articles will last two, three or five years depending upon the educational qualifications of the articled clerk, and he must also pass the examinations set down by the Law Society. No person may practise as a solicitor until he has had his name entered on the Roll of Solicitors and has obtained a certificate that the Law Society is satisfied that he has completed his articles and examinations and is also morally fit to be an officer of the Supreme Court.

The Law Society

The Law Society was founded under a Royal Charter in 1845 and is the controlling body for all solicitors. Although membership is voluntary, it has powers given to it by statute in respect of all solicitors over certain matters, such as articles, examinations and the handling of clients. In addition to this control, the Law Society administers the Legal Aid and Advice Service.

The Disciplinary Committee for Solicitors

This is a body, independent of the Law Society, which is constituted by the Master of the Rolls. It is a judicial tribunal which hears, among other matters, complaints against solicitors based on disciplinary offences involving professional misconduct. It has the power to strike a solicitor's name off the Roll, suspend him from practice or order him to pay a fine. There is an appeal from a decision of the committee to a Divisional Court of the Queen's Bench Division and from there to the Court of Appeal (Civil Division).

The Work of Solicitors

In order to carry out their practice, solicitors may work alone or, as is more usual, form partnerships with other solicitors. They usually employ a staff of clerks or legal executives to assist them. A person who wishes for legal advice or assistance in any matter goes to a solicitors' office (not to a barrister); for this reason a solicitors' office usually holds itself out as practising in all branches of the law. If it is a large office, many partners will specialise in certain branches of the law.

The practice of a solicitor will consist of a great deal of work which does not involve litigation (i.e. will not involve court proceedings): for example, the making of wills and conveyancing concerning houses and land. In legal disputes which will require a court hearing, such as divorce, the solicitors have the responsibility for the preparatory stages of the case. This will involve taking statements from witnesses and arranging the evidence.

In a few courts solicitors have a right of audience as advocates. This right is generally confined to the County Court and Magistrates' Courts, but in certain cases they may appear in the Crown Court. If the case is to be heard in any other common law court, the solicitor must 'brief' a barrister on behalf of his client.

Barristers

To become a barrister a student must have joined one of the four Inns of Court—Gray's Inn, Lincoln's Inn, Inner Temple or Middle Temple—where he must have kept eight terms. Furthermore, he must have passed the examinations laid down by the Council of Legal Education. He may then be called to the Bar, but will not practise until he has completed a year's pupillage with a barrister who has been in practice five years.

A 'junior' is a barrister who has not 'taken silk'. A 'junior' barrister with a substantial practice may apply to the Lord Chancellor for appointment as a Queen's Counsel: this is known as 'taking silk'. From the Queen's Counsel barristers the majority of the higher judicial offices are filled.

Barristers do not form partnerships but practise alone, each on his own account and each responsible for his own work. They do, for practical purposes such as office work and business accommodation, associate in chambers and employ a clerk.

As barristers are those lawyers who specialise in matters which are the subject of court proceedings, they have a right of audience in all the common law courts. They do not hold themselves out to be employed directly by a client, but only act through a solicitor. Thus, in litigation where a solicitor has no right of audience before the court, the solicitor will employ a barrister on behalf of his client, to advise on, or to conduct, the particular case. If a solicitor or his client wishes to obtain the services of a Q.C. they must also employ a 'junior'.

Many barristers specialise in particular aspects of the law and spend as much of their time acting as advisers and consultants on different matters brought to them by solicitors as they do arguing contested cases in court.

It has been mentioned that it is the solicitor who employs and pays the barrister on behalf of the client. The procedure for payment is for the solicitor to arrange the fees with the barrister's clerk. The barrister himself does not discuss his fees with the solicitor employing him and cannot sue one who fails to pay him. He may, however, report the solicitor to the Law Society who may order him to pay the fees on fear of suspension from practice.

Barristers abide by Bar Rules which regulate their relations with their instructing solicitor, between each other and with the public. Their professional conduct is subject to the scrutiny of the General Council of the Bar, and disciplinary measures are taken by the Senate of the Inns of Court.

The Constitutional Position of Lawyers
If a democratic government is to be effective and enduring, it is essential that the laws passed by the elected representatives of the citizens should be upheld justly. Therefore, there must not only be courts of law but judges and lawyers who deserve the confidence of the citizens. So that they are able to administer impartial justice, the functions of the judiciary and the legal profession within the British constitution are independent of any influence from the government.

(a) The Judges
The Lord Chancellor is the only judicial appointment made on a political basis, and he will resign from office with the resignation of the government. He is head of the English judiciary and is Speaker of the House of Lords.

The Monarch, acting on the advice of the Prime Minister or the Lord Chancellor, is responsible for all other appointments to the judiciary.

The appointments to the highest judicial offices, the Lords of Appeal in Ordinary (for the House of Lords), the Lord Justices of Appeal (for the Court of Appeal), the Lord Chief Justice (head of the Queen's Bench Division), the Master of the Rolls (for the Court of

Appeal) and the President of the Family Division, are made on the recommendation of the Prime Minister.

The Lord Chancellor recommends to the Sovereign the appointment of the High Court judges (puisne judges), the County Court judges, the Circuit judges and the Recorders (for the Crown Court), as well as the Metropolitan and Stipendiary Magistrates. Also, the Lord Chancellor appoints, on behalf of the Monarch, the Justices of the Peace (after receiving advice from the county or borough in which they are to serve).

With the exception of the Justices of the Peace, all appointments to the judiciary are made from persons who have qualified as a barrister or, in a few cases, as a solicitor. Justices of the Peace need no legal qualifications; in fact they are chosen for their integrity and under-standing and as being broadly representative of the community in which they will serve as J.P.s. On appointment they undergo a basic training in law, rules of evidence, procedure and sentencing to equip them for their work in Magistrates' Courts.

In order to safeguard the independence of the judiciary, the superior judges may only be removed from office by the Sovereign on an address presented by both Houses of Parliament. Judges of inferior courts, such as County Court judges and Justices of the Peace, may be removed from office by the Lord Chancellor.

(b) The Lawyers
It has been pointed out that it is essential to the British constitution that there should be an independent judiciary. Accordingly, it will be appreciated that if this is to work properly there must also be a legal profession which is free from any pressure or restraint from the government.

In this country the independence of the legal profession makes it possible for lawyers to challenge freely any unlawful acts of the State in a way that State lawyers or civil servants would be unable to do. They are able to act without governmental bias in the interests of an individual who claims that his rights have been unjustly threatened by the State, or that he has been treated unlawfully by some executive action.

Legal Aid and Advice
Although a State may be commended for its independent legal profession, this would be of little advantage to the individual if he could not afford the good services that were being offered. A legal problem if taken to a lawyer, even if not to the courts, can be expensive.

The Legal Aid and Advice Act, 1949, and various subsequent Acts brought into operation a scheme to make the services of a lawyer available to any individual who cannot afford the type of legal service that a reasonable man is expected to need. The scheme is aimed to ensure that every individual is able to consult a solicitor of his own choice to obtain legal *advice* as soon as any problem confronts him. The scheme also provides legal *aid* to ensure that a solicitor and, if necessary, a barrister will be available to resolve disputes and to appear in court for any individual, whether or not he can afford personally to pay the fees.

Legal Advice

Oral advice on legal problems is available at a reasonable fee to individuals who have only limited means. Advice can be obtained free of charge by those who are receiving social security benefits. This scheme is administered by the Law Society and the advice is given only by practising solicitors, who will be paid out of the Legal Aid Fund.

There is also a voluntary scheme whereby any individual, whatever his financial position, may ask advice from any solicitor on the legal aid panel. Provided the solicitor agrees, the advice will be for as long as thirty minutes and cost no more than £1.

Legal Aid

Legal aid in the resolving of a dispute differs according to whether the case is a criminal or civil matter.

(1) Criminal proceedings. Legal aid is available to the accused in any of the criminal courts, if it appears that he requires financial help in meeting the costs of the proceedings. This assistance is granted by means of a legal aid order made at the discretion of the court concerned 'where it appears to the court to be desirable in the interests of justice'. In the case of someone charged with murder, the court must make an order for legal aid. The court has power to order applicants to pay a reasonable contribution towards the cost of the case according to their means.

The cost of legal aid in Magistrates' Courts is paid out of the Legal Aid Fund, and in the higher courts the money is reimbursed by the government.

(2) Civil Proceedings. Free legal aid is available to individuals with very limited means and capital. Contributory legal aid is given to those of a more moderate income. The applicants for legal aid in a civil case must show that they have reasonable grounds for asserting or disputing a claim. Certain types, such as defamation, are outside the scheme.

The whole of the legal aid scheme is administered by the Law Society and is assisted by an advisory committee. It is operated by area committees and local committees composed of barristers and solicitors.

The cost of the scheme is met by the Legal Aid Fund, whose financial resources consist of an Exchequer grant, costs recovered from a court case and contributions from persons who have been assisted.

Law Reform
In General
If a particularly important aspect of the law fails to keep pace with the development of society, it will often raise a general public outcry and become a live political issue which will lead to parliament introducing legislation to remedy the defect. Instances of this have been the reform of the abortion, hanging and homosexuality laws.

However, apart from the areas of the law that are of general public interest, there are also small technical parts of the law, often called 'lawyers' law', which may not come to the attention of the public. If these narrow or more technical points in the law fail to keep abreast of the times, perhaps because the precedent of a case has become stagnant and is incapable of adaptation, it is the individual in his particular legal action who will suffer the injustice. Therefore, it is important that the legal profession should be continuously involved with questions of law reform and not leave all the initiative to the public and parliament with its legislation, Royal Commissions and committees. For this reason, lawyers often form societies or groups to enable them to carry out their responsibilities in law reform. For example, 'Justice' (the British Section of the International Commission of Jurists) 'was formed through a common endeavour of lawyers representing the three main political parties to uphold the principles of justice . . . without regard to consideration of party or creed or the political character of governments whose actions may be under review'. 'Justice' intends, among its objects, 'to assist in the maintenance of the highest standards of the administration of justice and the preservation of the fundamental liberties of the individual' and 'to keep under review all aspects of the Rule of Law and to publish such material as will be of assistance to lawyers in strengthening it'. This particular organisation, which consists of lawyers interested in law reform, has from time to time produced numerous reports on various aspects of the law which they consider to be in need of reform. These reports, some of which have led parliament to reform the law, have included such subjects as the Press and the Law, compensation for victims of crimes of violence, and trial of motor accident cases.

Official Agencies for Reform
The Law Reform Committee, the Criminal Law Revision Committee and the Law Commission all have a duty to keep under review the growth and the direction the law is taking so that they can recommend

any change according to the needs of society.

The Law Reform Committee and the Criminal Law Revision Committee are part-time committees of judges and lawyers appointed by the Lord Chancellor and the Home Secretary. The committees, respectively, examine such aspects of the civil and criminal law as may be passed to them by the government.

The Law Commission, established in 1965, is a permanent body consisting of lawyers who have the duty of scrutinising the law with a view to its systematic development and reform, including the possibility of codification, repeal of obsolete and unnecessary laws, and the simplification and modernisation of the law in general.

The Commission submits programmes of reform to the Lord Chancellor and it may recommend further examination of certain topics by a committee or a Royal Commission. The Law Commission submits an annual report on its proceedings and may also draft Bills for prospective legislation. Two results of their work are the Criminal Law Act, 1967, and the Animals Act, 1971.

B. THE POLICE SERVICE

The Royal Commission on Police, 1962, said: 'The Police in this country are the instrument for enforcing the rule of law; they are the means by which civilised society maintains order that people may live safely in their homes and go freely about their lawful business.'

There is no State-run or nation-wide police force in Great Britain. The police service is organised into a number of police forces on a local or district basis. It functions through a threefold relationship between the Home Secretary, the police authority and the police force itself.

Control by the Home Secretary
The Home Secretary has the ultimate responsibility for the preservation of law and order within England and Wales (the Scottish police service is separate), and he therefore has the overall control of the organisation and operation of the police forces. He is kept informed and advised on all matters concerning the police by Her Majesty's Chief Inspector of Constabulary and a number of Inspectors. The Inspectors are responsible for the annual inspection of the different police forces (excluding the Metropolitan Police) and they must be satisfied that they are being run efficiently. The Chief Inspector of Constabulary makes an annual report on the overall running of the police forces and the statistics of their work.

If the Home Secretary is not satisfied that a police force is running efficiently, he may withhold the government grant of finances to the particular police authority concerned. He also has to approve of the appointment of a Chief Constable by a police authority, and has the power to require an authority to retire a Chief Constable in the interests of the overall efficiency of the force. The Home Secretary also has the power to order an inquiry into a particular force and to call upon the Chief Constable to submit a report on any matter within his force.

The Police Authority
Each of the police forces is maintained by a police authority. In the counties the authority is a Police Committee and in the county boroughs it is a Watch Committee. Both types of committee are formed from the local council consisting of Justices of the Peace and councillors. Where police districts have been amalgamated, the police authority consists of a committee from the combined areas. Each police authority finances its police force partly from local finances and partly by a government grant.

The duties of the police authority are to provide and finance an effective policing of its area. It has power, subject to the approval of the Home Secretary, to appoint and retire the Chief Constable who actually runs its police force. It also has a say in the number of men needed to police its area.

The policing of the Greater London area is the direct responsibility of the Home Secretary. In charge and responsible for the day-to-day working of the Metropolitan Police is the Commissioner of Police of the Metropolis, who is appointed by the Crown on the recommendation of the Home Secretary.

The Police Forces
'The primary object of an efficient police force is the prevention of crime. Next, that of detection and punishment of offenders if crime is committed. To these ends all efforts of the police must be directed.'

In England and Wales there are five county police forces, six county borough police forces, thirty-four combined forces, the Metropolitan Police Force and a separate police force for the City of London.

Each Chief Constable is responsible for the running of his police force, and for the appointment, promotion and discipline of all ranks of police officers.

Although each police force has a separate area for policing, there is constant co-operation between them in such matters as training, regional crime squads, criminal records, research and planning.

The Police Officer
(a) The Functions of the Constable.

The Royal Commission on the Police in 1962 said: 'The policeman works in a changing society, and there is nothing constant about the range and variety of police duties, just as there is nothing constant about the pattern of crime, the behaviour of criminals, the state of public order or, at deeper levels, the hidden trends in society that dispose men to crime, to civil and industrial unrest, or to political demonstration. The emphasis on particular duties varies from one generation to another.' In the carrying-out of their work the police are given certain powers to assist them, either under the common law or granted to them by statute.

Firstly, the police officer has a duty to maintain law and order and he has been given common law and statutory powers to assist him. For example, under the Public Order Act, 1936, a police officer has power to arrest persons committing certain offences at public meetings; he also has a common law power of arrest for such crimes as unlawful assembly and riot.

Secondly, police officers must protect the life and limb of individuals and have been granted powers under many statutes. For example, under the Offences against the Persons Act, 1861, they have a power of arrest for such offences as causing grievous bodily harm and assault, and under the Sexual Offences Act, 1956, for rape and so on.

Thirdly, in his duty to protect the property of individuals, the constable has powers of arrest under such Acts as the Theft Act, 1968. He also has certain powers to search individuals and their houses.

Another function of the constable is the detection of criminals and his work in interrogating suspects. To assist him in this he has been granted powers of arrest which he may use even on a suspicion that a person has committed certain crimes. Advice has been set out for him by the Judges' Rules for the interrogation of suspects.

(b) Legal Status of Police Officers

A police officer, or constable, is an officer of the peace who swears allegiance to the Crown to 'preserve the peace by day and by night . . . '. He is an officer of the Crown exercising rights given to him by common law and by statute.

Although the police officer swears allegiance to the Crown and is paid by the local police authority, he is neither a civil servant nor a local government officer. The rights and powers that he has been granted are given directly to him by the law; they have not been delegated to him by the government or the local authority. A constable will be personally liable for the torts that he may commit while in the execution of his duties (see 'False Imprisonment', p. 114 below). However, the Police Act, 1964, states that the Chief Officer of police will be liable, jointly with the constable, in respect of torts committed by a constable in the course of his duties while under his direction and control.

C. THE JURY

In Criminal and Civil Cases

Under the criminal law, if a person is charged with an indictable offence he has the right to a trial by jury in the Crown Court. This means that the question of the accused's innocence or guilt will be decided by twelve 'good and lawful men of the body of his county' (Juries Act, 1825).

There are still a few civil cases which may be heard in the County Court or High Court before a jury of eight. Overall, however, the jury system has almost disappeared in civil cases, and the right to claim a hearing before a jury is now restricted to cases of defamation, fraud, false imprisonment and malicious prosecution. In all other civil cases a jury trial will only be allowed in exceptional circumstances at the discretion of the judge.

Qualifications

Most householders, male and female, are eligible for service on a jury, provided they are British subjects, between the ages of twenty-one and sixty and are on the register of electors. Persons in certain professions may claim exemption from serving; these include policemen, clergymen and lawyers. Furthermore, certain persons are disqualified from jury service, for instance persons with criminal records.

Summoning the Jury

Since the Courts Act, 1971, the Lord Chancellor is responsible for seeing that persons eligible for jury service are properly summoned. This work, together with the preparation of jury lists (i.e. jury panels), will be carried out by the administrative staff at each Crown Court centre. Persons named in the panel will be informed on what day and at which court they are to attend for jury service.

The actual jury of twelve is selected by ballot from all those summoned on the panel for that day. As each juror's name is drawn he is individually sworn in as a juryman or jurywoman, unless his presence on the jury is challenged.

Challenges by the Accused, without Reason

Before each individual juror is sworn in, the accused has the right to challenge his or her presence on the jury which will hear his case. The accused has the right to do this seven times with prospective jurors without giving any reason for the challenge. This is often done in cases when the accused wishes to obtain an all-male jury. Should the accused wish for any further challenges, he must state a good reason for making them.

Challenges by Prosecution or Accused, with Good Reason

These challenges are available to either party who shows good reason why an individual should not serve on the jury. The reason must be on the grounds that he will not be impartial: for example, if the juror is a relative of the accused or perhaps a friend of a prosecution witness.

Challenging the Array

These cases mentioned above are where the accused or the prosecution challenges the presence of individuals as members of the jury. Such challenges are called 'challenging to the polls'.

Where an accused wishes to object to the whole panel of jurors on the basis that the Crown Court has not made a disinterested selection of members of the community, he does so by 'challenging the array'.

'Praying the Tales'

It is possible, though not probable, that a court may find itself with too few jurors: for instance, if the accused has exhausted the panel by his challenges. In such cases the court may require anyone in or near the court, who has the qualifications, to become a member of a jury. This is called 'praying the tales', and such a member of the jury is known as a 'talesman'.

Number of Jurors

The first twelve jurors who are not successfully challenged are sworn in separately and go into the jury box where they will be present throughout the whole of the trial. If a juror drops out, for such reasons as illness or death, the case will continue, provided the number of the jury does not fall below nine. A substitute juror cannot be sworn in because he would not have been present throughout the whole of the evidence.

Verdict of the Jury

At the end of the evidence and after the summing-up of the trial by the judge, the jury will consider their verdict as to whether they think the accused is guilty or innocent of the crime with which he has been charged. They are not allowed to separate until they have reached their verdict, yet they need not retire from the courtroom unless they wish to discuss the matter between themselves.

The verdict in most cases need not be unanimous. If there are eleven or more jurors, then ten must be in agreement. The foreman, who has been appointed by his fellow-jurors, will give their verdict to the judge. If the accused has been found guilty, it is the judge who will decide on the punishment.

If the jury fail to reach even a majority verdict the case will be reheard before a different judge and a new jury. When two separate juries fail to agree after two trials, the prosecution, in practice, offers no evidence at the third trial and the accused will go free.

1. Compare the profession of a barrister with that of a solicitor.
2. Explain the independence of lawyers and judges within the constitution.
3. If a law is found to be out of date, what methods exist for reforming it?
4. Explain the workings of the legal aid and legal advice service in Britain.
5. What is the legal position of the police constable within the constitution?
6. Explain the working of the jury system in criminal cases.
7. Describe the present system of legal education for those wishing to become either solicitors or barristers.
8. After making enquiries with a firm of solicitors, describe one day in the life of either (a) a Legal Executive, or (b) a Solicitor's Clerk.
9. It is argued that more money is spent on giving legal aid in divorce cases than is spent on keeping up the marriage-guidance service. By enquiry and the use of published statistics, show whether this statement is right or wrong.
10. By using current pamphlets, enquiry and interview, explain the legal aid and advice systems: (a) for criminal cases, and/or (b) for civil disputes.
11. Research into the functions of either a Citizens' Advice Bureau, or a Community Law Centre.

Write short notes on:
(1) the Law Society
(2) the Law Commission
(3) the control of the Home Secretary over the police service
(4) challenges, in relation to the appointment of jurors.

5. The Sources of Law

The phrase 'sources of law' is used in two different senses.

Historical Sources
The word 'source' in a wide historical context means the origin from which a rule of law developed. In this sense it can be said that the historical sources of many rules of English law are to be found in the customs of the Anglo-Saxons, that the law relating to land has developed from the Norman feudal system of holding land, and that many other laws are due to changes in religion and social morality.

Authoritative Sources
In the second sense the word 'source' is used to refer to the authorities in any particular legal system which are able to declare a rule as being a law. These are the sources from which rules gain their legal force and validity, and they are known as 'authoritative' sources. For example, there is a law that makes it a crime to commit bigamy. The authoritative source of this law is the Offences Against the Person Act, 1861, yet the historical source of this rule can be traced back through the common law to the rules of the medieval Christian Church. It is only the authoritative sources of a rule of law that we are concerned with in this book, and this chapter sets out the sources that make these rules law.

The authoritative source of law in the majority of Continental countries is one legal code. A code consists of a formal document, enacted by the legislature of the State, incorporating all the laws of that State. Those countries that have codified their laws are said to have a legal system of civil law because they are derived from, or greatly influenced by, the civil law code of the Romans.

In contrast to the Continental legal systems, the English law is not contained in one authoritative code but has two main authoritative sources. Firstly, an *unwritten* source, known as 'judge-made' or 'case' law, which consists of the decisions of a vast number of legal cases decided by the courts of law and which are continuously being developed by further decisions. This 'case' law is divided into two parts, common law and equity, which together make up the bulk of English law. The second main authoritative source is legislation or *written* law. Although legislation is the supreme source of English law, because it can overrule common law and equity, it does not form the bulk of the law.

The whole English system of law, consisting of these two main sources, and a third called custom, is known as the common law system. Although at first the common law system was exclusively an English development, it has spread to, and is now the foundation of, the legal systems in many Commonwealth countries and also the United States of America.

To summarise, there are two main legal systems in the West: the civil law system, predominant on the Continent, with a codified system of law, and the common law system originating in England and consisting mainly of unwritten law and supported by written law. The law of Scotland is a hybrid system of law which is largely Roman law in origin, as in the Continental countries, yet it has not been codified.

A. WRITTEN LAW

I. Legislation

Legislation is law-making by parliament. It has already been mentioned that the Queen in Parliament is the sovereign legislative authority in the United Kingdom. As well as being an authoritative source for new law, legislation from time to time modifies or repeals existing laws, whether laid down by a previous parliament or declared by the courts of law.

The Process of Legislation
The items on a particular topic intended to be made law are contained in a Bill. The Bill usually has an introduction stating the reasons why the proposed law should be made. After passing through the various legislative processes of parliament the Bill becomes an Act of Parliament. The introduction of Bills is mainly under the control of the government and more specifically the Cabinet. It will be remembered that any Bill, excluding a Money Bill, may be introduced into either House. The pressure on parliamentary business leaves little time for Private Members' Bills, which are Bills introduced by an M.P. outside the Cabinet or government departments.

A Bill consists of a series of numbered clauses usually prepared at the request of the government by parliamentary draftsmen. It is introduced into parliament by the appropriate Minister who is from then onwards responsible for it.

Each Bill has to go through three 'readings' in each House. The First Reading is purely formal in nature. Permission for the Bill to be introduced is given by the House, the title of the Bill is read and then a formal motion is passed for the Bill to be printed and circulated to the members. There is no debate and, if the motion is carried, a date is agreed upon for the Second Reading.

At the Second Reading there is a debate and discussion on the Bill. This, however, is limited to the explanation, appreciation and criticism of the Bill on broad principles only. There is no discussion of its detailed and technical provisions. If a majority of the House passes the Bill on the Second Reading it is then referred to a Committee of the Whole House, or a Select or Standing Committee. It is at the Committee stage that the Bill is scrutinised in detail, clause by clause, and any proposed amendments debated. When the clauses of the Bill have been approved in its Committee stage it is 'reported' to the House which may, after debate, accept the report with or without its alterations.

The next stage is the Third Reading by the House. Here again the debate is confined to the general principles of the Bill and only minor amendments may be made to it. When a majority of the House has passed the Bill at the Third Reading it is endorsed as having passed through that House. It is then sent forward to the other House, where a similar process is carried out.

If a Bill passes both Houses it is then submitted for Royal Assent. After this the Bill becomes an Act of Parliament and is part of the law of the land from the date that has been laid down for it to come into operation.

Statutory Interpretation

The Act of Parliament is the authoritative source of the law and the actual words contained in the statute are the law. Therefore, when a court has to enforce the statute it must refer only to the words within the statute. In theory this should be straightforward, but in practice there are often difficulties. The courts frequently find that if sections or words of the statute are applied according to the 'letter of the law', they would produce a result completely inconsistent with the idea behind the statute, or would lead to ambiguities or injustices which were never intended by parliament. So the courts are permitted a certain amount of latitude in their interpretation of the statute and there are specific rules laid down for this purpose and many presumptions that the courts are entitled to make.

Different Types of Statutes

The majority of statutes lay down new laws or repeal or modify the old laws, and these are binding on all people. Some statutes give to officials and Ministers power to make rules by what is called delegated legislation; other statutes are of a purely administrative nature, such as those for the establishment of a new court or for changing the system of local government.

Some statutes are called *consolidating* statutes because they combine all previous statutes on a certain topic into one Act of Parliament. The purpose of consolidation is to make the law on a particular subject more immediately accessible where previously it required searching through many different written and unwritten sources.

Furthermore, some statutes are known as *codifying* statutes, which means that the whole of the unwritten law together with any previous statutes on a particular topic are gathered together under one statute. Examples of codification are the Sale of Goods Act, 1893, which incorporates all the previous case law on the sale and purchase of goods, and the Animals Act, 1971, which has codified all liability in tort concerning animals.

Although some Acts have codified parts of case law, it does not mean that England has a code of law. In England there has merely been codification of various topics or branches of law, not the whole legal system. The majority of English law is still case law; legislation, of whatever kind, merely supports or supplements the unwritten law. The unwritten law, consisting of decisions given in common law and equity cases, is capable of standing and developing as a complete system of law on its own, whereas statute law, in its present stage of development, is only fragmentary in its application and cannot be called a complete system; and completeness is the essence of a code.

II. Delegated Legislation

Another authoritative source of written law is delegated legislation. This takes place when parliament has delegated its law-making powers to some subordinate authority. The reason for delegation is because the business of parliament covers such a wide range of activities concerning the modern State, and the problems to be dealt with are often so complex and so technical, that it is impracticable for parliament to deal with them all personally by legislation.

This practice of delegating certain law-making powers to the executive originated towards the end of the nineteenth century, and it enables parliament to devote more time to general policy and the running of the State. Furthermore, the work in narrow and specialised fields such as science and engineering and the welfare services is best dealt with by experts employed by the appropriate government department who are more qualified in such matters than the majority of M.P.s. A further advantage of delegated legislation is that it enables greater flexibility in the making, amending and repealing of rules. This is because the procedure under which a Minister or government department makes rules is far simpler and shorter than the legislative procedure of parliament. The power given to the subordinate authority to make law is usually given in the form of a general statute passed by parliament and known as a 'parent' Act. The 'parent' Act sets out the provisions under which the subordinate authority is permitted to make its rules. If it is found that these powers are being misused, parliament can withdraw the 'parent' Act. Apart from the above advantages, it has been found that with the necessity for delegating legislative powers certain disadvantages have also arisen.

Delegating legislation is seen by some to be a threat to the sovereign legislative power of parliament. Soon after the practice of delegating to the executive began, it was seen that the number of statutory rules, regulations and by-laws made by subordinate authorities far out-numbered the statutes being passed by parliament and, for reasons such as the expansion of the welfare State, these rules have been increasing. Therefore, rules are now proliferating under an authority other than the legislature, by a procedure which does not have the safeguards of debate, discussion and, ultimately, the consent of the electorate.

In delegating powers to the executive, parliament has created a rival not only to itself but also to the judiciary. The courts of law are being confronted with the growth of a new form of law which is often outside, or has been removed from, their control and enforcement and placed in the hands of administrative tribunals. However strongly the courts believe in the principle that all the laws made within the State should be subject to their enforcement, they find they cannot exercise the same measure of control over public authorities and government departments as they do over individuals, nor can they always ensure protection for the individual under the rules that are made by such authorities. The control which parliament and the courts of law do have over delegated legislation will be shown later. It is now necessary to mention the various forms which delegated legislation takes.

Forms of Delegated Legislation
(a) Orders in Council
These Orders are passed by the Privy Council, consisting of the Monarch and Privy Councillors, under power given to them by an Act of Parliament.

In practice the Orders are drafted by the particular branch of the executive concerned with the subject-matter of the Order. The passing of the Order by the Privy Council is a formality. The idea of requiring certain forms of delegated legislation to be approved by the Queen in Council is probably due to the dignity given to Orders in Council, which are often used for matters of national importance and concern. For example, on the outbreak of war the Emergency Powers (Defence) Act, 1939, provided for the Minister to act by Order in Council, independently of parliament.

(The term 'Order in Council' also refers to Orders made by the Queen in Council under the inherent prerogative of the Monarch: for example, Orders legislating for colonies and the Queen's Regulations for the armed forces. Such Orders, which have been mentioned earlier, are 'original' legislation independent of parliament, and therefore are not delegated legislation.)

(b) Ministerial Orders
This is the most widely used form of delegated legislation. Ministers and departments make rules, regulations or orders within the scope of the authority given to them by general Acts of Parliament. For instance, the Secretary for the Environment has been given powers to make rules and orders under the Town and Country Planning Acts, 1962 and 1968.

There is no generally accepted distinction between a rule, a regulation or an order, but most of them fall within the comprehensive term 'statutory instrument'.

(c) By-Laws
Local authorities and many public authorities have power given to them by various statutes to make by-laws. For example, by the Public Health Acts, 1875 to 1939, local authorities have powers to enact by-laws binding upon the public generally; the British Transport Commission has powers given to it under statute to make by-laws and inflict penalties on persons who travel by rail in breach of the regulations.

Local authorities produce the greatest number of by-laws. They do not have complete discretion concerning the by-laws they wish to make. The power is delegated on a specific topic and the authority is required in most cases to submit its draft by-laws for inspection and confirmation to the central government department mentioned in the 'parent' Act. For example, the Public Libraries and Museums Act, 1964, gives power to local authorities to make by-laws regulating the use of libraries, museums and art galleries subject to initial confirmation by the Secretary of State for Education and Science.

In many cases the Ministry responsible for confirming the by-laws will issue model by-laws covering what is generally required in the local authority by-laws. In this way a large measure of uniformity is maintained throughout the country.

Control of Delegated Legislation
It was mentioned at the outset that the delegation of powers to the executive is a violation of the separation of powers because it takes a certain amount of legislative authority away from parliament, and that many of the orders and regulations that are made exclude the operation of the courts. However, delegated legislation is, perhaps, a necessary

evil, and in order that the functions of parliament and the courts are not usurped, certain controls are imposed upon subordinate bodies in the exercise of their powers.

(a) Control by Parliament

The sovereignty of parliament is, in theory, unlimited, Therefore it may retract any power it has given to a subordinate authority by repealing the 'parent' Act. This measure, however, would only leave parliament to do the work for itself, so parliament attempts to check the use of the power it has delegated by effective *control* of the subordinate bodies. Apart from motions of censure on the Minister responsible for the statutory instrument, debate and questions put to the Minister by M.P.s, there are the following controls:

(1) Laying before parliament. The Statutory Instruments Act, 1946, requires that some orders and regulations must be laid before parliament. The procedure is that certain kinds of statutory instruments that are laid before parliament have to be approved by a resolution of the House before they take effect. Others do not actually have to be approved, but will come into effect after a specified time if they have not been annulled by a resolution of the House in the meantime. The purpose of this procedure is to inform members of what is being done by a Minister and to allow their objection or approval to these orders.

(2) The Scrutiny Committee. The Select Committee on Statutory Instruments, usually referred to as the 'Scrutiny Committee', is required to report to the House of Commons on any order or regulation which deserves their special attention, for such reasons as imposing a tax, excluding the jurisdiction of the courts, or making some unusual use of the delegated power.

(3) Publication. The Statutory Instruments Act, 1946, requires that all statutory instruments are to be printed, put on general sale, and that Her Majesty's Stationery Office must publish lists showing the date on which every statutory instrument printed was first issued. The Act further states that it shall be a defence for an individual to prove that the instrument had not been issued by H.M.S.O. at the date of his alleged contravention of the instrument. The theory behind this is that an individual should not be punished for an offence which he had no possible means of knowing about, and this would be the situation if it had not yet been issued.

(b) Control by the Courts

The usual method of control by the courts over delegated legislation is by the doctrine of *ultra vires*. Delegated legislation must be carried out within the authority given by the 'parent' Act. The courts will declare any order, regulation or by-law void and ineffective which is beyond the power (*ultra vires*) of the person or body making it. This can be so, either because of the procedure by which the rule is made, or owing to the actual law that it sets out. In *Attorney General* v. *Wilts United Dairies*, a fee that had been imposed for the issue of a licence was held to be *ultra vires* as there was no power to charge a fee, although there was power to issue a licence.

III. Sources of Community Law

The European Communities Act, 1972, provides that the main treaties and secondary legislation are to become part of the law of the United Kingdom. Such legislation usually covers matters like customs duties, agriculture, movement of workers and other aspects of industry.

Secondary legislation includes Regulations, which are directly binding on all member States, and Directions, which require a member State to incorporate the law into its domestic laws by its own law-making procedures, for instance by statute and statutory instrument.

B. UNWRITTEN LAW

I. Case Law

Case law forms the larger part of the English law and consists of law that has developed through the decisions of judges given in the courts of law. Although these decisions have for a long time been recorded in law reports, case law is considered to be an unwritten source of law. In the written sources it is the words themselves laid down in the statutes or statutory instruments which actually *constitute* the law. However, in case law the words that the judges use in their decisions do not in themselves constitute law; the judges only *describe* in the clearest way possible what they consider the law to be in the particular case before them. As one eighteenth-century judge said: 'The reason and spirit of cases make law, not the letter of the particular precedent.'

The system of case law functions according to the doctrine of judicial precedent, which means that a judge, when coming to his decision in a particular case, will rely on previous decisions in similar cases for his answer. These previous cases are known as 'precedents', and by applying them to the problem before him the judge's task is made easier and he is also strengthened in his decision by knowing that he is making use of past authorities. There are the additional advantages of 'precedents' in that by following previous decisions certainty and consistency is attained in case law.

Within the doctrine of judicial precedent it will be seen later that there is a narrower doctrine of *stare decisis*. It is this latter doctrine that makes the English system of case law and judicial precedent different from any system of precedent on the Continent, and it is this doctrine that makes case law an authoritative source of law. The purpose of *stare decisis* ('standing by previous decisions') is that judges will, in many circumstances, be absolutely bound by the decisions of the previous cases from certain courts and will be obliged to follow them.

It was said at the beginning of this chapter that the substance of case law is made up of two branches of law which have been given the technical names common law and equity. It is now necessary to mention more of these two branches before going on to explain the working of judicial precedent and the ways in which some cases will be binding upon others.

The Common Law

The expression 'common law' has already been used in the context of the common law legal system as distinguished from the civil law codes of European countries. In this sense, common law refers to the whole body of English law.

Apart from this first meaning, within the English legal system itself the phrase 'common law' has two further meanings. In the first sense, it refers to all case law, or unwritten as distinguished from statute law. In the second sense, within the branch of case law the expression 'common law' is used in its narrowest sense to mean the law developed from the common customs of England through the decisions of the ordinary courts, as distinguished from the law known as equity, which emerged from the decisions of the Chancellor in a special court known as the Court of Chancery. It is in this last, narrower, sense, as a branch of law distinguished from equity, that common law is now explained.

During the Anglo-Saxon times there was no system of law or structure of courts that was common throughout England. The law that did exist was administered in local courts and consisted of customs that had grown up in that particular area. Thus, what was an offence in the north of England was not necessarily so in the south. After the Norman conquest the law over the next two centuries developed away from local custom and became a uniform body of rules which had been built up through cases heard by the King's judges. These laws were applied equally throughout the whole of the country through a system of royal courts that had been established on a national structure. These laws, which were common to all England and were administered through a regular court system, were called the common law. This name was used in order to distinguish these laws from the remaining local customs and certain rules that referred exclusively to certain classes of persons such as ecclesiastics and merchants and which were administered in special courts. The common law, which included such branches of law as contract, tort and crime, has continued to develop through decisions of judges in ordinary courts of law up to the present day, assisted by the doctrine of judicial precedent which is explained below.

Thus, in its simplest terms, the common law of England evolved spontaneously from the rules of custom which had been shaped and formalised into a uniform system of law by the decisions of judges through a uniform system of courts.

Equity

Although by the end of the thirteenth century it could be said that there was a common law, there were imperfections in this system of law. Firstly, there were gaps in the actual law itself which meant that individuals who thought they had been wronged would find no remedy in the common law courts. Secondly, the common law only gave damages (i.e. compensation) as a remedy and in many situations this was found to be inadequate. Also, the procedure for claimants wishing to bring a case to the courts was considered to be inflexible and unjust.

A system of law grew up to remedy these defects in the common law. This was known as equity and it evolved from the practice whereby persons who failed to gain satisfaction in the common law courts petitioned the Monarch or his council (as the 'fountain of justice'). These petitions were handled by the Chancellor. At first he made recommendations to the King, but soon he began to take decisions on his own initiative and presently this mode of justice became so popular that petitions were addressed direct to the Chancellor and a Court of Chancery was established by the beginning of the fifteenth century to hear these petitions. The justice that the Chancellor gave was called equity because, rather than base his decision on the common law, he did justice between the parties in the light of good conscience and fair dealing.

In certain cases the Court of Chancery recognised rights which the common law had not entertained. In other matters it would give a remedy where no remedy had previously been available under the common law, or it would give an alternative and more effective remedy to replace a common law remedy which was inadequate. Thus the Court of Chancery afforded an improved system for attaining justice, although wherever possible it was the policy of equity to follow the common law.

In the centuries that followed, the Court of Chancery became more inflexible and conservative in its outlook and began to administer equity according to a system of judicial precedent, the same as that used by the common law courts. The result was that by the eighteenth century equity had become a system of law as inflexible as the common law. By the nineteenth century there was little to choose between the two systems except that they were administered in entirely separate courts, heard different claims and gave different remedies. They had both become very slow and formal in their procedure and long delays were frequent, especially if an individual had to take his claim through both court systems. (For an example of this in literature, see *Jarndyce* v. *Jarndyce* in *Bleak House* by Charles Dickens.)

The Judicature Acts, 1873 and 1875, reorganised the whole structure and procedure of the courts into the system which is basically the same today. The courts of common law and equity were fused into one structure, known as the Supreme Court of Judicature, and it was laid down that each court had the power to apply both common law and equity even, if need be, in one case. In order to overcome the difficulty that might have occurred when a judge was faced with two conflicting rules, one common law and one in equity, it was stated that in such a situation the rule of equity was to prevail.

Judicial Precedent

Thus English law developed through the rules and principles of law declared by the judges in the courts of common law and equity. All this was made possible by the doctrine of judicial precedent.

To put it in its simplest form, a system of precedent means that a question or dispute should be decided in a certain way because a similar case was decided that way previously. Judicial precedent, in the sense that previous cases are used as guides for present decisions, is a doctrine that exists in all civilised legal systems, even in countries where the laws have been codified. The peculiarity of the common law system is not, therefore, in the fact that it applies precedent, but rather in the fact that precedent is linked with the doctrine of *stare decisis*. The doctrine of *stare decisis* means that certain precedents of certain courts act as a binding force which judges, usually of lower courts, are obliged to follow. The Continental judge may and usually does consult past decisions to assist him, but he does not feel himself bound to follow them and may ignore them. The English judge, on the other hand, if certain conditions are satisfied, knows that he is bound and must follow the previous decision. Judicial precedent will give a degree of uniformity to the law, but it is the doctrine of *stare decisis* which makes case law an authoritative source of law.

Applying Judicial Precedent

There are three major points that must be taken into consideration when applying a judicial precedent.

(a) The Law Report

There is no rule that a past case can only be relied upon or cited as a precedent because it has been reported. For instance, any judge may rely upon a precedent of which he is aware, even though the decision has not been reported. In fact, in the early development of the English law this was the general practice, that the reference to past cases depended entirely upon the personal experience and recollection of the judges and lawyers. However, the memory of individuals is so transient and fallible that this practice could not possibly form the basis of a workable system of case law. It is for this reason that the entire foundation of case law and precedent depends upon a reliable system of recording and publishing judicial decisions. Although the origins of law reporting go back as far as the thirteenth century, it is only since 1865 and with the creation of the Incorporated Council of Law Reporting for England and Wales that there have been official reports. The Council is responsible for issuing reports of important decisions of the superior courts, and these are labelled according to the year and the court making the decision. Before they are printed, the lawyer reporting the case submits his notes for examination and amendment to the judge whose decision is to be reported. Apart from the official reports, there are many bodies producing private reports which are considered sufficiently reliable for use in citing precedents.

The courts will normally require the report to be the best available on the case. However, because the case is old does not in itself weaken its authority as a precedent, provided the point of law it decided has not altered.

(b) The Court

The doctrine of judicial precedent also depends for its effectiveness on a definite structure and hierarchy of law courts. This is because the doctrine is based on the rule that the cases of higher courts bind lower courts.

The decisions of the House of Lords are binding upon all other courts, and until 1966 it considered itself bound by its own previous decisions. The present position can be seen by the statement that was made by the Lord Chancellor in 1966 on behalf of the Lords of Appeal in Ordinary:

> Their Lordships regard the use of precedent as an indispensable foundation upon which to decide what is the law and its application to individual cases. It provides at least some degree of certainty upon which individuals can rely in the conduct of their affairs, as well as a basis for orderly development of legal rules. Their Lordships nevertheless recognise that too rigid adherence to precedent may

lead to injustice in a particular case and also unduly restrict the proper development of the law. They propose, therefore, to modify their present practice and, while treating formal decisions of this House as normally binding, to depart from a previous decision when it appears right to do so ...

The Court of Appeal (Civil Division) is bound by the decisions of the House of Lords. It is not bound by the Criminal Division but it is bound by its own earlier decisions, with three exceptions:

1. If two of its earlier decisions conflict, it must choose which to follow.
2. It will not follow one of its own earlier decisions if it is inconsistent with a House of Lords decision.
3. If an earlier decision was given *per incuriam*, for instance in ignorance of a statute or other binding precedent, the court is not bound by it.

The Court of Appeal (Criminal Division) is bound by the decisions of the House of Lords and usually by its own decisions.

Each division of the High Court is bound by the House of Lords, the Court of Appeal and by a Divisional Court of the same division of the High Court.

The Judicial Committee of the Privy Council is not bound by its own decisions or by those of the House of Lords, nor does the court bind the lower English courts. However, because the bench consists of Law Lords, its decisions have a great *persuasive* authority. A persuasive authority is one that is not strictly binding, but is usually followed unless there is good reason why it should not be. For example, persuasive precedents include decisions of the High Court with regard to their effect on the Court of Appeal, and the Court of Appeal's decisions in the eyes of the House of Lords.

(c) The Decision

Each judge in a case will give his judgment, and it is not every part of the judgment that acts as a judicial precedent. It is therefore important that a judge who is using a case as a precedent should be able to recognise that part of the previous judgment which is binding upon him.

The portion of a previous judgment that is binding is called the *ratio decidendi* ('the reason for deciding'). This consists of the proposition of law which was essential to the judge in coming to his decision. In other words, it is the principle of law behind his decision.

Frequently in the judgment of a case the judge will make a comment concerning legal principles which are not directly relevant to the matters at issue in the case. These comments are known as *obiter dicta* ('matters spoken by the way'). The *obiter dicta* of a case are not binding on a future case although some carry persuasive authority, depending on the status of the judge.

Once a judge has found what he considers to be the *ratio decidendi* of a previous case, he will either:

1. *Follow* it by applying the *ratio decidendi* to the case before him; or
2. *Distinguish* his present case from the facts of the earlier case. In this way, by finding a distinction between the two, he may avoid following the *ratio decidendi* of the previous case, which would otherwise have been binding on him; or
3. *Overrule* the previous decision. This can be done by a higher court deciding that an earlier decision of a lower court is not good law.

II. Custom

The second authoritative source of unwritten law is custom.

Custom is the original source of common law. The latter was formed by welding into one system the law created by judges and the customs of England. Hence a statement that was made as early as 1350, 'common usage is common law'. As the law developed, the majority of customs received judicial notice and now practically all the general customs are either part of case law or statute law. However, it is still possible for custom to be a source of law, especially in specific localities.

Local custom consists of the habitual practices, rules and traditions of people in a particular locality. Such customs may become law even though they are not common to other areas, provided they have existed since 'time immemorial', they are not contrary to any existing statute or the common law, and they are reasonable.

1. What are the main sources of English law?
2. Describe the operation of the doctrine of judicial precedent in English law.
3. Distinguish between (a) common law (b) equity and (c) statute law.
4. Explain the different meanings of the words common law.
5. Explain the ways in which the English law is able to develop in order to keep abreast of the times.
6. What is the purpose of law reports?

7. What is meant by delegated legislation and what are its advantages and disadvantages?
8. What control does parliament and the courts of law have over delegated legislation?
9. After looking at the Health and Safety at Work Act, 1974, answer the following:
   (a) What is the preamble?
   (b) Explain what is meant by a Section and a Subsection.
   (c) How does the format of the statute make easy reference possible?
10. After reading the case *Lewis* v. Averay, [1972] 1 Q.B. 198; [1971] 3 All E.R. 907, answer the following:
   (a) In which court was it first held?
   (b) In which court did Lord Denning hear the case?
   (c) Who were the judges sitting with the Master of the Rolls?
   (d) Who read the judgment in the case?
   (e) Give the names of some cases that were cited during the hearing?
   (f) Name the solicitors and counsel for the plaintiff and defendant.

What is meant by the following:
(1) 'sources' of law
(2) *ratio decidendi*
(3) *obiter dicta*
(4) a code of law
(5) By-laws
(6) Orders in Council
(7) written and unwritten law.

6. Persons Subject to the Law

Legal Personality

Just as a Sovereign must have subjects or a State its citizens, each legal system must have persons who are subject to its laws. If a person, or a group of persons, has 'legal personality', it means that he is subject to the laws of a particular legal system. The rules of each legal system will lay down the types of persons whom it considers should possess 'legal personality'. The English legal system recognises not only human beings but also some 'artificial persons' as having 'legal personality'.

A. NATURAL PERSONS

Human Beings as Legal Persons

As laws are for the regulation of human conduct, naturally, each human being has legal rights and freedoms, as well as obligations, under the law. In other words, the law gives legal personality to each human being.

Broadly speaking, within the English legal system the legal personality of a human being begins at birth and ends at death. However, certain sections of the law do recognise and grant protection to the unborn child. This can be illustrated by the crime of child destruction. Furthermore, certain aspects of the law take an interest in the rights of a human being after his death; the law will respect and carry out the wishes that the deceased has made in his will, and in a few cases the offence of criminal libel will protect a deceased's reputation. Although it is not so in England today, in some legal systems certain human beings have been denied legal personality and consequently all rights and freedoms under the law. At one time in England a human being who had been declared an 'outlaw' ceased to be a legal person and was declared to be outside the protection of the law, even to the extent that killing him was not murder.

'Things' as Legal Persons

Some legal systems in the past have considered things and even animals as being worthy of a legal personality similar to humans. For instance, such 'things' as idols who have received goods or land from generous devotees have been able to keep the gifts in their own name.

Conversely, some legal systems have even held that some humans have a legal position no greater than 'things'. For example, slaves under the Roman law were considered as no more than a man's goods or chattels.

Status

Although all human beings have legal personality, certain categories of humans within the English legal system, such as aliens, married persons, minors and mental defectives, are subject to special rules based on the category to which they belong. These special rules are sometimes known as rules of *status*, which regulate a person's standing in relation to the law and the State.

(a) Nationality

An individual's nationality determines his status as a citizen or subject of a particular State. An individual who is not a national within the State has the status of an alien and is, as such, subject to restrictions concerning entry and employment after entry into the country, registration with the police and the rules regarding deportation.

The major part of the law relating to British nationality is set out in the British Nationality Acts, 1948 to 1965.

British subjects

British subjects are divided into two main classes:

(1) Commonwealth citizens. Citizens of the independent nations of the British Commonwealth (usually referred to as 'Commonwealth citizens') have a status that is regulated by the laws operating in their own country.

By the Commonwealth Immigrants Acts, 1962 and 1968, power has been given to the United Kingdom government to refuse admission to this class of citizen on various grounds and to deport them in certain circumstances.

(2) Citizens of the United Kingdom and Colonies. The main ways of acquiring this status are by:

(i) *Birth.* With a few exceptions, every child born within the United Kingdom or Colonies acquires 'British citizenship', irrespective of the nationality of the parents.

(ii) *Descent.* Any child, wherever born, whose father is, at that date, a citizen of the United Kingdom and Colonies, acquires citizenship by descent.

(iii) *Registration.* A citizen of one of the independent Commonwealth countries, or of the Republic of Ireland, may, if of full age and capacity, apply for registration as a British subject, provided certain residence requirements have been satisfied.

(iv) *Naturalisation.* Aliens and British Protected persons may apply for a certificate of naturalisation. The conditions for granting this are at the discretion of the Home Office, and the applicant must be of full age and capacity, of good character, have knowledge of the English language and satisfy certain residence requirements.

A citizen may either renounce his citizenship of the United Kingdom and Colonies or he may be deprived of it. In the case of *renunciation* the fact must be registered with the Home Office. *Deprivation* of citizenship only applies to those individuals who, in the first place, have acquired their citizenship by registration or by naturalisation, and in these cases it may be ordered by the Home Secretary for serious misconduct.

British Protected Persons
These are members of Protectorates, Protected States and Mandated or Trust Territories. They have neither the status of 'British citizenship' (but may become so by naturalisation) nor are they aliens (because they are not subject to the Alien Restriction Acts).

(b) Married Persons
A marriage is 'The voluntary union for life of one man and one woman to the exclusion of all others'. It is a change in legal status that in some ways affects the rights and obligations of the individuals involved. For instance, a husband is, as a general rule, bound to support his wife financially and, furthermore, unless they are judicially separated, they are under a duty to cohabit.

As well as increased obligations, the law allows various privileges to the married. In certain court proceedings husbands and wives should not be compellable as witnesses against each other. Also, what is said between husband and wife about other persons cannot generally be the subject of an action for defamation.

However, in many branches of the law a husband and wife are in the same position as other individuals. They may own property separately, they may in certain cases sue each other in contract and in tort, and they may be prosecuted for stealing each other's property.

(c) Minors
In certain areas of the law there is a need to treat persons who have not yet reached adulthood in a way that is different from persons who are considered to be of full age and capacity. Since the Family Law Reform Act, 1969, the age at which an individual becomes an adult is, for most purposes, eighteen. Any person who has not yet reached this age is a 'minor' (who before the 1969 Act was known as an 'infant').

The following are some of the distinctions made by the law between a minor and an adult:

(1) Marriage. A minor who is under sixteen years of age cannot marry. Minors between sixteen and eighteen years of age need the consent of their parents, guardians or a magistrate before they can marry.

(2) Voting. Under the Representation of the People Act, 1969, the voting age for parliamentary and local elections is eighteen years and over. Minors have no right to vote.

(3) Land and goods. A minor cannot hold a legal estate in land, yet his toys will be his own because he has the same rights of ownership of goods and personal property as an adult.

(4) Wills. As a general rule, a minor cannot make a will.

(5) Court proceedings. In civil cases, such as those involving contract or tort, a minor cannot bring an action in the courts himself, but can only do so through his 'next friend', which will usually be his parent or guardian. A minor has to defend an action through his guardian *ad litem.*

In respect of minors taking the oath before giving evidence in court, the situation differs according to whether the case is a civil or criminal one. In civil cases, under the common law, a child is only competent to give evidence if the judge is satisfied, after questioning him, that he understands what it means to take an oath. In criminal cases under the Children and Young Persons Act, 1933, a child may give unsworn evidence if the judge is satisfied that, although the child does not appreciate what is meant by an oath, he does understand that he has to tell the truth.

(6) Crimes. A child under ten years of age is not criminally liable for any offence and therefore will not be prosecuted. A child between ten and fourteen years old is presumed by the law to be incapable of forming an intention to commit a crime, but if the contrary is proved, he may be found guilty of the crime. Over fourteen years of age a young person is considered old enough to be liable for his criminal behaviour.

(7) Torts. A minor will be liable for the torts he commits in the same manner as any adult. However, where liability in tort depends on some special mental element, such as malice or carelessness, the court may find that he is too young to have formed that mental element. For example, in *Walmsley* v. *Humenick* the plaintiff and defendant, who were both five years old, were playing cowboys and Indians and during the course of the game the plaintiff was shot in the eye by one of the defendant's arrows. The court held that the defendant was not liable because he 'had not reached that stage of mental development where it could be said that he should be found legally responsible for his

negligent acts'. However, in *Gorely* v. *Codd* the court held that the defendant aged sixteen and a half was sufficiently old to be liable when he negligently shot the plaintiff with an air-rifle while 'larking about'.

As a general rule, parents will not be liable for the torts of their children, except where they have authorised the tort or the child's tort was really due to the parent's negligent control of the child. In *Bebee* v. *Sales* a father had given his fifteen-year-old son an air-gun and even allowed him to use it after he had broken the windows of a neighbouring house. Therefore, the court held that the father was liable when his son shot out the eye of another boy. However, in *Donaldson* v. *McNiven* the defendant's thirteen-year-old son had promised to use his air-gun only in the cellar. Without his father's knowledge the son took his air-gun out of doors and, when shooting it, put out the eye of the plaintiff. In this case it was held that the father himself had in no way been negligent.

(8) Contracts. Although relatively early on in life a person is expected to know the difference between right and wrong sufficient to be held responsible in tort, in the world of commercial transactions the law of contract takes more care to protect a minor from making a bad bargain. In some cases the contracts of a minor will be binding upon him, in other cases they will not. This subject will be dealt with in greater detail when explaining contracts in general.

B. ARTIFICIAL PERSONS

Offices and Groups as Legal Persons

Quite apart from granting legal personality to each human being, the English law applies the concept of legal personality to certain entities which it considers capable of exercising legal rights and incurring legal liabilities. Therefore, there are certain offices and also groups of human beings which act as a single legal entity and are regarded by the law as having a legal personality separate from the individuals who make up its corporate entity. For example, certain offices such as a bishopric have a legal personality separate from the person who, at the time, holds the office. Also, various towns, cities and universities have been granted a Royal Charter which has made them distinct and independent legal persons. Furthermore, the Crown is an important legal entity within the framework of the English legal system and is endowed with legal personality although it is not a human being. It has been shown earlier that, under the Crown Proceedings Act, 1947, the Crown may sue and be sued in many activities in the same way as any individual.

In the last one hundred years or more the law has developed a large body of rules providing for the creation of companies with independent legal personalities separate from its members. This branch of the law is known as company law, and consists of rules for the formation or creation of these corporate legal 'persons' and also rules concerning their operation and termination. These rules will be mentioned in greater detail later in this book.

Very often the same rules of law are applicable whether directed to legal persons who are human beings or to legal persons who are not. For example, an individual, a company and the Crown are all subject to the rules regarding the making of contracts and all are capable of committing certain torts. Naturally, however, there are some areas of the law that apply solely to human beings; for instance, the crime of rape or the tort of trespass to the person.

Corporations

An entity which has been given a corporate legal personality is known as a corporation. Such corporations have a legal personality which is completely separate from the individuals that form them, and they have a life that will continue irrespective of the death of their individual members. Corporations are created and ended by operation of the law.

Types of Corporation

(1) Corporation sole. A corporation sole is an office or position held by one individual. Offices such as the Crown, bishops and parsons and the Public Trustee are corporations sole, and they have a legal personality independent of the legal personality of the individual who, for the time, holds that office. For example, a man may hold the office of the Bishop of Winchester. In his private capacity he has the rights and duties of an ordinary private citizen, but in his public office he is only the present representative of that office.

(2) Corporation aggregate. This type of corporation is made up of certain groups of individuals who combine to make an entity with a separate legal personality from its members. For instance, a borough is a corporation aggregate consisting of the mayor, aldermen and councillors. A trading company is also a corporation consisting of its members and shareholders.

Creation of a Corporation

(1) By Royal Charter. The Monarch has power to create a corporation by the granting of a Royal Charter. The British Broadcasting Corporation was created by this means in 1926, as also are boroughs and universities.

(2) By special statute. Parliament may create a particular corporation by passing a statute specifically designed for this purpose. For example, the Independent Broadcasting Authority was created by the

Television Act, 1954, and the National Coal Board was formed by the Coal Industry Nationalisation Act, 1946.

(3) By general Act of Parliament. Certain Acts of Parliament have laid down that groups of persons who comply with certain legal formalities set out in the Act may gain a corporate legal personality. For instance, the Companies Act, 1948, laid down the rules to be followed by any group who wished to form a trading company or other type of company.

Termination of a Corporation

(1) Where the corporation has been formed by Royal Charter it may be terminated by voluntary surrender of its charter to the Monarch or by forfeiture of the charter due to some default.

(2) By particular Act of Parliament, in the same way as it was created.

(3) Where there is a general statute, which lays down a way of creating certain types of corporations, the Act will also lay down the ways in which such corporations can be terminated. For example, the Companies Act, 1948, states that companies are dissolved by means of 'winding up' in such situations as where it is unable to pay its debts or where a court of law decides that it is 'just and equitable' that it should be wound up.

Unincorporated Associations

Some groups of individuals associate together for a common interest yet have not become incorporated, in which case they have no corporate entity or legal personality of their own. In the eyes of the law they are simply groups of separate individuals.

There is an enormous variety of unincorporated associations. They may be small, informal groups such as a nature club or a college debating society, or they may be larger associations such as cricket, croquet or social clubs. Business partnerships are also unincorporated associations, which are in some respects recognised by the law; for this reason they are dealt with in another chapter.

1. Explain the meaning of (a) legal personality and (b) corporate personality.
2. In what ways may a person become a British subject?
3. In what ways does the law treat minors differently from adults?
4. What is the difference between (a) a corporation sole and (b) a corporation aggregate?
5. What are the ways in which a corporation can come into existence?

7. Individual Freedoms under the Law

A. THE NATURE OF FUNDAMENTAL FREEDOMS

The Need for Restrictions and the Need for Freedoms

Man does not live by himself or for himself alone, but has always needed to associate and co-operate with his fellow-men. In order that he may exist peacefully among others in a community, he must accept many types of restrictions, either because he must respect the rights of other individuals or through the demands of society as a whole. He must, for example, abide by the traffic laws if he wishes to travel by car, and must participate in such schemes as compulsory education and welfare services. The State cannot allow him to withdraw from such schemes, because by doing so he would upset a necessary system that is established for the majority's benefit.

Absolute freedom for an individual, therefore, neither exists nor would it be practical, and the more complex a society becomes, the greater the inroads that are made into a citizen's rights by duties that are imposed upon him by social laws. However, it is not these social obligations, which are imposed upon the individual in his everyday routine, that are dealt with in this chapter. We are concerned here with freedoms that are far more fundamental to every individual's existence.

Although a certain amount of regulation of an individual's life for the benefit of others and society is reasonable and to be expected, man also has a strong instinct for individuality and self-assertion, and has always considered himself entitled to certain fundamental freedoms. In any community an individual expects to possess these freedoms, and not to be denied them by the authority of the State.

These freedoms, which are often referred to as liberties, human rights or the inalienable rights of man, relate to a wide range of activities. They secure for him such rights as his personal freedom to move about as he wishes, and his freedom of speech to communicate his news and express his ideas to others. They safeguard his right to worship under a religion of his own choice and his right to assemble and associate with others; he is also given the fundamental right to choose who shall govern him.

This chapter sets out to cover these basic rights of an individual and to explain how they are safeguarded against any wish or attempt of the State to deprive him of them.

The Guarantee of Freedom for the Individual

There has always been a struggle between authority with its maintenance of order within the State on the one side, and the respect that
should be shown for human feeling and liberty on the other. The
problem has been to keep the correct balance between the two, and to
prevent the possible tyranny of an authority that wishes, perhaps for
political reasons, to restrict such rights of the individual.

In most States the citizens are now assured of their fundamental
rights at a national level. Most States set out to guarantee such liberties
either by including them in a written constitution, which has become
the practice followed by the new States, or by protecting them through
ordinary legislation and case law which is known as the Rule of Law.
For example, in the United States of America the guarantees of human
rights form part of their written constitution, while in the United
Kingdom, which has no written constitution, individual freedom is
protected by the common law and Acts of Parliament.

Safeguard by Constitutional Guarantees

With many States it has been found that the most effective way to
protect the fundamental legal rights of the individual and to limit the
interference by governmental power is by guarantees expressed in their
written constitutions. Such constitutions are more rigid and less
susceptible to change than the ordinary laws of the State, because they
usually involve a more elaborate procedure for alteration. Therefore, by
uniting the fundamental freedoms of the individual with the constitutional document, the former are thought to be more secure.

The United States of America in 1791 added to their written
constitution the first ten amendments, known as the Bill of Rights.
These amendments are designed to make wholly secure such basic rights
of individual liberty as the free exercise of religion, which includes
complete separation of Church and State; freedom of speech and of the
Press; the right of peaceable assembly and association; the security of
the people in their homes, of their papers and other belongings against
unreasonable searches and seizures; no deprivation of life, liberty or
property without due process of law; the speedy and public trial of all
criminal prosecutions by an impartial jury; and the right of the accused
to be informed of the nature of the accusation against him and to be
confronted with the witnesses against him.

As a further example, these fundamental rights are well set out in
the first clause of the New Zealand Bill of Rights, as follows:

(1)   It is hereby recognised and declared that in New Zealand there
      exist and shall continue to exist, without discrimination by
      reason of race, national origin, colour, religion, opinion, belief,

or sex, the following fundamental human rights and freedoms, namely:

(*a*)   The right of the individual to life, liberty, and security of the person, and the right not to be deprived thereof except in accordance with law.

(*b*)   The right of the individual to equality before the law and the protection of the law.

(*c*)   The right of the individual to own property, and the right not to be deprived thereof except in accordance with law.

(*d*)   Freedom of thought, conscience and religion.

(*e*)   Freedom of peaceful assembly and association.

Protection under the Rule of Law

Because the United Kingdom is without a written constitution, there are no formal guarantees of individual liberty such as those laid down in the constitutional documents mentioned above. Instead, it is the supremacy of the Rule of Law that secures the rights of the individual.

The term 'Rule of Law' is used to describe the whole process of the English tradition of government according to the ordinary law of the land. This means according to the rules that have been laid down by Acts of Parliament (enacted by the usual procedure for statutes) as well as decisions given by the ordinary courts of law. Thus, officials of the State and the liberties of the individual are all established as part of the ordinary law. This means that they are outside the direct control of the State and are therefore not subject to arbitrary interferences by the State. Although it has been said that a written constitution is more rigid and less susceptible to change, it is basically no more than a legal document and it could be withdrawn or suspended in times of emergency, whereas if the rights of the individual and the functioning of the government are inherent and inseparable from the ordinary law of the land, neither can be taken away or drastically altered without changing the whole structure of the English way of life.

Professor Dicey in his book *Introduction to the Study of the Law of the Constitution* has used the expression 'Rule of Law' to describe three important elements that are fundamental to our constitution and to the security of individual freedoms.

1. That no individual can be punished unless he has committed an offence against the ordinary law of the land and has been tried before an ordinary court of law. In this sense the Rule of Law protects the individual from the arbitrary will of an authority that might impose laws upon an individual that are inconsistent with the laws of the land, and establish special courts for the

hearing of such offences.

2. That all persons are equal before the law. Not only shall no individual be above the law, but every man, whatever position he may hold within the State, is subject to the ordinary law and the courts of law. For example, all government officials or persons in authority in England may be brought before the law courts to answer for their actions; and such complaints may be brought by any private individual.

3. The constitution and the fundamental freedoms of the individual are based on the ordinary law of the land. They are not rules that have been especially enacted by special procedure, but rules derived in part from ordinary Acts of Parliament and in part from case law created by the courts of law. There is no formal code or Bill of Rights to safeguard individual liberties, as it is considered sufficient if each individual is allowed equal access to the courts of law and to the ordinary remedies of the civil and criminal law that are available.

The Universal Rule·of Law for the Protection of Human Rights

In recent times the term 'Rule of Law' has taken on a second meaning. It is wider than the meaning used by Dicey and refers to a concept which means more than just the supremacy of the ordinary law, at a national level, within the constitution of a State. The second meaning refers to the universal movement to secure for each individual in every State, whether based on a written constitution or otherwise, the basic rights and liberties which every individual should possess in a civilised society. Therefore, through this movement an attempt is being made to establish human rights by the supremacy of the Rule of Law on an international level which no State, by its own domestic laws, is entitled to deny to its subjects.

This concept of a universal Rule of Law is being attempted in a number of ways. For example, the United Nations Charter, in its Preamble, states that one of its aims is to 'reaffirm faith in fundamental human rights', and in 1948 the United Nations adopted a Universal Declaration of Human Rights and proclaimed the Declaration as 'a common standard of achievement for all peoples and all nations' and stated that 'every individual and every organ of society, keeping this Declaration constantly in mind, shall strive by teaching and education to promote respect for these rights and freedoms and by progressive measures, national and international, to secure their universal and effective recognition and observance'. The provisions of the Declaration have been applied constantly by the United Nations in practice and in their criticism of the States who violate its principles. For instance, in 1963 the Security Council requested South Africa to cease forthwith its policy of racial discrimination and repressive measures which were contrary to the purpose of the Charter of the United Nations and were in violation of the Universal Declaration of Human Rights.

The member States of the Council of Europe (which includes the United Kingdom), on the example set by the United Nations, passed in 1950 the European Convention on Human Rights, with one of their aims being 'the maintenance and further realisation of Human Rights and Fundamental Freedoms'. The European Court of Human Rights was established at Strasbourg with a jurisdiction to pronounce on any violation of human rights that takes place within a member State. In the last decade the Court has given many decisions in favour of individuals who have been denied their fundamental rights by a member State.

Thus, it is generally considered that in a relatively short time, since the end of the Second World War, the universal concern for human rights has become a part of a Rule of Law superior to any domestic law that a State itself may make to guarantee fundamental freedoms.

B. EXAMPLES OF FUNDAMENTAL FREEDOMS IN ENGLAND

As the fundamental freedoms in this country are considered to be inherent in the Rule of Law, there has never been a need for them to be set out formally. It is only the restrictions, which it has been necessary to make, that have been laid down by the law. Therefore, the examples of our liberties must be looked at from the restrictions that the law has placed upon them and from the aspect of what we cannot do, rather than from the aspect of what we are entitled to do.

I. Personal Liberty

Introduction

The general rule of law is that no person will be deprived of his liberty without his consent unless by the authority of a warrant of a court of law, or when a court has passed lawful sentence of imprisonment after his trial.

The main exception to this rule is that in some situations the law recognises that it may be impracticable to wait for a court order before detaining someone; so in such cases Acts of Parliament have given a power of arrest without warrant provided the person arrested is taken before a court at the first practical opportunity.

Therefore, it can be seen that one of the objects of an arrest is to deprive a person of his liberty in order to bring him before the court. Only in cases of serious emergency will parliament permit a person to be deprived of his liberty without his being allowed any access to a court, and even these rare occasions have been the subject of strong criticism. For instance, in order to maintain national peace the police or army are sometimes given powers to intern without trial persons suspected of being responsible for national unrest.

When any person has been wrongfully deprived of his liberty, whether by persons in authority or by another private individual, his remedies are with the ordinary courts of law. If the individual is seeking actual release, he, or any person on his behalf, may apply to the High Court for issue of a writ of habeas corpus ('you have the body'). This writ requires the imprisoner to bring his captive before the court immediately so that it can decide whether the imprisonment is lawful or whether the prisoner should be released. If the individual is only seeking compensation for having been unlawfully detained, he will bring a civil action under the tort of false imprisonment (see Chapter 9).

Arrest with a Warrant

A warrant is a direction of the court, issued by a Justice of the Peace, ordering the person named in the warrant to be arrested and brought before the court to answer the charges that are mentioned in the warrant.

The issue of a warrant will be made in such circumstances as where the individual has failed to answer a summons to attend the court, or where there was no power of the police to arrest him without a warrant but it is necessary to detain and bring the individual before the court rather than have the delay in issuing a summons. A summons is a document signed by a Justice of the Peace, requiring the person to whom it is addressed to appear at court at some time to answer the offences mentioned in the document.

A warrant is addressed to all constables and its execution takes place when the accused is found and arrested, then taken to a police station or before a court.

Arrest without a Warrant

A general power to arrest without a warrant is given to police officers and to private individuals by the Criminal Law Act, 1967, section 2(2)–(5).

2(2)   Any person may arrest without warrant anyone who is, or whom he, with reasonable cause, suspects to be, in the act of committing an arrestable offence.

(3)   Where an arrestable offence has been committed, any person may arrest without warrant anyone who is, or whom he, with

reasonable cause, suspects to be, guilty of the offence.

(4) Where a constable, with reasonable cause, suspects that an arrestable offence has been committed, he may arrest without warrant anyone whom he, with reasonable cause, suspects to be guilty of the offence.

(5) A constable may arrest without warrant any person who is, or whom he, with reasonable cause, suspects to be, about to commit an arrestable offence.

Arrestable offences are offences or attempts to commit offences for which the sentence is fixed by law or for which the maximum sentence on first conviction is five years or more.

It can be seen that the power to arrest is slightly less in the case of private individuals. They have no power under subsection (4) and (5). Before a private individual can make an arrest an offence must be taking place or have actually been committed.

Moreover, some statutes, such as the Sexual Offences Act, 1956, or the Customs and Excise Act, 1952, give a specific power of arrest without warrant for offences committed under the Act.

Duties of the Arrester

Where a police officer or private person makes an arrest, the general rule is that he must tell the person the *true* reason for his arrest. This will not be necessary if, for practical reasons, the task is impossible, for example where the suspected person is running away, or where the reason for the arrest is obvious as when the thief is caught 'red-handed'.

The prisoner must be taken either before a magistrate or a police officer as soon as practicable. For instance, in *John Lewis & Co. Ltd* v. *Tims*, Mrs Tims was arrested by a store detective immediately after she had left the store. She was told the reason for her detention and she was kept in the store while the managing director decided whether or not to prosecute and send for the police. She was found not guilty of theft and brought an action for false imprisonment, but the court held that the store detective had reasonable suspicion for arresting her, and that the police had been informed as soon as reasonably practicable.

The Judges' Rules

These are rules that have been laid down by judges of the Queen's Bench Division for the general guidance of police officers when dealing with a person who is being detained. The rules lay down the procedure that should be followed when cautioning him, the form which a written statement should take and the conditions under which the statements should be taken. For example, the rules state that a person, when arrested and when charged with an offence, should be cautioned in the following manner: 'Do you wish to say anything? You are not obliged to say anything unless you wish to do so, but whatever you say will be taken down in writing and may be given in evidence.' When an arrested or suspected person is being questioned, adequate breaks for rest and refreshments should be given. If the Judges' Rules are disobeyed it does not necessarily make the arrest unlawful, but a disregard of the rules may prevent any statements or conversation being admissible as evidence in court.

Bail

Once a person has been deprived of his liberty, a decision will have to be made as to whether or not it is necessary to keep him in detention. This decision may have to be taken at the police station or by the court, but in each case the primary concern is as to whether or not the prisoner will turn up at court on the appointed day if he is to be released on bail.

Bail means the security given by another person that the accused will attend at the court on the appointed day. When the accused is granted bail he is released from the detention of the police or the court and entrusted to the custody of persons known as sureties. The sureties promise to produce the accused before the court or otherwise forfeit the sum of money that has been specified. Before this, they must have satisfied the police officer or the court that they have sufficient means to pay the sums in which they are bound. As the surety is given the custody of the accused and has a duty to the court to produce him on the named day, he has the power to arrest the accused if he fears that he will fail to turn up.

Bail by Police

If an individual has been arrested without a warrant he may be released by the police on bail to appear before a Magistrates' Court on a certain day. If it is not possible for the police to bring the accused before the court within twenty-four hours, their duty to grant him bail is higher.

In cases where a person is arrested on the authority of a warrant, the warrant is often 'backed for bail'. This means it states that the accused must be given bail provided he is able to comply with the conditions specified in the warrant.

Bail by Magistrates

Magistrates have the power to grant bail and may do so, for example, where they are committing the accused for trial and there will be some wait before his trial is heard, or where they wish to adjourn the case until a future date.

The application for bail is made by the accused, and the police are asked if they have any objection. If the police have no objection the court may grant bail after it has considered such points as the following:

1. Has the accused previously been released on bail and failed to turn up?
2. Has the accused a permanent address and has his identification been confirmed?
3. Is the accused likely to commit an offence if he is released on bail?
4. Is it better for the public safety that he should not be given bail?
5. Is it better for the accused's own protection that he should not be granted bail?

When a Magistrates' Court has refused to grant the accused bail or has offered him bail on unreasonable terms, he has the right to apply to a High Court judge for bail.

II. Freedom of Association and Assembly

Whether to give stronger voice to his opinions, or for security and better conditions at work, or purely for social reasons, an individual is entitled to associate and join together with other individuals for their common benefit, provided that neither the purpose of the association nor the means it employs are in any way unlawful. The types of associations that individuals usually form, such as companies or partnerships, trade unions or social clubs, and their position and responsibilities under the law, are dealt with elsewhere.

Here, mention is going to be made of the individual's right that is closely connected with that of association, his right of assembly. According to the common law there is a freedom of assembly; that is, any number of persons may meet or assemble peacefully, provided that the object is lawful.

Public Meetings and Assemblies

The law does not give a right to hold a public meeting, nor does it prevent such means of free expression or demonstration of opinion. In general, the law remains neutral until the actual meeting or assembly is being held, and then it will intervene only if the gathering contravenes some aspect of the criminal law or behaves in some way which amounts to a civil wrong.

(a) Place of Meeting or Assembly

There is no place where an individual has a right to hold a public meeting. In the case of public buildings, parks or squares, permission always has to be granted, whether by a local authority or some other body who is responsible for their upkeep. Even in the case of Trafalgar Square and Speaker's Corner meetings are merely tolerated; there is no right to hold a meeting there. The only occasion on which there is a right to demand a place for a public meeting is during general election time when a candidate uses local authority premises for his election speeches, provided he pays a reasonable fee.

The law also states that the highway must be used solely for the purposes of passing and re-passing. No person has a right to stand still and make speeches or gather around a speaker. If he does, in theory he will be guilty of the civil wrong of trespass against the highway authority and probably the criminal offence of obstructing the highway. In practice, an action for trespass is rarely used, and the police will intervene from the criminal aspect only if there is substantial interruption of traffic or pedestrians or if the conduct of the assembly makes their meeting unlawful.

(b) The Meeting or Assembly Itself

If the public place where the meeting is being held has not met with objection, the conduct in which it is carried out or which it incites from the audience may make the gathering an unlawful meeting.

(1) Common law. Generally, the common law prohibits three types of unlawful meetings: unlawful assembly, rout, and, the most serious, riot. The difference between these crimes is the degree to which their conduct is likely to cause a breach of the peace and create anxiety to persons in the neighbourhood. Depending on the seriousness of the assembly, the police may take any action that is reasonably necessary to prevent a disturbance. They may only find it necessary to disperse the assembly, or they may have to arrest persons who refuse to go, but in every case it is the duty of the police to prevent all breaches of the peace, and they may call upon private persons to assist them.

Unlawful Assembly. The common law crime of unlawful assembly is where three or more persons gather together with intent either to commit a crime or to execute a common purpose, whether lawful or unlawful, in a manner likely to cause reasonable persons in the neighbourhood to fear an imminent breach of the peace. It is an offence to participate in an unlawful assembly. An assembly, which is lawful to begin with, might become unlawful if it later embarks upon a course of conduct likely to result in a breach of the peace. However, an assembly will not be unlawful merely because it provokes other people or a rival meeting to act unlawfully or cause a breach of the peace. In *Beatty* v. *Gillbanks* the Salvation Army assembled for a lawful purpose and marched through Weston-super-Mare. They were violently interrupted on several occasions by the Skeleton Army, who were a rival organisation. The police, in order to prevent future breaches of the peace, reported the Salvationists for unlawful assembly. The magistrates bound them over to keep the peace, and they appealed. The Queen's Bench Division held that the Salvationists were not guilty of unlawful assembly as the interference and the likelihood of disturbance had been caused not by them but solely by their opponents.

Rout and Riot. The common law offence of rout is a disturbance of the peace by three or more persons who are assembled together to do an unlawful act and who take steps towards carrying it out. This offence is the preliminary step before a riot. A common law riot or riotous assembly consists of three or more persons who assemble together, without lawful authority, with an intent mutually to assist one another, by force if necessary, against anyone opposing them in the carrying out of their common purpose, and who in fact carry out that purpose in such a manner as to alarm at least one person of reasonable firmness and courage. The court held in *Ford* v. *Receiver of Metropolitan Police* that all the elements of a common law riot were present. On Peace Night 1919 an over-zealous crowd engaged in celebrations had lit a bonfire. To acquire more fuel they broke into an empty house and stripped the woodwork, and in doing this they caused the next-door neighbour such alarm that he dared not stop them through fear of being killed.

(2) Statutory restrictions. As well as the common law offences of unlawful assembly, rout and riot, the freedom of assembly has also been restricted by a number of statutes in the interests of law and order. Thus, the Riot Act, 1714, provides for the dispersal of riotous assemblies consisting of twelve or more persons and for the punishment of those detained after 'the reading of the Riot Act'. The Seditious Meetings Act, 1817, makes unlawful any assembly of more than fifty persons within one mile from Westminster Hall for the purpose of petitioning during the sitting of parliament. The final example is the Unlawful Drilling Act, 1819, which forbids all meetings and assemblies for the purpose of training or drilling in the use of arms or of practising military exercises, unless under lawful authority.

Apart from the above crimes that may arise from the conduct of an assembly of people, there are other offences designed to regulate individual conduct at public meetings. Under the Public Meeting Act, 1908, it is an offence for anyone to act in a disorderly manner or incite other persons to act in that way at any lawful public meeting with the intention of preventing the transaction of the business of the meeting. The freedom to hold a peaceful assembly is further reinforced by the Public Order Act, 1936, which states that it is an offence to indulge in any offensive conduct such as using threatening, abusive or insulting words or behaviour at any lawful public meeting with the object of provoking a breach of the peace.

Public Processions

Generally, in the case of public assemblies there is no power to prohibit them in advance of their taking place, but only a power to stop them once they have begun and are in some way unlawful. However, with public processions there is power given under the Public Order Act, 1936, to prohibit processions and marches even before they take place. A chief officer of police with the consent of the local authority may ban any class of public procession for a period not exceeding three months. If such a drastic measure is considered unnecessary, the police, nevertheless, have power to impose conditions on the holding of the procession, such as the restricting of the display of flags, banners or emblems, and may regulate the route it must follow or re-route it for the preservation of public order.

III. Freedom of Speech or Expression

The freedom of speech or expression is the right to express views and to communicate ideas and opinions to others. However, as with other freedoms, the individual's right to say what he likes or write exactly what he feels is not an absolute right; it is subject to legal restrictions imposed by the criminal and civil law.

As will be seen by the restrictions to follow, what amounts to a denial of the freedom of speech may depend not only on what the individual says, but where he says it or the type of employment he has. For instance, a person may be guilty of defamation or even criminal libel if he says something among his friends, but the law may allow him to make the same remark in a court of law or, if he is an M.P., under the privilege of parliament. Also, where it may be perfectly natural and legal for an individual to talk freely about his work, if he happens to be employed by the government or within the police service he is bound, in certain aspects of his work, by the Official Secrets Acts.

The types of restriction that the law places on the freedom of speech take two forms. Firstly, in some cases the law considers that certain statements should never be made and some views never expressed; this kind of prohibition is called 'censorship'. Secondly, the law will allow an individual to state his mind or express his views provided that in doing so he does not offend another person. For example, the Official Secrets Acts actually censor some persons talking about certain matters, but the tort of defamation does not censor remarks that an individual is going to make; it only requires him to pay compensation to any person who is injured by the remark he actually does make.

Civil Law Restrictions
The main restriction which the civil law imposes on the freedom of speech is the tort of defamation. This is designed to prevent one individual damaging another's reputation by telling lies about him to others. The defamatory remark takes the form of slander or libel. The former is when the remark is made by speech or gesture, and the latter is when the statement is in some more permanent form, such as writing, a film or tape-recording. As defamation is a tort which has to be studied in greater detail, it will be dealt with separately in a later chapter. However, as libel may be a crime as well as a tort, the criminal aspect of libel will be mentioned below.

Criminal Law Restrictions
Criminal Libel
The purpose of libel as a tort is to protect an individual's reputation, whereas the criminal libel is intended to prevent statements being made about another person which are likely to lead to a breach of the peace. This difference between the two forms of libel can be seen from the fact that a person may be guilty of a criminal libel even if his statement is true, provided it is likely to lead to a disturbance, whereas in the tort of libel it is a complete defence to prove that the statement is true. Furthermore, the tort of libel requires that the defendant's statement must have been communicated to a third person, but the crime of libel is complete even if the statement is made only to the person concerned without a third person hearing of it.

Sedition
Although every individual is allowed to discuss all matters of public concern quite freely and air publicly any grievance he might have, he must not do this in such a way as to incite a revolt among Her Majesty's subjects.

The crime of sedition forbids an individual to say or write anything, whether true or false, which is intended to disturb the peace of the State by creating ill-will towards the Monarch, parliament or any of the established institutions, such as the courts of law.

Official Secrets Acts, 1911–1939
The Official Secrets Acts affect any person who holds a public office, such as Ministers, civil servants, members of the armed forces or the police. The Acts are designed to prohibit the passing-on or disclosing of any information which has been entrusted to them in confidence during the course of their work.

This information may be of national importance, in which case a disclosure might prejudice the safety of the State, or it may simply be the kind of information ordinarily given in confidence to any civil servant. Thus, the Acts cover a variety of situations, from espionage to the unauthorised disclosure of the contents of an income-tax form.

The government therefore requires all civil servants to sign a document saying that they will not disclose any information acquired in the course of their work. In this way the government exercises wide powers of censorship over its work and activities. However, there is a check on the abuse of this censorship in that the consent of the Attorney-General is necessary before any prosecution can be brought under the Acts.

Obscenity and Horror

The State has restricted the freedom of speech not only by making laws for its own protection, in such cases as the Official Secrets Acts and sedition, but also by legislating to prevent harm to its citizens. Two instances of this are the Obscene Publications Acts, 1959 and 1964, and the Children and Young Persons (Harmful Publications) Act, 1955.

The Obscene Publications Acts have made it a crime for an individual to publish an obscene writing, film, picture or tape-recording whether or not it is done for profit. The test that the courts must apply in order to discover whether an article is obscene is to find out if the article, taken as a whole, tends to deprave and corrupt persons to whom it is communicated or made accessible.

This censorship of obscene matter, and the power given under the Acts for magistrates to order the destruction of any such matter, is only intended to prevent the harm that can be caused by allowing obscenity for obscenity's sake. It is not intended to, although unwittingly it may, censor matter that is in the interests of science, literature, art or in some other way for the public good.

The Children and Young Persons (Harmful Publications) Act, 1955, sets out to censor the publication and circulation of horror comics. These are stories told mainly in pictures which show acts of violence, cruelty, the commission of crimes, or portray incidents of a repulsive and horrible nature in such a way that they are likely to corrupt their young readers.

Theatre Censorship

By the Theatres Act, 1968, the censorship of plays performed on the stage has been abolished.

Before the 1968 Act the main censor of stage plays was the Lord Chamberlain, who often restricted productions which included reference to the Royal Family, public figures and religious themes. Also, there was a form of censorship exercised by local authorities, who would refuse to grant theatre licences unless their conditions as to the type of play to be performed were complied with. Now, since the Act, both forms of censorship no longer exist.

However, the 1968 Act makes it a criminal offence to present an obscene play in public or in private. An obscene play is one which tends to deprave and corrupt any individual who is likely to attend the performance, and prosecution is at the discretion of the Attorney-General. There is a defence to this charge of obscenity if the producers or directors can prove that the performance is for the public good: for example, that it is of dramatic or literary worth.

Cinema Censorship
There is no official or State censorship of films. The censorship and classification of films that does take place is carried out by the local authorities and the British Board of Film Censors.

Under the Cinematograph Acts, 1909 and 1952, premises for the showing of films must be licensed by the local licensing authority. These authorities are usually the county or county borough council, and frequently the power to license is delegated to the local Justices of the Peace. By this power to grant and withdraw licences the local authorities exercise a control over all films that are intended to be released for showing in their area.

In deciding whether a film is suitable for release the local authorities usually, though they are not obliged to, rely on the judgment and classification of the British Board of Film Censors. This Board, which is voluntary and unofficial, was set up by the film industry in 1912 with one of its aims being to ensure a uniform standard of censorship on a national scale. Each film is seen by two or more members of the Board, who are not connected with the film industry. Their job entails seeing whether the film is suitable for public release and classifying and granting a certificate to the film. The film passed by the Board receives one of four classifications:

'U' Certificate:	suitable for any person not less than five years old.
'A' Certificate:	suitable for any person over five years old, but containing some material that some parents might prefer their children not to see.
'AA' Certificate:	suitable for persons over fourteen years of age.
'X' Certificate:	suitable for persons over eighteen years of age.

Broadcasting
The authority to broadcast is granted by licence issued by the Minister

of Posts and Telecommunications.

Radio broadcasting services for Britain and overseas are provided by the licence granted to the British Broadcasting Corporation (B.B.C.). Television services are provided under licence granted to the B.B.C. and to the Independent Broadcasting Authority (I.B.A.).

The B.B.C. is a corporate body created by Royal Charter. The governors are appointed by the Crown on the advice of the Prime Minister. The I.B.A. (formerly I.T.A.) is a corporation which was set up by the Television Act, 1954, and its chairman and members are appointed by the Minister of Posts and Telecommunications.

The B.B.C. and the I.B.A. are required to provide a 'public service' and are independent authorities in the day-to-day operation of broadcasting, including the programmes and administration. The government, however, retains ultimate control through the Minister of Posts and Telecommunications who has the power to withdraw their licences. The Minister is answerable to parliament for general questions of policy, and he may issue directions to the B.B.C. and the I.B.A. on a number of subjects.

Both organisations are expected to show balance and due impartiality in their general presentation of programmes, particularly where matters of public policy or controversial subjects are concerned. As far as possible, they must ensure that a programme neither offends against good taste and decency, nor encourages crime. Although most censorship of the B.B.C. and the I.B.A. is internal self-censorship, there is a final power of censorship in the Minister who has the authority to prohibit the broadcasting of any particular matter.

The Press

It is important that there should be a free and responsible Press with journalists who accept that both the liberty of the subject and the security of the State have to be protected. If the Press lost sight of either of these interests, their work would become biased and any standard of the truth would be lost. A Press that relied wholly on information given to it by the government, without making independent inquiry, would lead to totalitarianism; a Press that considered only the interests of the individual, to the extreme, would work to the detriment of the good and safe government of the country.

As a general rule, the law does not interfere directly with the problem of balancing, on the one side, the need for the freedom of the Press to publish what it regards as being in the public interest against, on the other side, the occasional higher interest of restricting publication for the security of the State.

The Press and the Law

Basically, the Press has the same freedom of speech and expression as the individual. This is to say and communicate what it likes and express whatever opinions it has, provided the criminal or civil law is not broken. There is no specific law for the Press, and it will be liable for publishing anything which is libellous, seditious or which offends the Official Secrets Acts, in the same way as any individual would be.

There have, naturally, been a few areas where the law has had to make special provision for the Press. For example, the Criminal Justice Act, 1967, for the benefit of the accused and a fair trial, severely restricts the right of the Press (as well as radio and television) to report on any criminal proceedings which take place before the actual trial of the accused. At committal proceedings in a Magistrates' Court the report may contain only the name of the accused, the offences with which he is being charged and other minor matters. Furthermore, the Press may report on certain matters such as parliamentary proceedings and court trials and, provided it gives a true and accurate account of such matters, it has the defence of privilege under the tort of defamation. As regards printing matter that might be defamatory of an individual, it has the defence of unintentional defamation.

The Services, Press and Broadcasting Committee

There is no overall governmental or legal censorship of what the Press may wish to publish and, unlike the broadcasting authorities, the Press is not legally bound to be politically impartial. However, agreement has been reached between the Press and the government that the former will not publish matters that genuinely affect national security. This censorship in the interests of the general public is achieved through the Services, Press and Broadcasting Committee. This committee consists of representatives of the government, the Press and the broadcasting services. Any matter that the committee considers unsuitable for publication is issued with a 'D' notice, which prevents the information from being released to the public. If certain information has not been protected by a 'D' notice and the Press is still doubtful as to whether its reporting would be in breach of the Official Secrets Acts, it will ask the advice of the committee before publication. If the Press publishes matter which is covered by a 'D' notice, the remedy of the government, or the individual affected by the publication, is by bringing a prosecution in the ordinary courts of law.

The Press Council

The General Council of the Press, originally set up in 1953 and reconstituted in 1963, consists of members of the Press, independent persons and a lay chairman (who is usually a judge). Among its functions are the regulation of the ethics within the profession itself, the giving of advice concerning the general standard of information that should be printed, and the suggesting of means by which the Press should gather its information. In this way the Press Council exercises a certain amount of censorship within the profession. The Council issues annual reports which are available to the public, and it also possesses a means for considering any complaints that may be made by the general public.

IV. Freedom of Worship

'That religion, or the duty which we owe to our creator, and the manner of discharging it, can be directed only by reason and conviction, not by force or violence, and therefore all men are equally entitled to the free exercise of religion, according to the dictates of conscience . . . ' (United States Declaration of Rights, Virginia, 1776).

In Britain today an individual has the freedom to follow any religion or to worship any god he chooses. He may express his faith openly and propagate his beliefs in speech and in writing without any fear of interference from the law.

As a general rule the law does not discriminate against an individual because of his religious beliefs. His religion should be of no hindrance in his obtaining work, a house or a spouse (provided it is only one spouse).

Although the law exercises religious toleration, the Monarch must still, for historical reasons, be a member of the Church of England and must promise on accession to uphold this established religion of the State.

V. The Right to Vote

The idea of democracy is government by the people. As in practice it would be impossible for every individual to take a direct part in governing, each individual has a right to participate indirectly by voting for a person to represent him in parliament.

Any British subject, eighteen years old or over, is eligible to vote in the constituency where he resides, provided he is recorded on the register of electors.

Each elector has one vote which must normally be cast at the polling station on the day set aside for the election. However, members of the armed forces, Crown servants of the United Kingdom and various other employees and their families at the time resident overseas may vote by proxy.

The Representation of the People Acts, 1949 to 1969, state that the following persons are not permitted to vote: aliens, minors, peers, persons serving a long prison sentence and persons who have been found guilty of corrupt practice at elections.

1. Do you consider that each individual should have an absolute freedom to do and say what he likes, or do you think that it is necessary to have certain restrictions on the complete freedom of the individual?

2. Do you consider that the protection of individual rights in Britain is helped or hindered by the constitution being unwritten?

3. How does the British constitution safeguard the liberties of the individual compared with the constitution of the United States of America?

4. How far is the freedom of speech restricted by the laws involving (a) cinema censorship (b) official secrets and (c) theatre censorship?

5. What is meant by the expression 'The Rule of Law' within the British constitution?

6. To what extent is the law concerned with the freedom of the Press?

7. Explain the general view of the law with regard to (a) the freedom from arrest and (b) the freedom of worship.

8. (a) What legal redress is available to a person who has been wrongfully deprived of his freedom of movement?

    (b) In what circumstances may a person who has been arrested be released on bail? What redress has he got if his application for bail is refused?

9. A local organisation for the expansion of motorways has decided to hold a meeting in its town. The organisation is hated by the majority of townsfolk. The organisation advertise that the gathering will be (a) in a private house (b) in the town square and (c) by way of a procession through the streets. Explain what powers the police have to prevent such gatherings of the organisation.

10. What are the ways, under U.K. law, for establishing something as a 'freedom'?

11. Do you consider there are any areas where there are needs that should be recognised as fundamental freedoms but which at present are not so recognised?

Write short notes on the following:
(1) the meaning of 'Human Rights'
(2) arrest with and without warrant
(3) the importance of the Judges' Rules
(4) the writ of habeas corpus
(5) the Services, Press and Broadcasting Committee.

Explain the following crimes in relation to the freedoms of the individual:
(1) unlawful assembly
(2) common law riot
(3) sedition
(4) publishing obscene matter
(5) criminal libel.

PART TWO

PART TWO

8. The Nature of Torts

The Reason for the Law of Torts

'Tort' is the French word for 'wrong', and in English law it is used to cover certain kinds of civil wrongs and the rules which prohibit them.

The law of torts is designed to protect the interests of the individual from the wrongful acts of other individuals. It does this by requiring that the wrongdoer shall pay compensation for the injury he has caused. For example, the law of torts considers that an individual has an interest in keeping his good reputation, so if some person harms it, the individual is entitled to bring an action for compensation under the specific tort of defamation.

The more complex a society becomes, the more varied and numerous become the interests of the individual; correspondingly, the more individual interests there are that could be injured by the wrongful behaviour of others. Therefore, the law of torts is a branch of civil law that is for ever extending its horizons in order to cover new situations where an individual considers he should be protected from the wrongful or socially unreasonable behaviour of another individual.

The following are examples of the types of interest the law of torts protects, some of which will be described in detail in the following chapters.

Examples of Interests Protected by Torts

Interests in Body and Mind

The primary interest of any individual is the protection of himself. From a very early time this was recognised under the tort of trespass to the person, which made it tortious to interfere directly with an individual's interest in personal safety and freedom of movement. Trespass was, and still is, concerned only with *physical* harm. However, probably because of the sophistication of society, it has been clearly established by the courts in the last ninety years that it also constitutes a tort intentionally to inflict *mental* injury upon a person, even though it does not come within the tort of trespass. For example, in *Wilkinson* v. *Downton* the defendant, as a practical joke, falsely told the plaintiff that her husband had met with a serious accident and had broken both his legs. The plaintiff believed him, and as a result was so violently shocked that she suffered a nervous illness for some weeks. The court held that as a result of his wrongful behaviour the defendant was liable to pay her compensation. The creation of this new branch of wrongful behaviour under the law of torts is understandable when a society is so preoccupied with mental health and nervous disorders.

Interests in Reputation

The individual also has an interest in what other people think of him, and he therefore has a corresponding right not to have others wrongfully say or write lies about him. This right is protected by the tort of defamation, which entitles a person to his true reputation in the eyes of his fellow-men. The law will not protect a false reputation, so it will not amount to defamation to tell the truth about another person even if it is unpleasant.

Material Interests

An individual's various interests in 'things' are as much protected as his interest in himself. For instance, with regard to his goods or chattels, under the tort of conversion a person has a right not to have his ownership or title to goods denied him, and under the tort of trespass he has a right not to have his possession of goods interfered with. Furthermore, in the case of his land, the individual has many interests. For example, the tort of nuisance protects a person's interest in using and enjoying his land, and the tort of trespass will protect him from unwelcome trespassers.

Business, Commercial and Economic Interests

There are some torts, which have been firmly established in the last one hundred years, that make it wrongful for a person to damage an individual's commercial interests or his right to carry on his trade. Although these torts are not within the scope of this book, they are worthy of a brief mention. For instance, it is a specific tort wrongfully to interfere with someone else's contract, especially in a contract of employment, by inducing employees to leave their present employment by breaking their contracts. It amounts to the tort of passing-off for a trader to represent or pass off his goods as being those of someone else. Also, in some situations it will be tortious for one person to cause another person financial loss by a careless statement. For example, Mr A gives advice about investments in his professional capacity. When Mr B asks him about investing in C Co., Mr A must take care not to give negligent advice. If he does not take such care and Mr B acts on this wrong advice and invests in C Co., Mr A will be liable if Mr B loses all his investments, because of his negligent misstatement.

Fault

The normal rule is that the defendant, before he is liable under a tort and has to pay compensation for the damage he has caused to the plaintiff's interest, must have acted in some blameworthy manner. This is usually referred to as being at 'fault'.

Intention and Negligence

The defendant may be at fault because he has committed the tort 'intentionally', which means that he did the act deliberately and was fully aware of what the consequences would be. However, the kind of fault that most commonly leads to liability in tort is 'negligent' behaviour. This is where the defendant did not intentionally cause the injury, but instead had not used reasonable care and foresight in the way he had behaved; if he had done so he could have avoided damaging the plaintiff's interest.

For example, an individual might intentionally wish to set fire to a haystack, in which case he would light a match and put it to the hay with the intention that it should burn. On the other hand, a camper might light his pipe and discard the lighted match in such a way that it sets fire to the haystack. In the latter situation his mental attitude will be one of carelessness or negligence.

Strict Liability

Although they form no part of this book, there are some torts where the defendant will be liable for his own conduct even though he is not at 'fault'. In other words, there are some situations where the defendant will be responsible to pay the plaintiff compensation even though he has not intentionally or negligently done anything wrong. These torts are called torts of strict liability and usually concern dangerous activities, such as the manufacture or handling of dangerous substances, the keeping of dangerous animals or the accumulating of anything, such as large quantities of water, on land which, if it escapes from the land, is likely to cause damage.

Vicarious Liability

A further example of liability without 'fault' is where an individual is liable for acts that are not his own. The law lays down that, in certain situations, one individual will be liable for the torts committed by another person, even though the individual himself has not done anything wrong. This situation, which is known as vicarious liability, exists in certain special relationships. One example is that a master is vicariously liable for the torts which his servant commits while carrying out his master's work. The topic of vicarious liability is dealt with in greater detail in Chapter 16.

Insurance

Owing to the widening of the scope of insurance during the past century, it is not always the person who is at 'fault' who has to pay the compensation. In some situations the person who has committed the tort may be insured against causing such damage to the plaintiff. For instance, every person who uses a motor vehicle on a road is required to take out a policy of insurance. This insurance is to indemnify him in respect of certain liabilities that might arise out of his use of the vehicle. Therefore, if a driver drives so negligently that he injures a pedestrian or another motorist, the plaintiff may bring an action for compensation directly against the insurance company as well as the driver.

Remedies Available for Torts

The law of torts is designed to protect the interests of the individual, rather than the public, and its aim is to compensate him for the loss he has suffered. Therefore, the individual's main remedy is to bring an action for *damages* against the person who has wronged him. An action for damages is a claim for financial compensation to be awarded by the court.

In some cases the courts have allowed the plaintiff to protect his own interest by what is called *self-help*. In other words, he is entitled to remedy the wrong himself: for example, by ejecting a trespasser from his land or by abating a nuisance.

There are other cases where the plaintiff will not only require compensation but will ask the court to put a stop to the defendant's behaviour. This the court may do by issuing an *injunction*: for example, by ordering the defendant to stop causing a nuisance.

All these remedies are dealt with in greater detail under the specific torts to be covered later.

Defences to Torts

Some defences are restricted to particular torts; for instance, the defence of fair comment is peculiar to the tort of defamation, and the defence of lawful correction is a defence restricted to trespass to the person. These specific defences, and others, will be mentioned when covering the particular tort in question.

There are, however, certain defences that are generally applicable to all torts. These include consent, statutory authority, necessity and inevitable accident. These general defences, like specific defences, will be explained later in the context of the particular tort discussed.

Torts Distinguished from Other Branches of Law
Tort and Contract

The law of torts is designed to protect certain interests of individuals from various kinds of harm. These protected interests and the obligations not to violate them are laid down by the law. The obligations imposed by the law of torts are binding by law upon every individual for the benefit of every other individual.

The law of contract is designed to protect agreements that individuals make with each other. In a contract the interests that are protected and the corresponding obligations exist only because the parties who make the contract consent to them. Obligations in contract are not imposed by the law, they are imposed by agreement between the parties. Contractual obligations are only enforced by the law.

For example, an individual undertakes to build a house for another person in return for payment. If he fails to build it he will be liable to pay compensation for his breach of contract. He will be liable, not because the law imposes an obligation upon everybody to build houses for others, but because he agreed to build the house for the other person in the first place. On the other hand, if an individual, while driving his car negligently, runs somebody down, he will be liable to pay his victim compensation. This is not because of any contractual agreement the driver had made with his victim not to run over him, but because the law imposes upon all persons an obligation in tort not to cause such injury. (This act of negligent driving will, no doubt, also amount to a criminal offence. This is because the State also wishes to prevent such types of behaviour on behalf of the community as a whole.)

Tort and Crime

A tort is a civil wrong and is not, therefore, the same as a crime, although the two have various points in common. For instance, they both differ from contract law in that their obligations are imposed by law rather than by agreement.

However, the difference between the two lies in the interests they are designed to protect. A crime is an offence against the public as a whole for which the State, on the public's behalf, will prosecute the offender. This criminal prosecution is primarily concerned with punishing the offender and not with compensating the individual for his injuries. The civil action of tort, however, is commenced by the injured person himself with the object of receiving compensation for the damage incurred.

As tort and crime are completely different branches of law yet may arise from the same event, as in the example of negligent driving mentioned above, it is possible for two separate court cases to arise from one set of circumstances. In order to eliminate the need for many facts to be proved on two separate occasions, the Civil Evidence Act, 1968, has stated that a conviction that has been obtained in the criminal court may be used as evidence in any civil proceedings that might eventually be taken over the same matter.

The aim of punishing the offender is the object of the criminal law and it usually does not enter into the law of tort. However, damages may be awarded as a punishment for a tort if the behaviour of the defendant was outrageous or malicious. Such damages are called *exemplary* or *punitive* damages, and are given to the plaintiff over and above the compensation for the actual loss he has suffered. For example in *Cassell* v. *Broome*, Mr A wrote a book about one of the great naval disasters of the Second World War, entitled *The Destruction of Convoy P.Q.17*. The book placed the blame for this disaster on Broome, who was the officer commanding the escort ships at the time of the disaster. In writing the book Mr A knew fully what he was doing and persisted with it in spite of repeated warnings from authoritative sources that passages in the book were defamatory of Broome. The first publishers whom Mr A approached refused to publish the book because they had been advised that it 'reeks of defamation'. Mr A then offered the book to Cassells who agreed to publish it. The original publishers warned Cassells of its libellous contents and so did Broome. Nevertheless, Cassells published the book and Broome then brought an action for the tort of defamation. He was successful. The jury awarded Broome £15,000 compensatory damages and £25,000 punitive damages. The House of Lords upheld the award of these damages and said that damages by way of punishment of the defendant in excess of those necessary to compensate the plaintiff for the injury done to him might be awarded to a plaintiff in the case of certain torts, and defamation was one of them.

1.   Study the influence of insurance on the law of tort. In doing this you should refer to Law Reports, Reports from Tribunals and Arbitration, statements from Law Reform Agencies, and other textbooks.
2.   Read generally the Occupiers' Liability Act, 1957, either from a textbook or H.M.S.O. Then set out what is meant by 'Common Duty of Care'. State to whom this duty is owed. Note the situations that are covered by the Act.

9. The Tort of Trespass

The Semi-Criminal Nature of Trespass
The object of the criminal law is to preserve the peace of the community, and this is achieved by an efficient police force. In the Middle Ages the policing system was not so strong as it is today and much peace enforcement was left in the hands of the individual. In the cases of minor, yet obvious, wrongs involving a breach of the King's peace, it was left to the victim, as a substitute for private vengeance, to bring his own culprit before the court. This the victim would do under an action of trespass.

Once the wrongdoer had been brought before the King's court and found guilty, he would be punished under the sanctions of the criminal law by fine or imprisonment. Only as an afterthought and incidentally to these criminal proceedings was compensation for his injuries awarded to the injured person. At a much later date the close association between the law of crime and the tort of trespass was broken, though by this date the semi-criminal character of trespass had become firmly established.

Injury Must be Direct
Trespass is the remedy for *direct* and immediate injury to an individual, whether caused to his body, his goods or his land: in short, against the type of conduct which was, in the Middle Ages, most likely to lead to a breach of the peace by provoking retaliation. If the injury is indirect, and only consequential, the injured person has no remedy in trespass, because in those days it was considered that it was an act's directness that was likely to lead to retaliation.

Damage Need not be Proved
Trespass is one of the torts that is said to be actionable *per se* ('in itself'), which means that the person injured by a trespass need not prove that he has suffered material damage. The explanation for this is probably to be found in its criminal flavour, in the fact that conduct of a direct forcible nature was so likely to arouse violent resentment that it was wise to provide a remedy in the interests of the King's peace, even though the outraged victim could not prove actual damage. Thus trespass is still today one of the few torts that are exceptions to the fundamental rule of civil actions that damage must be proved before compensation can be awarded.

The Mental Element in Trespass

The early concept was that a wrongdoer would be guilty of trespass merely by his doing the wrongful act, irrespective of his state of mind: for instance, whether he acted intentionally, negligently or purely by accident. Nowadays the state of the wrongdoer's mind is important. Since the development of the separate tort of negligence, most cases of unintentional conduct are now brought under this more recent tort. Therefore, trespass, in practice, is usually reserved only for situations where the wrongdoer has *intentionally* caused direct interference with an individual's interest in bodily safety or the security of his goods or land. Depending on which of these interests has been violated, he will bring an action for trespass under one of its divisions, trespass to the person, to goods or to land.

A. TRESPASS TO THE PERSON

1. General

The first concern an individual has is for his own personal safety. If some person has violated this interest without justification, the individual will be able to bring an action for trespass to the person. This branch of trespass has laid down that a person's right to bodily safety can be violated in one or more of three ways: firstly, by his being threatened or menaced in such a way that he fears he will be physically injured; secondly, by his actually suffering some bodily harm; and lastly, by having his right to freedom of movement restricted. These three interests are protected by actions for assault, battery and false imprisonment, respectively.

Assault and battery are crimes as well as torts, and because of some criminal statutes that have been loosely worded, in popular language assault and battery are often treated as synonymous under the general word 'assault'. Yet in their strict legal sense they are separate wrongs, standing for two quite distinct types of behaviour. Shooting a man is different from only threatening to shoot him, and therefore the law recognises a difference between physical contact, which is a battery, and the mere apprehension of it, which is an assault.

In some situations a person may be guilty of both assault and battery in quick succession: for instance, where a man threatens another with a stick and then strikes him. If, however, the person was struck from behind without warning there would only be a battery, and no assault. It is because these branches of trespass to the person can exist separately that they must be given separate consideration.

2. Assault
An assault is a threat by one individual to inflict unlawful force upon another.

Must be Fear of Battery
The essence of this tort is the effect the *threat* creates upon the mind of the victim. This effect must be the *fear* or apprehension of an *immediate* battery. If this is present, the tort is complete. Naturally, it is possible for the threatener to create a fear of bodily harm in a person even when he does not intend to carry out his threat or has not the ability to do so. For instance, a man may point a gun at someone not intending to shoot or knowing that it is unloaded, but the person he threatens may still have the *fear* of being shot—in which case there is an assault.

Injury Feared Need not be Serious
As will be seen later, the contact necessary for a battery may be either heavy or light. Therefore, in an assault the anticipated contact need not amount to a threat of grievous harm. It may be an assault to threaten to touch, to throw water on or set a dog upon someone, just as much as it may to brandish an axe or mallet menacingly.

Fear Must be Reasonable
So, the tort of assault is designed to cover situations where, metaphorically speaking, a dog's bark can be as bad as his bite, provided the threatened person can *reasonably* expect to be bitten. If it is not reasonable to expect a battery, then there is no assault. This would be the case where one person in a passing train shakes his fist at a motorist who is stationary at a level crossing, or where someone is threatened by a gun he knows for certain is a toy. In each case the person threatened should know that the threatener has not the present ability to put his threat into practice.

3. Battery
A battery is the application of force to the person of another without his consent.

Degree of Force Necessary
Battery takes place when there is an *actual application* of force to another individual. The force must result in some *direct* contact with the body, whether it is by the landing of a missile or of a punch. The degree of force used, and the insult that may accompany it, may make a difference to the damage that the individual suffers, and this will affect the amount awarded in compensation. But provided there is

bodily contact, whether the force be great or ever so small, there will still be a battery, because the civil law does not set down degrees of violating the sanctity of the person.

Thus, it has been held by the courts that it would be as much a battery to cause insult by an undesired kiss or the wrongful taking of fingerprints as it is to cause serious hurt by a vicious blow or to sterilise a person without their consent. In *Nash* v. *Sheen* a hairdresser was found guilty of battery for applying a tone-rinse when the client asked only for a permanent wave. Other examples that have been sufficient violation for a battery are the spitting in a man's face, the cutting of his hair, and the firing of a pistol so close to him that he is burnt.

Presumed Consent to a Battery
Battery, therefore, protects the individual from any force involving physical contact. Whether 'a coward does it with a kiss, the brave man with a sword', such force need not be applied in anger or hostility provided the individual can prove something over and above the force that is received during the hazards of everyday life. For the courts have held that everyone is expected to tolerate a reasonable, even if unwelcomed, amount of physical contact from such persons as the rush-hour hustler, the jovial backslapper or the over-enthusiastic handshaker.

4. False Imprisonment
It is false imprisonment to impose direct physical restraint upon an individual without justification.

Meaning of Imprisonment
Trespass to the person protects an individual not only from the threat and menaces of injury and uninvited physical contact, but also from being wrongfully deprived of his freedom to move about as he wishes. Imprisonment need not be incarceration in a dungeon; it is sufficient if the plaintiff has been in any manner completely and wrongfully deprived of his personal liberty: for example, where a person, without his consent, is kept in an office lift, or prevented from leaving his house, his car or even a ski-lift.

Total Restraint
This bodily restraint must be total. If it is incomplete, as would be the case where the off-side door of the car is locked but the passenger door is left unlocked, there would be no false imprisonment, provided it would be reasonable to expect the person to try the other door. In *Bird* v. *Jones* the defendants fenced off part of the public footway on Hammersmith Bridge, put seats in the enclosure for the use of

spectators to a regatta on the river and charged for admission. The plaintiff insisted on passing along that part of the footway and climbed over the fence without paying the fee. The defendants refused to let him carry on, but told him he might go back and cross by the other side of the bridge. He declined to do so and remained in the enclosure for about half an hour. The defendants were found not guilty of false imprisonment because the plaintiff was not totally deprived of his freedom of movement. He could turn back and go another way.

Unlawful Arrest

One of the objects of an arrest is to restrain a person's liberty of movement, and in Chapter 7 the powers and procedure for making an arrest were set out in detail. Here the matter of arrest is dealt with only in the context of false imprisonment, for if either a police officer or a private individual, when making an arrest, acts outside these powers or without following the correct procedure, the arrest becomes unlawful and will leave the person responsible for the arrest open to an action for false imprisonment.

Person Responsible for the Arrest

The person responsible for the arrest, and liable for any action for false imprisonment, is not always the person who has physically detained the prisoner. For instance, if an individual tells a constable to arrest a man for stealing his wallet and on this individual's word the constable arrests, the officer will merely be acting on behalf of the complainant and it is the latter who is responsible for having the prisoner arrested. However, where an individual merely states his suspicions to a constable and the latter, after making inquiries, decides to make the arrest, it is the officer who is responsible for making the arrest, for the arm of the law has been required to use its discretion. In *Austin* v. *Dowling*, a police officer refused to take responsibility for arresting a prisoner on an accusation made by an individual. Eventually the officer did make the arrest when the individual agreed to sign the charge-sheet. The court came to the decision that it was the private individual who would be liable for false imprisonment.

The rules of procedure that accompany an arrest are as important as the power under which the arrest is made. For instance, it has been pointed out in Chapter 7 that in normal circumstances the prisoner must be told the *true* reason for his arrest, and also that he must be taken either before a police officer or a magistrate as soon as reasonably practicable. *Christie* v. *Leachinsky* was a case that arose prior to the Criminal Law Act, 1967, when a police officer had a general power of arrest without warrant for offences which were called felonies, but no such power for minor offences which were called misdemeanours. In this case the police officer, Christie, and another officer arrested L. without a warrant for an alleged misdemeanour under the mistaken belief that a specific statute gave them powers to do so. When they were sued for false imprisonment the police officers pleaded that they had reasonable grounds for suspecting that L. had also committed the felony of larceny (now called theft). Their plea did not succeed and they were found guilty, because if they were arresting him for suspected larceny they should have told L. of this charge when he was being arrested, and this they had not done.

B. TRESPASS TO GOODS

This tort consists of committing any act of direct physical interference with any goods in another's possession.

Types of Interferences Protected

An individual has a right not only to personal protection, but also to the security of the goods in his possession. In the earliest cases this branch of trespass only protected the possessor from having his goods *carried off* or taken out of his possession, for example in the taking of a horse from its stable. Later, the tort was extended to cover cases where the goods were *damaged* but not necessarily removed; and later still, trespass to goods developed to include cases where an individual's possession of goods was *interfered* with, even though no damage may have been caused. Thus, today it is trespass to move from one place to another, damage or destroy, or merely to interfere with or make unpermitted use of, the goods in someone else's possession.

The range of goods that are capable of possession is vast, and the ways in which one can trespass against them are countless. It will be trespass to use a car without permission even if no harm has been done; or to take a tyre from a car on exhibition and replace it with another one (even if the replacement is better). Also, it has been held a trespass to shoot a racing pigeon, to chase cattle and to poison pets.

Tort against Possession

The action for trespass is solely concerned with protecting actual possession. To deprive someone of their title or ownership in goods may overlap with trespass, but this is mainly dealt with under the separate tort of conversion. Anyone in possession of the chattel at the time of the interference can maintain an action in trespass. For instance, either the finder of an article or a person having illegal possession may bring an action against any person other than the true owner. This rule as to actual possession has been relaxed in a few situations in favour of a person with a right to possession whose servant, agent or bailee has actual possession, and with regard to personal representatives and trustees.

Actionable *per se*

The main remedy for trespass to goods is an action for damages, and in most cases some form of injury will be proved for which the complainant can be compensated. However, as trespass is actionable *per se*, it will be as much a trespass to meddle with museum exhibits and feed sweets to the animals in the zoo as it is to daub another's car with paint.

C. TRESPASS TO LAND

This tort consists of any unjustifiable interference with another's possession of land.

Trespassers Cannot Usually be Prosecuted

An individual in possession of land is protected from all direct and unjustifiable interferences with his occupation of it. Trespass is a tort which may give rise to a civil action; it is not a crime, and therefore trespassers cannot be prosecuted. If, however, the trespassing on land is accompanied by damage, such as the breaking of fences or the treading down of crops, the action may also amount to a separate crime. However, in an action for trespass alone there is no need to prove such damage.

Tort against Possession

As in all branches of trespass, it is a tort which is essentially a violation of the right of possession, not the right of ownership. Ownership unaccompanied by possession is protected by other remedies. Thus a landlord cannot sue for a mere transitory trespass to land in the occupation and possession of his tenant; such an action can only be brought by the tenant. Moreover, the fact that a person merely has the use of land does not necessarily make him a possessor: this rule will usually prevent an occupier of a bed-sitter, the boarder at a hostel, the lodger or the guest from suing in trespass.

The general heading 'trespass to land' is divided into surface, subsoil and airspace, because a person is as much entitled to possession of the ground itself as he is to the space above and the earth beneath.

Types of Trespass to the Surface of Land
(a) By Abuse of Right of Entry
Some persons may have permission either to enter certain parts of another's land, or to enter on to the land for a specific purpose; if they abuse this right of entry by going where they are told not to go or doing something they are told not to do, they will become trespassers: for example, the sightseer to a stately home who fails to keep to the prescribed route of the tour, or takes photographs when this has been expressly forbidden.

(b) Trespass ab initio *(from the outset)*
This form of trespass was created to provide a remedy against abuses by persons in authority which might lead to oppression of the individual's interest in the sanctity of his home: for example, by the abuse of a search warrant. It applies to persons who enter another's land under the authority of the law and, while there, act outside the realm of their authority. They will then be trespassers, not merely from the time when they start abusing their right, but retrospectively, from the time they *initially* entered on to the land.

(c) By Placing Objects on Land
Trespass by walking across land is obviously different from trespass caused by depositing rubbish upon it. The latter is likely to remain there longer and is called a 'continuing trespass' for which successive actions will continue to lie until the offence is removed.

Trespass Above and Below the Surface
Possession of land may carry with it the right to the space above and the earth beneath. As in the case of all trespass, the interference must be *direct*; if it is not, another remedy will have to be found. For example, the burrowing of roots from a tree and the encroachment of overhanging branches have been held by the courts to be indirect and will give rise only to an action for nuisance.

It has been held a trespass to airspace to place an advertisement in such a position that it occupies space above the premises of someone else, and to swing the jib of a crane so that it passes to and fro over another's land.

The Civil Aviation Act, 1949, applies to the situation of civil aircraft passing over land. The Act provides that no action in trespass to airspace or nuisance will lie for flights over any land at a reasonable height.

Trespass to the subsoil would exist if an individual were to mine for coal, or to lay pipes or construct sewers in another's land.

D. DEFENCES TO AN ACTION FOR TRESPASS

It has been mentioned in Chapter 8 that there are certain general defences that are available for any tort; for example, consent will be a complete defence in any tort if it can be proved that the injured person consented to the wrong being committed against him. The general defences that are mentioned below, that is, consent, necessity, inevitable accident and statutory authority, deal with situations that have arisen or may arise in connection with the tort of trespass.

Some torts, because of their particular nature, have certain defences which are applicable only to them. In the case of trespass such specific defences mentioned below are self-defence, defence of goods and lawful correction.

Consent

Consent to a person's conduct is willingness that it shall take place. Persons who indulge in sports or contests are presumed to consent to physical contacts consistent with the rules of the game. If such rules are broken and injury is caused, there will be an action for battery. For example, in football you do not consent to be punched and in boxing you do not consent to be kicked. In each case the act is beyond the rules to which you are presumed to have consented.

In other cases, for instance with surgical operations, express written consent may be given. When such consent has been granted, it is only a defence where the conduct is of a substantially similar nature to that to which he consented. For instance, it would be a battery to amputate a leg when permission had been given to operate on a toe; but it was not a battery to remove parts of Fallopian tubes during an appendectomy. Likewise, it would be trespass to goods to injure a horse by taking it over jumps when permission to ride was only granted provided it was kept on the straight; and permission to dump a few articles on land is not permission to strew it with rubbish.

Self-Defence

A man who is attacked should be allowed to take reasonable steps to prevent harm to himself, for there is not always the time to resort to the slower processes of the law. Moreover, a man is not required to wait for his assailant to strike the first blow or until his imprisoner has turned the key, for perhaps afterwards it will be too late.

This right to self-help is limited to the use of *reasonable* force. The defender is not permitted to inflict a beating beyond that of self-protection, nor does the right extend beyond the heat of the moment, for then self-help has turned to retribution.

The right to resist an unlawful arrest is subject, in general, to the same rules of reasonable conduct.

Defence of Goods and Land

The interest in peaceful possession of goods or occupation of land also justifies protection by the defence of self-help. The possessor may resist the trespasser by any force which might, in other circumstances, have amounted to an assault, battery or false imprisonment. In *Harrison* v. *Duke of Rutland* the plaintiff was allowed to cross the defendant's land, but on one occasion he went on to the land with the intention of disturbing the grouse and interrupting the Duke's shooting party. The servants of the Duke took hold of the plaintiff and ejected him from the land. The plaintiff brought an action for assault and battery, but his action failed as it was held that the Duke was entitled to use reasonable force in ejecting the plaintiff who had trespassed by abusing his right of entry.

The force in defence must be reasonable in comparison with the force that is threatened. Moreover, it must be noted that the law has a higher regard for human safety than for the protection of things. An individual is not entitled to inflict serious injury when only in defence of his land or goods. Broken bottles on the top of walls and barbed wire may be justifiable for deterrence where spring-guns and man-traps are not.

Necessity

A person is justified in causing trespass in situations where the harm done is to prevent an even greater harm, for which neither of the parties are responsible.

A person may interfere with the goods of another and have the defence of necessity: for example, shooting a rabid dog or burning contaminated clothing. Also, this general defence may justify interference with a person or his land: for instance, in forcibly feeding a prisoner on a hunger strike to prevent the greater harm of his dying; and in *Cope* v. *Sharpe* where a gamekeeper was sued for trespass to land for entering on to the neighbour's land and starting a fire. This was to act as a fire-break to prevent a larger fire spreading to his employer's land. He was found not guilty of trespass even though such drastic precautions had not been necessary.

Lawful Correction

A parent or guardian may use corporal punishment, provided it is reasonable, for the discipline and control of their children. A teacher has the same authority for the maintenance of the morale and decorum of the school. In each situation the chastisement must be fair for the form of misbehaviour and moderate in how it is administered. If not, the harm will amount to a battery.

Inevitable Accident

An inevitable accident is an occurrence which could not have been foreseen or prevented by taking reasonable precautions: for instance, where a car driver has a heart attack and injures a pedestrian. It is a general defence to an action in tort to prove such an unusual occurrence. In *Stanley* v. *Powell* the defendant was a member of a shooting party and the plaintiff was employed to carry cartridges and any game that was shot. The defendant fired at a pheasant but the shot glanced off an oak tree and injured the plaintiff. It was held that the defendant was not liable for causing the injury as it was an inevitable accident.

Lawful Authority

The arrest of a person, the entry on to his land or the seizure of his goods may be carried out with lawful authority. This topic has already been covered in Chapter 7.

1. Explain what is meant by the tort of trespass and the kinds of interests this tort aims to protect.
2. What forms may trespass to land take? Who may sue under this branch of trespass and what remedies are available to him?
3. Trespass to the person protects an individual from the infliction of bodily injury, the fear of such injury and the unlawful interference with his freedom of movement. Explain and distinguish between these different forms of trespass.

Explain the meaning of:
(1) actionable *per se*
(2) 'force' in the context of battery
(3) injury must be 'direct' rather than 'consequential'
(4) 'reasonable fear', in relation to assault
(5) restraint must be 'total' in false imprisonment
(6) lawful correction
(7) trespass by abuse of right of entry
(8) trespass *ab initio*

What form of trespass, if any, has been committed in the following situations:
(a) D threatens to shoot P. D's gun is empty but P does not realise this.
(b) D, whilst P is asleep, locks P's bedroom door and then opens it before P awakes in the morning.

(c)   D, without P's consent, paints flowers over P's car.

(d)   D threatens to set his dog on to P.

(e)   T has lent his bicycle to P, and while in P's possession D lets the tyres down.

(f)   D, while looking around an art gallery starts fingering the paintings. There is a notice at the entrance saying this is forbidden. When D refuses to leave at the request of P, the curator, P locks D in his office until closing time.

(g)   D, a neighbour, tips all his rubbish at the bottom of P's garden.

(h)   P, whilst playing football, is kicked by D.

(i)   P and D are travelling to work on the bus in the rush hour. During a heated discussion D says to P, 'If this bus were empty I would hit you'.

10. The Tort of Negligence

The Different Meanings of 'Negligence'
'Negligence' has two different meanings in the law of torts. Firstly, it refers to an *attitude of mind* in which most torts may be carried out. For example, an individual may commit trespass negligently, or may negligently defame another person. In this sense, 'negligence' means carelessness.

In its second meaning 'negligence' is the name given to an actual tort, in the same way that defamation or trespass are independent torts. This chapter is concerned with this second meaning and, as such, the tort of negligence refers to a certain type of wrongful *conduct*.

The Nature of the Tort of Negligence
It has been said above that the specific tort of negligence refers to the conduct of an individual. This means the actual way he behaves and not his state of mind. The type of conduct that amounts to negligence consists of behaviour by one individual that exposes another individual to an unreasonable risk of injury.

Many things we do, if carried out in the wrong way, may lead to injury to others. If a motorist drives badly he risks injuring other road users; if a person leaves an open manhole unguarded he risks injuring pedestrians; also, if a mechanic fails to repair the brakes of a car properly he will risk injuring the driver and any passengers.

This tort of negligence is designed to prevent a person behaving wrongfully or unreasonably in any situation where he should foresee that he is likely to injure somebody. If his conduct does lead to injury, the injured person may bring an action for damages. It can be appreciated that negligence is an extremely wide and important tort, and it is for ever expanding to cover new situations where the courts consider that the defendant should pay compensation for his wrongful behaviour that has injured the plaintiff.

The courts have constructed a formula whereby the tort of regligence can be proved. This formula, which consists of the following elements, also serves as a rough definition of the tort. The courts have laid down that where:

(*a*)   the defendant owes a duty of care to the plaintiff, and
(*b*)   he breaks this duty by exposing the plaintiff to an unreasonable risk of injury, and
(*c*)   injury does result from this breach of duty,

the defendant will be liable to pay compensation to the plaintiff under the tort of negligence.

It is now necessary to examine each of these elements of negligence in greater detail.

A. THE DUTY OF CARE

Where an individual, in any situation, can reasonably foresee that what he is doing may expose other persons to a risk of injury, he owes those persons a duty of care not to injure them.

The courts have not laid down a list of situations where they consider that one individual owes a duty of care to another individual. New situations are constantly coming before the courts where the plaintiff has been injured by the defendant and the former considers that the defendant was under a duty of care not to injure him. The first point which the courts have to decide in each of these new situations is whether or not the defendant did owe such a duty to the plaintiff.

There are also many situations where the courts have already established, by previous cases, that one person owes a duty of care to another. For instance, a driver of a car owes a duty of care towards other road users, and a manufacturer owes a duty of care to make his product safe for consumers. It has also been established that a surgeon owes a duty towards his patient to operate with all the reasonable care and skill that can be expected of a person in his profession. Furthermore, a person who gives advice in the course of his business is under a duty to give reasonably sound advice to persons who approach him.

The 'Neighbour' Principle

But how do the courts decide that an individual owes a duty of care to another individual? In the situations where it has not already been established that a duty of care exists, the courts will often apply what is known as the 'neighbour' principle. This test was formulated by Lord Atkin in *Donoghue* v. *Stevenson*. In this case a friend bought some ginger beer for the appellant. The drink was in an opaque bottle, therefore the contents could not be seen. She poured and drank her first glass; then, when she was emptying the bottle into her glass, the decomposed remains of a snail floated out. She became seriously ill and wishes to claim compensation. The person most likely to be responsible was the manufacturer, because he had bottled and sealed the drink together with the snail. There was no contract between the appellant and the manufacturer so the former brought her action under tort, for negligence. As this was the first case between a consumer and a manufacturer involving this tort, the first problem was for the appellant to prove that she was owed a duty of care by the manufacturer. The

House of Lords held that the manufacturer did owe her a duty of care as it is his duty to the consumer to take reasonable care that his product is free from any defect likely to cause the consumer injury.

The important test that was laid down in this case for discovering whether a duty of care exists in each particular situation was stated by Lord Atkin as follows: 'You must take reasonable care to avoid acts or omissions which you can reasonably foresee would be likely to injure your neighbour. Who, then, in law is my neighbour? The answer seems to be, persons who are so closely and directly affected by my act that I ought reasonably to have them in contemplation as being so affected when I am directing my mind to the acts or omissions which are called in question.'

Therefore, if an individual can reasonably foresee that his conduct is likely to expose another person to an unreasonable risk of injury, he owes a duty of care to that person (his 'neighbour'). The application of this 'neighbour' principle can be seen in *Bourhill* v. *Young*, where a motor-cyclist drove so negligently that he collided with a stationary motor-car and killed himself. At the time of the accident, but a few vehicles in front, a pregnant fishwife was alighting from a tram-car. She was not in a position to see the collision, yet she heard the impact and afterwards went back to the scene of the accident and saw the blood left on the road. As a result of this she suffered severe nervous shock and gave birth to a stillborn child. She brought an action against the estate of the deceased motor-cyclist because of his negligence, but she was unsuccessful. The House of Lords held that the motor-cyclist did not owe her a duty of care as she was not at the time of the collision within 'the area of risk' of his negligent behaviour. It was not reasonable for the motor-cyclist to foresee that his negligent conduct was exposing a person in her position to a risk of injury.

In *Home Office* v. *Dorset Yacht Co. Ltd* the House of Lords found that the Home Office, through their servants and agents, owed a duty of care to persons who lived in the neighbourhood of an open borstal. In this case the Home Office kept an open borstal. A party of its boys was on a training exercise in Poole Harbour, and one night seven of them escaped and went aboard a yacht moored nearby. They caused it to collide with another yacht which suffered considerable damage. The court held that the taking of the yacht and the causing of the damage ought to have been foreseen by the borstal officers as likely to happen if they failed to exercise proper supervision of their trainees.

B. BREACH OF THE DUTY

The second element that must be proved is that the defendant has broken the duty of care he owed to the plaintiff. The defendant will not have broken his duty if the court considers that he has behaved reasonably or, in other words, if his conduct did not fall below the standard of care expected of him.

Standard of Care

The standard of behaviour which is expected of the defendant varies in each new situation. It is the task of the court to discover what sort of behaviour is reasonable in the defendant's particular situation, taking into account his knowledge and the standards of behaviour in the particular community at the time. In order to discover this, the court relies upon a standard of care which is based on the behaviour of the ordinary 'reasonable man' and what he would have done in the particular circumstances. What each court will ask itself in each case is whether an ordinary reasonable person would have behaved in the same way as the defendant did. If the conclusion they reach is 'no', then the defendant has behaved unreasonably and his conduct will have fallen below the standard of care expected of him.

The hypothetical 'reasonable man' is 'a man of ordinary prudence' or a man using 'ordinary care and skill'. As the courts use the test of the 'reasonable man' in each case to examine whether the defendant has behaved unreasonably or reasonably, the character of the reasonable man changes according to the circumstances of each defendant. If a case involves the negligent behaviour of a surgeon, the reasonable man will be endowed with the usual skills of this profession, so the test will be what a reasonable surgeon would do in the circumstances; in other situations, it might be the reasonable manufacturer or reasonable motorist. For example, if the defendant is a motorist accused of negligent driving, whether he has broken his duty will depend on what would be expected of the average competent motorist driving in those particular conditions, on that roadway at the time of the accident.

Some Factors Used to Determine a Breach of Duty

Whether there has, in fact, been a breach of duty of care may depend on many factors. In some cases the courts may have to consider one or more of these factors which are, basically, used to find out whether the defendant has acted reasonably in the circumstances.

(a) The Seriousness of the Risk of Injury

The defendant's behaviour will be judged against the seriousness of the risk of injury to which he has exposed the plaintiff. The more serious the injury that the plaintiff is likely to suffer, the more care the defendant should take to prevent it happening. This point is illustrated in *Paris* v. *Stepney Borough Council* where the defendants employed the plaintiff who had only one eye. He was employed on work that involved some risk of eye injury, but the risk of serious injury was not sufficiently great to require the defendants to give their ordinary workmen goggles. However, the plaintiff was blinded in the course of his work and claimed that the defendants broke their duty of care to him by not supplying him with protective goggles. The court held that the defendants had broken the duty they owed to the plaintiff as they must have known that the consequences of any injury to the eye would be more serious in the case of a one-eyed workman than to a normal-sighted employee.

(b) The Likelihood of Injury
The defendant need only take reasonable precautions to prevent a risk of injury to the plaintiff. What is reasonable in each case is discovered by comparing the likelihood of the injury with the precautions that the defendant has taken to prevent injury. The defendant is not required to be over-cautious by eliminating all possible chances of injury. This factor was considered in *Bolton* v. *Stone*, when the plaintiff was struck by a cricket ball hit out of the cricket grounds. There was evidence that a ball had been hit out of the grounds only six times in the last thirty years. For this to be accomplished, the ball had to travel at least 78 yards to the edge of the grounds and still be at a sufficient height to clear a protective fence which was approximately 17 feet above the level of the pitch. The court held that the plaintiff could not succeed under the tort of negligence because, although the defendants owed a duty to passers-by, they had taken reasonable precautions to eliminate the risk of injury to them. By acting reasonably the defendants had not broken their duty of care.

(c) Importance of Object to be Attained
In some cases the defendant may be in such a position that, in order to achieve an important object, he has to expose others to some risk of injury. The defendant will not have broken his duty if the courts consider that the risk of injury to which he exposed others while attaining his object was not unreasonable in the circumstances. In *Watt* v. *Hertfordshire County Council* a woman had been trapped under a heavy vehicle and the lifting-gear at the fire station was required urgently to save her life. The officer in charge of the station ordered the gear to be carried on a lorry that was not equipped for this purpose, but it was the only vehicle available. Because the lifting-gear was insufficiently secured, on the way to the accident it moved and injured a fireman who was travelling with it. He claimed damages for negligence. The court held that the risk taken by the fire officer was one which

might normally have to be taken in an emergency and was not unduly great in relation to the object it was hoped to achieve.

C. RESULTING INJURY

The third element in the tort of negligence is that the injury or damage suffered by the plaintiff must result from the breach of the defendant's duty. If the injury does not *result* from the breach of duty, the third essential is missing. In *Barnett* v. *Chelsea and Kensington Hospital Management Committee* the casualty officer failed to examine properly a night-watchman who went to the hospital complaining of stomach ache and vomiting. The man had been sent away and told to see his own doctor in the morning, but he died a few hours later of arsenic poisoning. Although the casualty officer obviously owed a duty of care to the patient and had broken this duty by failing to examine him properly, he was not liable under the tort of negligence because it was proved that the night-watchman would have died whatever action might have been taken at the hospital. Therefore, his death did not *result* from the breach of duty.

Damage which is Too Remote
Not all damage that follows from a breach of duty will be sufficient to establish the tort of negligence. The defendant is not liable for injury to the plaintiff that is too remotely connected with his breach of duty. In *Hobbs* v. *London and South Western Railway* the plaintiff and his family, through the negligence of a railway porter, were put on the wrong train and had to walk four miles home in the rain late at night. As a consequence of this walk, the wife caught a cold and received medical attention. The plaintiff brought an action against the porter's employers but the court held that the damage the plaintiff had suffered, which was the payment of his wife's medical expenses, was too remote a consequence from the porter's negligence to make the defendants liable.

Damage Must be 'Reasonably Foreseeable'
As a general rule, the only damage that will satisfy this third element of negligence is damage that could reasonably have been foreseen by the defendant. This important point is illustrated by a case that is commonly referred to as *The Wagon Mound I*. The defendants, while refuelling their ship called the *Wagon Mound* in Sydney Harbour, carelessly spilt some fuel oil on to the water. The oil spread to the plaintiff's wharf where welding was being carried out on another ship. As soon as the oil was noticed, welding was stopped until the plaintiff

had asked the defendants whether it was safe to continue. Both parties, and some experts that they consulted, believed that the oil was non-inflammable in its present state, so welding was continued. Two days later some molten metal falling from the plaintiff's wharf set fire to some cotton waste floating in the oil, and this, in turn, ignited the oil. As a result of this fire serious damage was done to the plaintiff's wharf. The Judicial Committee of the Privy Council held that the defendants were not liable in negligence for the damage because they could not have reasonably foreseen this.

It can be seen, therefore, that in most cases damage will not be considered too remote if the reasonable man, in the position of the defendant, could have foreseen the injury. If the damage could not have been foreseen by the reasonable man, then the defendant will not be liable.

D. *RES IPSA LOQUITUR*

It is a general rule in lawsuits that the plaintiff has to prove the wrong he is asserting against the defendant. The person who has to prove the wrong is said to have the 'burden of proof'. For example, in negligence the plaintiff has to prove all three elements of the tort.

However, in the case of negligence there is an exception to this rule. This exception arises where the plaintiff suffers injury and it is not within his means to prove that the defendant has acted negligently, yet it appears on the surface obvious that the defendant must have been negligent. In this situation the plaintiff is allowed merely to prove his injury before the court and then say 'the matter speaks for itself' (*res ipsa loquitur*) that the defendant has been negligent. By doing this it places the burden of proof on the defendant who must then show that he has not been negligent.

For example, in *Cassidy* v. *Ministry of Health* the plaintiff went into hospital to be cured of two stiff fingers and after an operation came out with four stiff fingers. The court held that *res ipsa loquitur* applied as it was obvious that the plaintiff could not show how it happened and the defendants would have to show that the two additional stiff fingers were not due to their negligence.

This reversal of the burden of proof will only be allowed by the court when there is no other reasonable explanation for the injury than that the defendants must have been negligent. For instance, in *Fish* v. *Kapur* the plaintiff claimed damages for a broken jaw which she alleged had been caused by the negligence of her dentist while she was having a tooth extracted. The doctrine of *res ipsa loquitur* did not apply because the possible negligence of her dentist was not the only reasonable explanation for her injury. The injury could easily have happened because she had a weak jaw.

The defendant will have discharged the burden of proof if he can show that he has not been negligent, or that the injury was due to the negligence of some other person. For instance, in *Birchall* v. *Bibby* the plaintiff, a carter, was loading bags of bran on to a wagon at the defendant's warehouse. The bags were moved by a sling and hoist system and when the control rope snapped, the plaintiff was struck by three bags and was injured. The court held that *res ipsa loquitur* applied and the burden was on the defendants to prove that they were not negligent. They proved that the rope was cut maliciously by some third person and this was sufficient to discharge their burden of proof. They did not have to show who actually did it.

E. DEFENCES TO NEGLIGENCE

Two important defences to the tort of negligence are consent and contributory negligence.

1. Consent
This general defence of consent or, as it is often called, *volenti non fit injuria* ('no injury is done to he who consents'), has already been mentioned under the tort of trespass, and the same principles apply when it is used as a defence to an action for negligence.

Express or Implied Consent
The plaintiff may have expressly or impliedly given his consent to run the risk of being injured. In *Hall* v. *Brooklands Auto-Racing Club* an onlooker at a race meeting was injured when a car left the track and crashed through the safety barriers. The court held that the defendants were not obliged to guard against obvious dangers in the sport which could be foreseen by spectators and to which they had impliedly consented by attending the meeting.

Knowledge of the Risk is not Consent to Injury
In order for the defence of *volenti non fit injuria* to be successful, it is not enough to show that the plaintiff *knew* he was running the risk; the defendant must also prove that the plaintiff *consented* to run it. This difference between consent and mere knowledge can be seen in *Smith* v. *Baker*. In this case a man worked in a quarry over the top of which a crane frequently swung heavy stones. The workman continued his work even though he knew these stones were being transported above him. On one occasion he was hit by falling stones, and the court held that

although he *knew* that there was a risk of injury, he had not *consented* to run the risk, at his own expense, of the employers being negligent. (See also *Nettleship* v. *Weston* below.)

'Rescue' Cases

The courts have held that the plaintiff will not have consented to run the risk of injury at his own expense, even though he knows of the risk, if he can prove that he was under a moral duty or that it was reasonable in the circumstances for him to run the risk of injury. For instance, in *Baker* v. *Hopkins* the defendants used the defence of *volenti* against the plaintiff in a case where they admitted negligence. Two of the defendants' employees were working down a well and were overcome by poisonous fumes from a petrol-driven pump. A doctor descended into the well to rescue the men, but was himself overpowered by the fumes and died. The court said that the defendants could not claim that the doctor had consented because, through their own negligence concerning the pump, they had placed their workmen in peril and it was foreseeable in such a situation that somebody would attempt to rescue them.

Therefore, if a person, by his own negligence, puts himself or others in such peril that it can be expected that someone will attempt a rescue, that person will be liable for the injury that is suffered by the rescuer. This is provided that the rescue attempt was reasonable. In *Haynes* v. *Harwood* the defendant had negligently left his horses and van unattended in the street. The animals bolted and this placed some children playing in the street in danger. The plaintiff, a policeman on duty in the police station, rushed out and was crushed in his efforts to check the runaway horses. It was held that his efforts were reasonable, and therefore the defendant could not plead the defence of *volenti non fit injuria*.

However, if the defendant does not put himself or anyone else in peril, then any 'rescue' would be unnecessary and unreasonable, as in the case of *Cutler* v. *United Dairies*. In this case the horse drawing the defendant's milk float careered off the road and into a field. The driver, while he was attempting to pacify the animal, called for help. The plaintiff, who went to his aid, was injured. The court held that the plaintiff had been unreasonable in his efforts as the milkman was in no real danger.

2. Contributory Negligence

In some situations the plaintiff's injury may not be entirely the defendant's fault, but may be partly due to the plaintiff's own negligence. In such circumstances it would be unjust for the defendant to be responsible for the whole amount of the damages the plaintiff is claiming. For example, a motor-cyclist and a car have a collision and the motor-cyclist claims damages. If the court finds that the motor-cyclist is three-quarters to blame for the incident, then the amount of damages that the motor-cyclist has claimed will be reduced by 75 per cent, because his negligence contributed to his own injury.

The Law Reform (Contributory Negligence) Act, 1945, provides that where the plaintiff suffers damage partly as a result of his own fault and partly due to the fault of the defendant, the amount of damages which the plaintiff is entitled to recover will be reduced according to what the court considers to be the plaintiff's share in the responsibility for his injury. Thus, in the above example, if the motor-cyclist had claimed £200 in respect of his damages, he would be awarded £50.

In *O'Connell* v. *Jackson* the court held that the failure by a moped rider to wear a crash helmet amounted to contributory negligence when, in a crash, he suffered severe head injuries. This case is of particular interest because the cause of the accident was due entirely to the car driver's negligence, yet because the moped rider failed to wear a crash helmet he was contributorily negligent in the amount of injury he suffered. If he had worn a crash helmet his injury would have been far less serious. His damages were reduced by 15 per cent.

Another interesting case is *Nettleship* v. *Weston*, where a driving instructor was injured while in a car being driven by a very inexperienced learner driver. The instructor claimed damages against the learner driver for a broken leg. In this case the court had to consider, firstly, the standard of care expected of a learner driver before it could establish negligence on the part of the learner driver; secondly, whether the instructor by being in the car had consented to run the risk of injury; and thirdly, the aspect that he negligently contributed to his own injury. The court held that the learner driver owed the same duty to the instructor as that owed to any passenger or to any other road user, because in all cases the standard of care expected of a learner driver is the same as that for the reasonable, competent and experienced driver. In dealing with the defence of *volenti* pleaded by the learner driver, the court held that although the instructor had *knowledge* of the driver's lack of skill and experience, he had not *consented* to run the risk, therefore this defence did not apply. On the third point, the instructor was held to be contributorily negligent. Although the driver had panicked, the instructor had also failed to act quickly enough to correct the error, because during this particular lesson he had been assisting the driver by moving the gear-lever, applying the hand-brake and occasionally assisting with the steering. He was found to be contributorily negligent to the extent of 50 per cent.

The Dilemma Principle

There are a few situations where the plaintiff will be partly responsible for his own injuries, yet will not have been contributorily negligent. These situations are where the defendant by his negligence has put the plaintiff in such a dilemma that in 'the agony of the moment' the plaintiff takes the wrong course of action and injures himself.

In *Jones* v. *Boyce* the plaintiff was a passenger on top of the defendant's coach which, through the defendant's negligence, had become out of control. The plaintiff, believing that the coach was in imminent danger of overturning, jumped clear and broke his leg in doing so. Although the coach did not overturn, the court held that the plaintiff had acted in a reasonable apprehension of danger and in the agony of this moment the method he used to avoid the danger was reasonable, even though it turned out to be the wrong course of action. Therefore he was entitled to damages.

The above case was applied in the more recent case of *B.S.M.* v. *Simms*. The defendant, while she was taking her driving test, negligently failed to give way at a 'Give Way' sign. The examiner, fearing an accident, applied the hand-brake which resulted in the car stopping half-way across the road junction and causing an accident. It was alleged that the examiner had been contributorily negligent. The court held that in the sudden emergency the steps which he took, although in the circumstances the wrong ones, were none the less reasonable because of the predicament in which he found himself.

1. (a) What three elements must the plaintiff prove against the defendant if he is to succeed in an action for negligence?
   (b) P. is standing looking in a shop window when, for some unknown reason, a car parked further up the street rolls down the hill into him. Discuss the nature of P's claim for damages.
2. D., without looking where he is going, steps out into the road. P., a motorist, brakes sharply to avoid hitting D. and, because he is not wearing a safety-belt, injures his head on the windscreen of his car. Discuss what the outcome of an action for negligence brought by P. might be.
3. The fire brigade receives an emergency call that three people are trapped in a burning house. On the way to the fire the fire-engine, which is exceeding the speed limit, collides with P., a motorist driving home. Discuss whether P. has an action for negligence.
4. D., who is a lecturer employed by Easysuccess Tutors, gives lessons based upon his lecture notes which are ten years out of date. P., a student who has relied entirely upon D's teaching, fails his exams. Has P. any remedy against D?

Explain the meaning of the following, illustrating your answers with cases where possible:

(1) *res ipsa loquitur*
(2) damage must be 'foreseeable'
(3) a duty of care
(4) the 'neighbour' principle
(5) the 'reasonable man'
(6) *volenti non fit injuria*
(7) Contributory negligence.

Explain the part played by negligence in the following topics:

(1) consumer law
(2) health and safety at work.

11. The Tort of Nuisance

The Two Forms of Nuisance

There are two separate forms of nuisance. The civil form is known as *private* nuisance and the criminal form as *public* nuisance. It is because of these two aspects that there has always been difficulty in giving nuisance an exact legal definition. However, in its literal sense 'nuisance' means 'annoyance' or 'inconvenience'.

A private nuisance is a tort and is restricted to the disturbance of the interests an individual has in the use and enjoyment of his land. The action for the tort of nuisance lies in the hands of the individual whose interests have suffered an unreasonable degree of annoyance or inconvenience.

A public nuisance is a crime which extends to virtually any form of annoyance or inconvenience which disturbs the rights of the community as a whole. Such disturbances may be as varied as the obstruction of a highway, the selling of food unfit for human consumption, or the sight of prostitutes soliciting in the street. The prosecution for the crime of public nuisance is in the hands of the State.

The two forms of nuisance have little in common, except that each causes inconvenience or annoyance and, in both its forms, the disturbance must be sufficiently substantial to cause an interference with the private or public interest involved. In neither form, civil or criminal, will the courts concern themselves with the insubstantial and trivial interferences which are nothing more than the result of everyday life in the community. Thus, an occasional unpleasant smell from a neighbour's dustbin will not be sufficient for a private nuisance; nor will the infrequent annoyance to the community of a weekend bonfire amount to a public nuisance.

A. PUBLIC NUISANCE

The Nature of Public Nuisance

A public nuisance is conduct which causes inconvenience or annoyance to the public; it is conduct which affects the interests of Her Majesty's subjects generally. It has already been said that it is a crime, and this prosecution is usually brought on behalf of the community by the Attorney-General, as it would be unreasonable to expect one person to take criminal proceedings to put a stop to a nuisance that has affected so many people. The usual remedies for this form of nuisance are punishment by a fine or an injunction to prevent the continuance of the nuisance.

Civil Actions for Public Nuisances

An individual can, however, bring a civil action in respect of a public nuisance where he suffers some special damage, peculiar to himself, which is over and above the ordinary damage caused to the public by the nuisance. For example, in *Iveson* v. *Moore* the defendant caused an obstruction of the public highway which amounted to a public nuisance. The plaintiff was a colliery owner and he brought a civil action to recover the profits he had lost because the obstruction prevented his workmen from coming to the colliery and the coal from being carted away. His action was successful as he had suffered some special damage over and above the general public nuisance to the other road users.

A further example of an individual being able to bring a civil action for what was essentially a public nuisance is *Campbell* v. *Paddington Corporation*. The plaintiff often let the rooms in her house to spectators at public processions. On one occasion Paddington Corporation constructed a stand which amounted to a public nuisance and also to a personal inconvenience to the plaintiff, as it obstructed the view from her windows. The court held that the plaintiff could recover for the special damage she had suffered. This amounted to the loss of her profits because she was unable to let her rooms.

If the interference which amounts to the offence of public nuisance also amounts to a private nuisance, then, naturally, the individual may bring an action for this separate wrong under the tort of nuisance.

Some annoyances have been made public nuisances by statute, for example the Clean Air Act, 1956, and the Noise Abatement Act, 1960.

B. PRIVATE NUISANCE

Nature of Private Nuisance

The essence of a private nuisance is an unlawful interference with an individual's use or enjoyment of his land. Virtually any disturbance of the use, comfort or enjoyment of a person's interest in land will amount to a private nuisance, provided the interference is substantial and unreasonable and would be a nuisance to any ordinary person.

(a) 'Use'

Examples of nuisances resulting from interferences with an individual's *use* of land are the killing of vegetation or cattle by poisonous fumes, or pollution of a river by noxious waste, or damage to a building caused by the vibrations from a factory's machinery.

(b) 'Enjoyment'

Examples of interferences with an individual's comfort and enjoyment of his land are unpleasant stenches from manure heaps or the continual distraction caused by the excessive tolling of church bells.

Substantial Interference

It has already been mentioned that in order for an interference to amount to a nuisance it must be a substantial interference with the plaintiff's interest in land.

Where the interference results in some *material* loss to the plaintiff, the courts will have little difficulty in establishing that the interference is sufficiently substantial for the tort of nuisance: for example, where an interference is with an individual's use of land, which prevents him growing crops, or where the interference causes structural damage to his buildings.

However, the courts have more difficulty in establishing that the interference is substantial enough for the tort of nuisance where there is no material loss caused to the plaintiff. This is the situation where the plaintiff is only claiming loss of comfort or enjoyment of his land. In such cases the courts will decide whether the interferences to the comfort or enjoyment of the plaintiff are substantial, judged alongside what would be offensive, inconvenient or annoying to the normal person in the community. The interference must be judged 'not merely according to elegant or dainty modes and habits of living, but according to plain and sober and simple notions among the English people'.

(a) Sensitiveness of the Plaintiff

In deciding upon the degree of discomfort caused, the court judges according to the standards of the normal person in the community, rather than the personal tastes or abnormal sensitivity of a particular plaintiff. Thus an individual cannot complain if the exotic flowers he cultivates in his garden are harmed by some interference of his neighbour, when ordinary flowers would not have been affected; nor can he complain of fumes merely because he has a hypersensitive nose.

In *Robinson* v. *Kilvert* the defendants began to manufacture paper-boxes in the cellar of a house, the upper part of which was occupied by the plaintiff. The defendant's business required hot and dry air and he heated the cellar accordingly. This raised the temperature of the plaintiff's floor and dried and lessened the value of the brown paper which he warehoused there; but this would not have damaged ordinary paper, nor did it inconvenience the plaintiff's workmen. It was held that the defendant was not liable for nuisance.

(b) Duration of the Interference

The duration of the interference is a further factor to be considered by the court when judging whether the interference is sufficiently substantial to amount to nuisance.

When the plaintiff is complaining of loss of *comfort* or *enjoyment* of his land, the interference, to amount to a nuisance, must usually have continued for some time, or must recur at frequent intervals. This is because the interference will not otherwise cause substantial interference to comfort or enjoyment.

However, if the plaintiff is complaining of *material* injury to his property, the interference will be substantial enough for nuisance even if it is temporary, occasional or momentary. In *Midwood* v. *Mayor of Manchester* an electric mains installed by the defendants fused. This caused an accumulation and explosion of gas resulting in a fire which damaged the plaintiff's goods. The defendants were held liable, and their argument that a sudden accident could not properly be called a nuisance was not accepted by the court.

Unreasonable Interference

The interference with the protected interest must not only be substantial, it must also be unreasonable. Every member of the community must put up with a certain amount of annoyance and inconvenience in order that life in the community can continue. So every individual is expected to tolerate a reasonable amount of interference from such unpleasant things as the noise and vibrations of traffic in towns, those nebulous smells that seem to be a natural part of everyday life, or the occasional mowing of the neighbour's lawn. The courts have realised that life within a community depends on the policy of 'live and let live', so compensation will only be awarded for the tort of nuisance where the interference is greater than the plaintiff might reasonably be expected to endure in the circumstances.

This policy of 'live and let live' that has been adopted by the courts indicates that the defendant has a right to make reasonable use of his land and that the plaintiff has the corresponding right to undisturbed comfort, enjoyment and use of his land. The courts have the problem of ensuring that neither of these interests should prevail over the other, and that a balance of reasonableness is maintained between the parties. Therefore, an action in private nuisance is very often a matter of adjustment, and this will always be according to what is reasonable in the circumstances.

The factors which the court may have to consider in order to establish what is reasonable may include how substantial is the harm inflicted as well as the sensitiveness of the plaintiff. Other factors may include the nature of the locality in which the nuisance is happening, and even the attitude of the defendant who causes the nuisance.

(a) The Locality and Reasonableness

Certain areas, because of their geographical character or the accident of community development, are devoted to certain types of activities. There are some districts that are devoted to heavy industry, others to agriculture, and others are planned purely as residential areas. What may amount to a nuisance in any particular district will depend on what is considered reasonable in that particular locality. In the words of one judge, 'What would be a nuisance in Belgrave Square would not necessarily be so in Bermondsey'.

Anyone wishing to devote his land to a specific purpose should try to do so in a suitable area: for instance, if a person wishes for a quiet retirement he should not make his home in the centre of a city, or if a person wishes to manufacture glue he should find a place other than a residential area for his factory. In *Adams* v. *Ursell* the defendant opened a fish-and-chip shop next door to the plaintiff. The plaintiff brought an action to restrain the nuisance caused by the smell and vapour from the defendant's premises. The court granted an injunction preventing the defendant from carrying on his business in that particular place. The judge said it did not follow that 'because a fried fish shop is a nuisance in one place it is a nuisance in another'.

The concern with the nature of the locality is only relevant when the interference is to comfort and enjoyment. The locality or character of the neighbourhood is not so important where the interference has caused material injury, because wherever a person may live it would be unreasonable to expect him to tolerate physical damage to his land. In *St. Helens Smelting* v. *Tipping* the plaintiff's trees and crops had been damaged by the fumes from the defendant's smelting works and he claimed damage under private nuisance. The defendant's plea that the locality was devoted to works of this kind failed. One of the judges in the House of Lords said: 'It appears to me that it is a very desirable thing to mark the difference between an action brought for a nuisance upon the ground that the alleged nuisance produces material injury to the property, and an action brought for a nuisance on the ground that the thing alleged to be a nuisance is productive of sensible personal discomfort.'

(b) Malice and Reasonableness

In order to establish the tort of nuisance the plaintiff does not need to prove that the defendant acted maliciously. The test is merely whether or not the interference is reasonable or unreasonable. However, if one party is malicious it will show that his conduct is not reasonable, and this may convert a situation that might otherwise have been a matter of 'live and let live' into an actionable nuisance.

In *Christie* v. *Davey* the parties lived in adjoining semi-detached houses. The plaintiff was a music teacher and the noise that arose from the lessons he gave annoyed the defendant so much that during the lessons he blew whistles, banged on trays, knocked on the communal wall and shouted. The court issued an injunction against the defendant to prevent him causing a nuisance by such malicious behaviour.

Plaintiff Must Have an Interest in Land

For the plaintiff to succeed in an action for private nuisance he must have an 'interest' in the land affected by the nuisance. It is usually the person in occupation who suffers the interference, and it is he who will bring the action. However, if the nuisance makes a lasting or permanent effect on land, an owner who is not in possession may be able to sue for his loss.

The 'interest' in land may be that of owner, mortgagor or tenant in possession. The courts have held that a person has no actual 'interest' in land if he is a lodger, visitor, guest, employee or even a member of the occupier's family. In *Malone* v. *Lasky* a water tank in the lavatory, owing to vibrations caused by machinery on adjoining land, fell upon and injured the plaintiff. The court held that she could not bring an action as she had no 'interest' in the land; she was only the wife of the occupier.

C. DEFENCES TO NUISANCE

It is no defence for the defendant to prove that he was there first and that the plaintiff came later to the nuisance. It would be unfair if an individual, who had just bought land in a certain locality, had to live there and tolerate the nuisance merely because it was there before he arrived.

Furthermore, it is no defence for the defendant to plead that the work he is carrying out is for the public good or is of general usefulness. The courts do not expect an individual to put up with a nuisance without compensation merely because the usefulness of the defendant's work outweighs the loss caused to the plaintiff.

Apart from the general defences to the law of tort, such as a nuisance being authorised by statute or being carried on with the consent of the plaintiff, there is the following important specific defence.

Prescription

If the defendant's activities have openly and without interruption been causing a nuisance to the plaintiff for twenty years or more, the plaintiff will not be able to claim that these activities are a nuisance to him.

The period of prescription (twenty years) only starts to run from the time that the activities become a nuisance to the plaintiff, not from the time that the defendant actually began his activities.

This difference can be illustrated by *Sturges* v. *Bridgman*. A confectioner had for over twenty years been using large pestles and mortars in the back of his premises which adjoined the garden of a physician. Then, the physician built a consulting-room at the end of his garden and, for the first time, found that the noise and vibrations from the confectioner interfered with his work. The physician succeeded in an action for nuisance because, although the confectioner had been carrying out his activities for over twenty years, the work only became a nuisance when the consulting-room was built.

This defence only applies to private nuisance; a public nuisance is never made lawful by prescription.

D. REMEDIES FOR NUISANCE

Provided it can be proved that a nuisance exists, the plaintiff has the following remedies.

1. Abatement

This occurs where the plaintiff puts an end to the nuisance himself, but he must take the risk that he is justified in doing so. This remedy is similar to 'self-help' in trespass, that is, it is used where a remedy quicker than the ordinary process of law is required. If the defendant delays unreasonably, the right to abate is lost.

The right must be exercised by the person who would be entitled to bring an action for nuisance, and the right allows him to enter another person's land in order to abate it. While abating the nuisance he must not cause wanton destruction, but only do sufficient to discontinue the nuisance.

2. Action for Damages

As in the case of all torts, the plaintiff can recover damages for his loss. In nuisance it will be the value of the comfort or enjoyment he has lost in his land, or the diminution in value of the land due to the interference, or the price of whatever use may have been affected: for example, loss of crops.

3. Injunction

In General

An injunction is an order of the court and its disobedience may be punished by imprisonment for contempt of court.

The most common form of injunction orders an individual not to do a certain activity or refrain from continuing with it. In this form the injunction is called *prohibitory*. For example, a prohibitory injunction may be granted to prevent the defendant continuing to trespass or cause a nuisance. In *Sturges* v. *Bridgman* the physician was granted an injunction to prevent the confectioner causing a nuisance by pounding his pestles.

An injunction may, in a very few situations, order an individual to do some positive act. In this form it is called a *mandatory* injunction. For example, in *Morris* v. *Redland Bricks Ltd* the defendant, by excavations on his own land, had caused the plaintiff's land to subside. The Court of Appeal issued a mandatory injunction ordering the defendant to shore up his land. It was estimated that this process would cost the defendant £30,000 and the loss to the plaintiff, who was a market gardener, was only about £1,600. On appeal by the defendant the House of Lords withdrew the mandatory order since the courts should have greater regard to the possible financial consequences of ordering an individual to do something.

An injunction is an equitable remedy, which means that it is issued only at the discretion of the court. No individual has a right to have one granted.

For Nuisances

An individual who asks the court to issue an injunction must first of all prove that the defendant has committed the tort of nuisance and that he has suffered some damage in consequence.

However, the courts will not issue an injunction for what they consider to be merely a trifling interference; for instance, in a case of trespass the court refused to grant an injunction to prevent a trespass by collectors who chased a butterfly on to the plaintiff's land. Furthermore, the courts will not grant an injunction where damages would be an adequate remedy in itself. For instance, in *Swaine* v. *Great Northern Railway* manure heaps which were normally inoffensive occasionally became offensive by a delay in their removal and because of the presence of dead cats and dogs. The court held that this was a nuisance, but as it only happened occasionally damages were a more appropriate remedy than injunction.

An injunction may be granted to restrain a public nuisance where there is a continuous disregard for the law or where a criminal penalty has proved inadequate.

1. What are the two forms of nuisance and how do they differ?
2. D has parked his car on the highway in such a way that it blocks the exit to P's house and prevents T passing along the highway in his car. What action may T and P take against D?
3. P's neighbour, D, holds noisy parties late into the night, to which P is not invited. Discuss the factors that the court is likely to consider in deciding whether D is causing a nuisance.
4. D is a 'Do-it-yourself' enthusiast and often P is disturbed by the sound of D's electric drill and saw. P approaches D about making less noise and D's only reaction is to make all the noise he possibly can. Advise P.
5. P keeps prize cats. These cats are highly sensitive to noise and are seriously affected by the sound of D's lawn-mower at weekends. Discuss the liability of D.
6. P buys a house next door to a small printing works. When P first moves in the noise does not bother him. As he grows older P becomes less tolerant. After thirty years of living next door to the works P wishes to bring an action. Advise P.
7. What are the remedies available to a person complaining of a private nuisance?

Write short notes on:
(1) prescription
(2) injunctions
(3) the importance of the locality in an action for nuisance
(4) the meaning of 'loss of use or enjoyment' of land
(5) the persons who are capable of bringing an action for nuisance
(6) the principle of 'live and let live'.

12. The Tort of Defamation

A well-known definition of this tort is that defamation is the publication of a false statement which tends to lower a person in the estimation of right-thinking members of society or which tends to make them shun or avoid that person.

1. 'Publication'

This simply means the communication of the untruths about the plaintiff to at least one person other than the plaintiff and defendant. Although for the plaintiff to succeed in an action for defamation he needs to show that the lie was told to, or had come to the notice of, a third person, if the defamatory statement was written on a postcard or telegram the plaintiff will not have to prove 'publication'; the courts presume that such messages have been read.

2. 'Shun or Avoid'

From the definition it can be seen that the tort covers not only the situation where a person's reputation has been lowered in the eyes of his fellow-men, but situations where he is shunned or avoided by them. For example, if the defendant untruthfully told others that the plaintiff was suffering from some unpleasant and contagious disease, or that he was insane, the plaintiff would possibly be shunned and avoided, even though nobody may think any the worse of him.

In *Youssoupoff* v. *M.G.M. Pictures Ltd* the plaintiff, a Russian princess, claimed that the defendants had falsely imputed in one of their films that she had been ravished by the notorious monk, Rasputin. She was successful in her action for defamation, for to imply that she had suffered such an experience tended 'to make the plaintiff be shunned and avoided and that without any moral discredit on her part'.

3. 'Right-Thinking Members of Society'

Whether a statement can be considered defamatory depends on the effect such a falsehood would have on the right-thinking members of society generally. The right-thinking member of society is the reasonable man. Among his qualities the 'reasonable man' has the attributes and feelings of the ordinary citizen: he is neither so prudish as to censor any small defect in the plaintiff, nor so permissive as to accept anything that may be said of the plaintiff. Naturally, the attitudes of the reasonable man will vary according to the ever-changing moral standards of the community. For instance, perhaps today the reasonable man would not tend to shun and avoid the plaintiff in

Youssoupoff v. *M.G.M. Pictures Ltd* because of the fate that was said to have befallen her.

In *Byrne* v. *Deane* the plaintiff was a member of a golf club in which there had been some illegal gaming machines. As a result of a complaint being made to the police the machines were removed. Shortly afterwards the following lampoon appeared on the wall of the club-house near to where the machines had stood:

> For many years upon this spot
> You heard the sound of the merry bell.
> Those who were rash and.those who were not,
> Lost and made a spot of cash.
> But he who gave the game away,
> May he Byrne in hell and rue the day.   Diddleramus.

The plaintiff brought an action against the proprietors of the club for libel. The court held that the words were not defamatory because the standard was to be judged according to the attitude of the right-thinking members of society, and the reporting of illegal behaviour to the police was not something that would lower the reputation of the plaintiff in their minds (even though members of the club may think worse of him).

Vulgar Abuse
For the statement to be defamatory it must be false, yet a statement that is untrue is not necessarily defamatory. For instance, if untruths are uttered in the heat of an argument, or sworn during a loss of temper, the court may consider that the words are merely abusive and not defamatory. In *Penfold* v. *Westcote* the defendant called out: 'Why don't you come out you blackguard, rascal, scoundrel, Penfold, you are a thief.' In this case, although the introductory words could be considered as merely vulgar abuse, the mention of the word 'thief' made the overall comment defamatory.

A. LIBEL AND SLANDER

Different Forms of Defamation
The law divides defamatory statements into those which are published in a permanent form and those which are in transient form. In the former case they are called libel and in the latter, slander.

Paintings, statues, printing and any form of writing are permanent forms, and will be libel. Furthermore, the Defamation Act, 1952, has said that defamatory statements broadcast by wireless or television are to be treated as libel.

Slander may consist of anything conveyed in speech or by gesture.

Libel, if it tends to provoke a breach of the peace, may be a crime. The requirements for criminal libel differ from the tort of libel and have been mentioned in an earlier section (see p. 95). Slander can only be a tort, although some words uttered may amount to a specific crime, such as sedition.

An important difference between these two forms of defamation is that libel is actionable *per se*, and slander is not. This means that in libel the plaintiff need not prove that he has suffered as a result of the defamatory statement. In a case of slander, bar four exceptions, the plaintiff must prove that he has suffered from the remarks.

The reason for libel being actionable *per se*, while slander is not, is possibly because a libellous statement can have more serious consequences. As libel is in a permanent form it means it could possibly do harm for longer and come to the notice of more people. Furthermore, as libel usually consists of the printed word, it is possible that more people will believe such statements; print seems to give a certain authority, and sometimes a false credibility, to a statement.

Slander Actionable without Proving Damage

In the following cases slander is actionable *per se*; therefore the plaintiff need not prove that he has actually suffered damage before he is able to bring a successful action.

1. Where the defendant says anything calculated to disparage the plaintiff by imputing dishonesty, unfitness or incompetence in any office, profession, calling, trade or business: for example, where the defendant says that the plaintiff, who is a solicitor, knows no law.
2. Where the defendant imputes that the plaintiff has committed a criminal offence which is punishable by imprisonment.
3. Where the defendant imputes that the plaintiff is suffering from a contagious or infectious disease which is likely to prevent other persons associating with him.
4. Where the defendant imputes that a woman is unchaste or adulterous.

B. FACTORS TO BE PROVED IN DEFAMATION

In every action for defamation, whether libel or slander, the plaintiff must prove, firstly, that the statement is defamatory; secondly, that the statement referred to him; and lastly, that the defamatory statement had been published to a third person.

1. The Statement Must be Defamatory

The statement may be defamatory in an obvious sense. For example, if an individual calls his neighbour a thief, the statement is easily recognisable as being defamatory and the plaintiff will have little trouble in proving this first point before the court.

Defamatory by Innuendo

Not every statement is obviously and at first sight defamatory. On some occasions statements that are perfectly innocent in appearance may, in reality, contain a hidden defamatory meaning. For example, although the statement that 'Mr A drinks' might be quite true and innocently stated, expressed in another way the same remark could carry defamatory implications.

Tolley v. *Fry* concerned an advertisement that was innocent on the face of it, but when the plaintiff proved further facts it could be appreciated that it was defamatory by *innuendo*. In this case the plaintiff was a famous amateur golfer, and without his knowledge the defendants used a caricature of him in an advertisement for their chocolate. The picture showed the plaintiff playing golf with a packet of the defendant's chocolate protruding from his pocket. Beside the plaintiff was a caddy who was explaining how excellent both the plaintiff's golf and the defendant's chocolate were. The plaintiff brought an action for libel and alleged that by innuendo the advertisement gave persons the impression that he must have been paid for the advertisement and therefore was breaking the rules of his amateur status. The court held that as the advertisement was reasonably capable of bearing the innuendo alleged, the plaintiff should succeed.

Where a statement contains an innuendo or hidden meaning, the plaintiff must show, in order to prove that the statement was defamatory, that a reasonable person could, and in fact did, interpret the statement in a defamatory sense. In *Cassidy* v. *Daily Mirror* the defendant's newspaper, under the heading 'Today's Gossip', showed a photograph of Mr Cassidy with Miss X. The caption to this picture said that their engagement had just been announced. Mr Cassidy was, in fact, already married and Mrs Cassidy brought an action against the newspaper. She proved that the article was defamatory by innuendo. It was reasonable for her acquaintances to believe that the defendant's article was true and assume that she could not have been married to Mr Cassidy but must have lived with him in immoral cohabitation.

2. The Statement Must Refer to the Plaintiff

When the court has decided that the statement bears a defamatory meaning, it must then consider whether the plaintiff has proved that the statement actually referred to him.

If the defendant's statement is intended to be about the plaintiff, it is obvious that he will have little difficulty in proving that it referred to him. However, the defendant may publish a statement which he does not intend to be about the plaintiff, but, nevertheless, other people think it does refer to him. For example, in *Newstead* v. *London Express Newspapers* the defendants published in their newspaper that Harold Newstead, a thirty-year-old Camberwell man, had been convicted of bigamy. Although this statement was true of a Camberwell barman of that name, it was untrue of another Harold Newstead, an unmarried man who was a hairdresser and lived in Camberwell. The latter successfully brought an action for defamation, saying that although this statement may have been intended to refer to another man it was understood by many persons as referring to him, and in this sense it was defamatory.

Before the Defamation Act, 1952, if a statement was innocently printed about one person but some people took it as referring to the plaintiff in a defamatory way, the plaintiff could bring an action. This was the case even if this statement told the truth about the original person (see Newstead's case), or even if the defendant intended the original character to be fictitious, as in the case of *Hulton* v. *Jones.*

In that case the Hulton Press published a humorous article about a motor festival in Dieppe and an account of the immoral behaviour of a Mr Artemus Jones, a churchwarden from Peckham. Artemus Jones was intended to be a fictitious character, but there was in fact a barrister of this name who did not live in Peckham, was not a churchwarden and who had not attended the festival. He brought an action for defamation and was successful, as he proved that some of his friends believed that the article referred to him.

Unintentional Defamation

The situations where a defendant was liable for his statement although he could not have foreseen that it could be defamatory of the plaintiff, or even where he had no idea that it could refer to the plaintiff at all, could not only lead to injustice but could also give rise to 'gold-digging' actions. A so-called 'gold-digging' action was brought by a person hoping to receive damages merely by showing that the statement happened to be defamatory of him or referred to him, even though he had not really suffered in consequence.

These situations have been modified by section 4 of the Defamation Act, 1952. Now, under this section, the defendant may make an 'offer of amends' for any statement that he has published 'innocently', 'unintentionally' and without being negligent, provided:

(*a*)   that the publisher did not intend to publish the words about the plaintiff and did not know how they could be understood as referring to him (see *Newstead* v. *London Express Newspapers* and *Hulton* v. *Jones*, above); *or*

(*b*)   that the words were not defamatory at face value and the publisher did not know how they could be considered defamatory of the plaintiff (see *Cassidy* v. *Daily Mirror* and *Tolley* v. *Fry*, above).

An 'offer of amends' means that the defendant may publish a suitable apology and correction for the plaintiff. Provided the defendant does this, an 'offer of amends' is a defence in any action, when:

(*a*)   it has been carried out and accepted by the plaintiff; *or*

(*b*)   if refused by the plaintiff, it had in any case been made as soon as practicable after the defendant realised the words were or might be defamatory of the plaintiff and the offer has not since been withdrawn.

3. The Defamatory Statement was Published

The essence of defamation is that an individual's reputation is lowered in the estimation of others. Thus, others must be aware of the defamatory remark. It would not be sufficient for one person to utter horrible untruths about another person to his face if no one else was present to hear the comment, or if a person wrote lies about somebody in his diary which no one else read. The defamatory statement must be 'published'; this means it must come to the knowledge of someone other than the person defamed—a third person.

However, the courts have held that in the following situations there has been no publication of the defamatory statement:

(*a*)   The law considers that if the person only communicates the defamatory statement to his or her spouse it has not been published. For example, if Mr A tells his wife something defamatory about Miss C, Miss C will not have an action for defamation against Mr A as this remark had not been published to a third person, but only to Mrs A.

(*b*)   Where a person makes the defamatory statement in a way that is unintelligible to the third party, there will be no 'publication': for example, if the defamatory remark was in a foreign language, a personal shorthand or, when the third party is deaf, by speech.

(*c*)   Where the maker of the defamatory statement has taken reasonable care to ensure that no third person knows of the statement, he will not be liable for its publication where the third party by some wrongful means gets to know of the remark. For example, in *Huth* v. *Huth* a defamatory letter was sent through the post and a butler without permission opened and read the contents out of curiosity. It was held that the defendant was not responsible for the publication.

(d)   A person will not be liable for publication if he merely distributes such matter as books, newspapers or magazines that he could not be expected to know contained defamatory remarks. Such a person is called an *innocent disseminator*, and in *Emmens* v. *Pottle* a newsvender was held not liable for publishing a defamatory statement which was in the newspapers that he had sold in the ordinary course of his business.

A library that lends out books that contain libellous statements will be innocent disseminators unless they should have known of the libel. In *Vizetelly* v. *Mudie's Select Library* the defendants lent copies of a book containing a libellous statement about the plaintiff and were held liable for its publication because they had overlooked a publisher's note requesting them to withdraw the books from circulation and return them.

C. DEFENCES TO AN ACTION FOR DEFAMATION

As well as the defence of 'unintentional defamation', mentioned above, which was created by section 4 of the Defamation Act, 1952, the defendant may have any of the following defences open to him.

1. Truth

However unpleasant and malicious his remarks may be, the defendant is justified in saying what is true about the plaintiff. It would be unjust if the plaintiff could stop the defendant saying truths about him, even if they are unflattering.

The statement that the defendant makes need not be absolutely true; it is sufficient if it is substantially accurate. In *Alexander* v. *North Eastern Railway* the defendants stated, on a notice, that the plaintiff had been convicted of travelling on the railway without paying his fare. For this, the notice went on to say, he had been fined or given the alternative of three weeks' imprisonment. The court considered that the defendant's statement was substantially true and that therefore they were justified in saying it.

2. Privilege

So far we have seen that the purpose of the tort of defamation is to protect the individual from having untrue remarks made about him. However, in certain situations the law has considered it more important to protect the interests of the person who made the statement rather than protect the reputation of the victim of the statement.

The law considers that in some places and in certain situations a person should be allowed to make statements without the fear of an action for defamation. For example, for the benefit of the working of government, all that is said in parliament is privileged (see 'Absolute Privilege'), and for the benefit of a future employer a present employer's character reference for an employee may be privileged (see 'Qualified Privilege').

Thus it will be seen that privilege may be either absolute or qualified. In the former the plaintiff has no action for defamation even if the untruth is outrageous or malicious. In the latter, the defendant is allowed to make the statement even if it happens to be untrue, provided he is not being malicious.

(a) Absolute Privilege
This includes:

1. Statements made by a member in either House of Parliament.
2. Publications made by the order of either House of Parliament.
3. Statements made by one officer of State to another in the course of official duties.
4. Newspaper and television reports of public judicial proceedings, provided they are fair, accurate and contemporaneous. Therefore, such reports will not be absolutely privileged if they are delayed, biased and inaccurate.
5. Statements made in the course of judicial proceedings. It does not matter whether the statement is made by the judge, member of the jury, counsel, witness or either party, provided it is relevant to the present proceedings.

(b) Qualified Privilege
It must be remembered that this defence will be successful only if the statement was made without malice or a desire that it should injure the other person's reputation. With this qualification in mind, the defence may be claimed in the following situations:

1. Statements made in situations where the law considers that an individual is under a legal, social or moral duty to say something about one person to another person. The person to whom the statement is made must also have a corresponding interest in hearing what has to be said. For example, in *Beach* v. *Freeson* the defendant was an M.P. and he had received a complaint from a

constituent about the plaintiffs, who were a firm of solicitors. The defendant passed the complaint on to the Law Society and sent a copy of his letter to the Lord Chancellor. The plaintiffs sued for libel but the court held that the defendant was protected by qualified privilege in both instances. The defendant was entitled to write to the Law Society, and the letter to the Lord Chancellor was also privileged because he has an interest in the conduct of solicitors as they are potential holders of judicial office.

2. Fair and accurate reports of judicial proceedings in situations that may not be covered by absolute privilege: for instance, if they are not contemporaneous and not by a newspaper, radio or television.

3. The Defamation Act, 1952, section 7, gives qualified privilege, in many different situations, to fair and accurate reports in newspapers or broadcasts. For instance, reports on meetings of public bodies or organisations will come within this section.

3. Fair Comment

An individual has a right to talk about matters or persons of public interest. Furthermore, persons of public interest are presumed to expect and tolerate such comments. Therefore, the law allows an individual to state his opinions on such matters or persons, provided that what he says is fair and unmalicious. The law will protect such persons from lies, but not from fair comment.

If the maker of a statement pleads the defence that his remark was an opinion on a matter of public interest and it was fair comment, he must prove the following:

(a)   That the subject of the comment was of public interest, national or local. For example, the subject may be any person from the Prime Minister to the local mayor, or any organisation from parliament to a local bazaar. This defence covers the public life and conduct of every public person, but will not include their private lives unless it reflects on their ability in public life.

(b)   The statement must be one of opinion. The opinion must be honestly believed and any facts upon which the opinion is based must be truthfully stated. If the facts are untrue the defendant cannot succeed in fair comment, even if his comment upon the false facts happened to be made honestly. For example, to say that a person did something is a statement of fact; to criticise this act by saying it was dishonourable or disgraceful is a matter of opinion and comment.

(c)   The comment must be fair. The defendant must show that his opinion on the true facts is a fair one, though it need not necessarily be reasonable. The law is liberal on the question of what is fair and what is not. There is no objective test as to what the 'reasonable man' would consider to be fair. If there was such a test, it would prevent any number of people, with varying views held at various levels of fanaticism, from expressing their opinions unless they coincided with the opinion of the 'reasonable man'—and this would be sad.

(d)   The comment must not be malicious. If the defendant's remark was prompted by some malicious or evil motive, the comment could not have been an honest opinion; and if it is not honest it cannot be fair.

1.   Explain the difference between libel and slander.
2.   What must the plaintiff prove in order to succeed in an action for defamation?
3.   What defences are available to an action for defamation?

Give brief answers to the following questions:
(1)   Is it a defence to an action for defamation to prove that one has told the truth?
(2)   Is it slander or libel if a person, who is being interviewed on a 'live' television programme, says something defamatory?
(3)   Would you consider it libel or slander if someone made a defamatory image of you in snow outside your front gate?
(4)   A radio programme untruly represents you as a traitor to your country. Is it libel or slander?
(5)   A newsvendor is selling newspapers which contain a defamatory article about you. Is he necessarily guilty of libel?
(6)   D sends by post to P a postcard that is defamatory of P. Does P have to prove that it has been published to a third person?

Which is the most likely defence to be used in the following situations:
(1)   Mr D, a member of parliament, in the course of a parliamentary debate makes a defamatory statement about P.Co.Ltd.
(2)   Miss P, a typist, has asked her employer, Mr D, for a reference. Her potential employer says that he cannot offer her the job because of her reference from Mr D, which states that she spends most of her working day gossiping.
(3)   A newspaper article says that Mr P, a member of parliament, has no right to be in charge of a ministry because of the inefficient way in which he has dealt with public matters in the past.
(4)   A local newspaper states that Mr P has been fined £100 for driving

under the influence of drink when, in fact, he was fined £50.

What is the meaning of:
(a) publication
(b) innuendo
(c) unintentional defamation
(d) innocent dissemination
(e) actionable *per se.*

13. The Law of Contract

A. THE NATURE OF CONTRACT

The Definition of a Contract
A contract is an agreement which the law will enforce.

We have seen that in the case of crimes and torts the duties imposed upon an individual are imposed by the law. The law makes it a crime to steal and the law says an individual must not make defamatory statements about another individual. However, the duties are basically different in the law of contracts. In contract law the individual is only obliged to do something because he has agreed with another individual that he will do it. For instance, the law certainly does not force an individual to sell his car; but if he has agreed to sell it to someone who has paid for it, then the law will enforce the agreement by making the individual pay compensation if he breaks his agreement.

So, the basis of a contract is the agreement that one individual makes with another; and the law of contract is the rules laid down which usually have to be followed if the parties to the agreement wish their transaction to be legally binding and enforceable in a court of law.

Simple Contracts
Contracts can be made informally or formally.

The contracts that can be made with the least amount of formality are called *simple* contracts, and it is these contracts that concern us in this chapter. Contracts that are formal are known as contracts *under seal*, and they are not valid unless the agreement has been made in writing and signed, sealed and delivered.

Simple contracts require little formality, which means the parties are able to choose their own way of making the agreement. The agreement may be made orally, for instance when buying a newspaper; or in writing, such as the purchase of clothes from a mail-order firm; or the agreement may be partly oral and partly in writing, as when one party writes his offer of the agreement in a letter and the other party accepts the offer by telephoning a reply. It is also possible for a simple contract to be created purely by the conduct of the parties: for instance, by putting money into an automatic machine to buy cigarettes or to park a car.

Nevertheless, there are several types of simple contract that do require an element of formality if they are to be enforced by the courts. These are, firstly, contracts of guarantee, and secondly, contracts for the sale of land, leases or mortgages. All these contracts require some written evidence of the agreement before the courts will enforce them.

Because of the relative freedom and informality in making simple contracts, the courts have laid down that certain elements must be present before they will consider the contract to be legally binding on both parties. Each simple contract must consist of an *offer* by one party, an *acceptance* of the offer by the other party, and both parties must have given some *consideration*. The court must also be able to find some evidence to show that both parties intended to be legally bound by their agreement.

B. THE CREATION OF THE CONTRACT

As just mentioned, there are three basic elements to the creation of a simple contract. Firstly, there must be an offer and an acceptance of the offer. For example, Mr A may say to Mr B, a garage owner, 'May I buy that car for £500?' Mr B may reply 'Yes.' In this case Mr A has made an offer, Mr B has accepted and there is now an agreement. However, an agreement, in itself, is not a contract; two further elements have to be present, the second element is consideration. This consists of what each party has given or promises to give. In the present illustration, the consideration of Mr A is that he has promised to pay for the car, in return for Mr B's consideration which is the car he promises to sell. The third element is that both parties must intend to be legally bound by the agreement, and in the case of Mr A and Mr B the courts would consider that over the sale of a car from a garage the parties must 'mean business' and intend legal relations.

It is now necessary to consider these three elements separately and in greater detail.

I. The Agreement

The Offer

The party who makes the offer is called the *offeror*, and the party to whom it is made is the *offeree*.

An offer is where one party offers to enter into a contract with the person who accepts. Therefore, the offer must be firm and definite, because the offeree must know exactly what the offer entails and that he is able and allowed to accept it. For example, there is no firm offer if a person is merely making tentative inquiries to see whether an article is for sale, or where a prospective buyer might ask for further information before he makes up his mind whether or not to make an offer. The courts will, in certain cases, make a distinction between what looks like a firm offer but what is only an 'invitation to treat'.

Invitations to Treat

An invitation to treat is not an offer, but only an invitation for somebody to make an offer. For example, where an article is displayed in a shop window with a price-tag on it, the courts have said this is usually not an offer to sell because if it was, the customer, by accepting, would make a contract binding on the shopkeeper. This would lead to difficulties if, for instance, the shopkeeper had mistakenly given the article the wrong price-tag or found it was the last of those articles in stock and he did not want to sell it.

Therefore, the courts have stated that a shop window display of goods, goods in shelves in self-service stores, and advertisements for the sale of goods in newspapers and the like, are not firm offers but merely invitations for a person to make an offer. For example, in *Fisher* v. *Bell* the court said that the display of flick-knives in a shop window was not an offer to sell them. The display was only an invitation to treat. The court said that it was the customer who makes the offer to buy the articles which the shopkeeper may either accept or refuse.

To whom the Offer May be Made

The offeror may make the offer to a particular individual. If he does, it is only that person who can accept.

The offer may, however, be made to a group of persons, or even to 'the world at large', provided the offer is capable of being accepted by only one of those persons. This rule was established in *Carlill* v. *Carbolic Smoke Ball Co.* The defendants had printed in a newspaper an advertisement which said that their carbolic smoke ball prevented flu. The advertisement went on to say that if any person bought and used a smoke ball in the proper way and was unfortunate enough to catch flu, the company would pay him £100. To show their sincerity in this, they said that they had deposited £1,000 with their bank for the purpose. Mrs Carlill bought and used the smoke ball and caught flu. The company refused to pay her, and when she sued them they claimed that the advertisement was not an offer but was only an advertising 'puff' which was not meant to be taken seriously. They further claimed that, even if it had been an offer, it was not made to any definite person. The court held that the advertisement was an offer because the depositing of £1,000 showed that they intended readers to take the proposition seriously; the court further held that this offer could be made to 'the world at large' and would be accepted by any individual who bought and used the smoke ball.

The Offer Must Include All the Terms

An offer is one whole side of the agreement, and as such it must contain all the terms that the offeror intends to be bound by. All these terms must be made known to the offeree before he accepts, because he cannot be expected to agree to terms he knows nothing about until after his acceptance. In *Olley* v. *Marlborough Court Hotel*, Mr and Mrs Olley paid in advance at the reception desk for their stay at the hotel. When they went to their room they saw a notice on the wall informing guests that the hotel would not be liable for any loss of valuables from the bedrooms. Mrs Olley left some furs in the bedroom and they were stolen. When Mr Olley sued the hotel for compensation the hotel said that they were not liable because of their notice. The court held that the contract between Mr Olley and the hotel was made at the reception desk and at this time he did not know about the notice. He was therefore bound by it and his claim was successful.

How an Offer Ends

Naturally, the offer will terminate if the offeree turns it down, or when the offeror withdraws his offer before the offeree has had time to accept it. Also, in most cases, the offer ends if either party dies before it has been accepted. There are two further ways in which an offer can be terminated.

Firstly, a *counter-offer* will cancel out the original offer. For example, Mr A offers his piano to Mr B for £500. Mr B, instead of accepting, makes a counter-offer by saying he will pay only £400. This counter-offer cancels out Mr A's original offer. So, if Mr A refuses to sell the piano for £400, Mr B, in theory, cannot then say that he will accept the original offer. But naturally, in practice, very few transactions are so rigid.

Secondly, it would be inconvenient commercial practice if an offer remained open indefinitely. Therefore the courts have said that if the offer does not state how long it is to remain open, the offer will lapse after a reasonable length of time. What is a reasonable length of time for an offer to remain open depends, of course, on the subject-matter of the contract. For example, it may be unreasonable to expect an offer to sell fresh mackerel to remain open for two weeks, but reasonable in the case of dried fruit. In *Ramsgate (Victoria) Hotel Ltd* v. *Montefiore* the court considered that it was unreasonable to expect an offer to purchase shares in a company to remain open for six months when the buying price of shares may fluctuate from day to day.

The Acceptance

The offer must be accepted by the person to whom it was made if there is to be an agreement. Also, the offeree must do something to show that he has accepted the offer. It is not sufficient if he remains silent or merely thinks to himself that he will accept. This is because the acceptance must be communicated to the offeror.

The offeree may inform the offeror he is accepting either orally or in writing, or he may show his acceptance by his conduct; for instance, in *Carlill* v. *Carbolic Smoke Ball Co.* Mrs Carlill accepted the offer by buying the smoke ball and using it according to the instructions. If, however, the offeror states that the offer has to be accepted in a certain way, for example by telegram, the offeree must comply with this term of the offer, otherwise there is no complete acceptance of the offer.

Acceptance by Post

Where the parties make the agreement by letters sent through the post, the rule regarding acceptance is different.

If Mr A posts a letter to Mr B offering to sell his car, the offer is made, obviously, when Mr B receives and reads the letter. However, the rule relating to acceptance by Mr B is less understandable: the courts have held that Mr B's acceptance of the offer takes place as soon as he posts his letter of acceptance to Mr A, not when it reaches Mr A.

It can be appreciated that certain problems may arise with this rule. For instance, the letter, although posted by Mr B, may never reach Mr A. In this situation there will still be an agreement, but Mr A will be unaware of the acceptance and might, in the meantime, have sold the car to somebody else, in which case he will still be liable to Mr B.

II. Consideration

Nature of Consideration

In every simple contract each party must contribute something of value towards the agreement in order to make the agreement binding on the other party. What the parties put into the contract is called 'consideration', whether it is money, goods or even a promise to do something.

In all simple contracts consideration is essential. For example, if Mr A offered his car to Mr B, and Mr B accepted, there would be an agreement but it would not be a contract. Mr B could not bring an action for breach of contract if Mr A later changed his mind about giving away his car, because Mr B has not supplied consideration.

The consideration between the parties may take the form of (a) actual money or money's worth, for example a car for cash or a car in return for a television set, or (b) mutual promises, for example where one party promises to paint a house next week if the other party promises to pay for the work and materials, or (c) a promise in return for an act, for example a promise to pay a reward to the finder of a lost dog.

If the consideration is actually carried out at the time of the agreement, it is called *executed* consideration: for example, the purchase of goods from a shop when the shopkeeper hands over the goods in return for the buyer paying the price.

If the consideration consists of the parties making promises to be fulfilled in the future, it is called *executory* consideration. *Executory* consideration is still sufficient to make the consideration given by both parties is executory because it has not yet been performed. For example, where a grocer promises to deliver goods next Friday and the householder promises to pay the account at the end of the month, the consideration given by both parties is executory because it has not yet been performed.

Consideration Must be of Some Value

The courts are primarily concerned to know that some consideration has been given. Therefore, in order that consideration can be recognised, it must be of some value for which the courts could award compensation. Once the courts see that some valuable consideration has been given, they are not concerned whether it is adequate or not. For example, money is obviously recognised by the courts as being of value, so it is sufficient consideration to pay £5 for a house however inadequate this may be in relation to its market value. It is the seller's own fault if he asks too little.

Where the consideration does not consist of money, but, for instance, of an act or a promise, it must still be of some monetary value. However, in the following situations the courts have held that the acts or promises are not of sufficient value to amount to consideration.

Firstly, if one party is already obliged to do something for the other party, he cannot make this obligation his consideration in another contract with that person. For example, in *Stilk* v. *Myrick* some sailors contracted to take a ship on a voyage and bring her back. During the course of the voyage two seamen deserted and the captain promised the remaining sailors the wages of these two men if they would work the ship home. The court held that the sailors were not entitled to the extra wages promised to them because they had supplied no consideration for this promise. They were already bound by their contract to work the ship home and they had not done sufficient extra work to amount to consideration. Similar to the above situation, it does not amount to consideration if a person promises to do something he is already bound by law to do. This point is illustrated by the case of *Collins* v. *Godefroy*, where the defendant promised to pay the plaintiff a sum of money if he would attend court as a witness. The court held that the plaintiff was not entitled to the money because he had supplied no valuable consideration. He was already bound by law to attend court.

Secondly, a promise to pay a lesser sum than is already owed to the other party does not amount to consideration in an agreement for the discharge of the whole amount. This is known as the rule in *Pinnel's Case* or the rule in *Foakes* v. *Beer,* and is best explained by example. If A owes B £20 and A pays or promises to pay £15 in return for B's promise to forgo the remaining £5, the rule states that A has supplied no valuable consideration. However, B's promise to accept less money does amount to consideration on his side of the agreement.

Thirdly, if an individual promises to do, or does, something which is only of moral worth, rather than of monetary value, the promise or act will not amount to consideration: for example, a promise to be of good behaviour, or to be someone's best friend, or a promise of love and affection.

Consideration Must not be Past

To amount to consideration, the act or promise must be given as part of the agreement. Consideration is past and insufficient for a contract if it is carried out before the agreement was contemplated. For example, Mr A, on his own initiative, digs Miss C's garden; then, at a later date, Miss C promises she will pay Mr A for his labours. If Miss C breaks this subsequent promise Mr A cannot claim because he gave no consideration in return for her promise; all his labours were done before he knew anything of her promise to pay and was past consideration, which is valueless.

However, where a person does something at another's request, and then at a later date the other person promises to pay for the services, the courts have held that the work is not past but good and valuable consideration: for instance, if Miss C asked Mr A to dig her garden and then, some time later, she promised to pay him for it. This was the situation in *Lampleigh* v. *Brathweight,* where the defendant asked the plaintiff to go on an errand which entailed travelling throughout the country. When the plaintiff returned successful the defendant promised to pay him £100 for his efforts. At a still later date the defendant refused to pay. When the plaintiff sued for the money the defendant said he was not bound to his promise because the plaintiff has supplied only past consideration. The court held that the plaintiff should receive his money because, even though he did not know how much money he would receive at the time he ran the errand, he had been asked by the defendant to make the journey

III. Intention to Create Legal Relations

Meaning of the Phrase

Even though there might have been an offer and an acceptance between the parties and some form of consideration given by both, the agreement is still not necessarily a contract.

For instance, Miss C offers to cook a meal for Mr A in return for his bringing a bottle of wine. Mr A accepts and when he arrives he finds she has not prepared a meal. In this situation it is not expected that Mr A would take legal action because presumably neither of them intended to be legally bound by their agreement.

Thus, the third essential element to a contract is that the parties intended to enter into an agreement that could be legally enforced by either of them through the courts of law if the other broke the agreement.

Domestic and Commercial Agreements

In the context of legal relations, it is not easy for the courts to discover what the parties actually intended by their agreement. For this reason the courts divide agreements into two categories.

Firstly, there are those agreements which the courts presume were not meant to be contracts and by which the parties did not intend to be legally bound. These are called *domestic* agreements, which include such agreements as those between husband and wife, friends and relatives.

The second category consists of *commercial* agreements. In these cases, which will include any business transactions or mercantile contracts, the courts presume that the parties did mean to make a contract and intend to create a legally enforceable agreement.

Rebutting the Presumption

These presumptions that the courts make on the nature of the agreement are not absolutely rigid. For instance, it is possible that what is presumably a domestic agreement may on further evidence be decided by the court to be legally binding in nature. This was the outcome in *Simpkins* v. *Pays*. In this case the plaintiff lodged with the defendant and her granddaughter, and each week all three entered a Sunday newspaper competition. The combined entry was sent in the defendant's name, but they all shared in the expenses that they incurred. One week the entry was successful. The defendant, as the entry was in her name, received £750, and refused to give the plaintiff his one-third share. When the plaintiff sued for his share the defendant said she was not legally bound to pay him as it was only a 'friendly adventure'. The court held that the evidence of sharing the expenses showed that they 'meant business' and it was a joint enterprise for which the plaintiff should receive his share of the prize.

Also, in some commercial transactions one of the parties often goes to great trouble to show the other party that he does not intend to be legally bound by their agreement. This is often shown by inserting what is called an 'honour clause' into the contract. For example, in *Jones* v. *Vernons Pools Ltd* the plaintiff sued for the money he alleged he had won with his football pool coupon, which the defendants stated they had not received. The court held that the agreement was not legally enforceable by the plaintiff because the defendants had printed on each coupon 'This transaction is binding in honour only'.

C. CONTRACTUAL CONSENT

The general rule is that an individual will be bound by what he has consented to. If he finds later that through his own foolishness he has consented to a contract that is disadvantageous, or the goods are not what he expected, he will still be bound to his agreement because the courts consider that he has only himself to blame for not making the best out of his bargaining. The rule *caveat emptor* ('let the buyer beware') is explained in Chapter 14.

However, the law recognises that in certain situations a party may have given his consent to a contract which it is unfair to hold him to, because his consent was not freely given. The most obvious is called *duress*, where a person is threatened by physical violence to enter into a contract. Naturally, in this situation there is no free consent. Another situation is where one person, by the position he holds over another person, *unduly influences* the other to enter into a contract.

Two important situations where there has been no free consent are when the party has made a *mistake*, and where he has been persuaded by some *misrepresentation* to enter into a contract. Both these situations must now be considered more fully.

I. Mistake

The Effect of Mistake
In the few situations where the law allows a mistake to affect a contract, the contract will be *void*. This means that the contract will be a nullity and will have no legal effect on the parties. So, where there has been a void contract, whatever has been done by the parties must be undone. Each party is returned to the position he was in before the contract was attempted. For example, if the contract concerned the sale of a car, the purchaser would receive his money back and the seller would have the car returned to him.

It would lead to great uncertainty and havoc in commercial practice if every time a party proved that he had made a mistake, however slight it might be, the contract could be declared void. Therefore, only a few types of mistakes have been recognised by the courts as capable of rendering a contract void. These are common mistake, mutual mistake and unilateral mistake.

1. Common Mistake

This is when both parties make the same mistake. The mistake common to both of them must concern some underlying fact which is fundamental to the existence of the contract. For example, in *Couturier* v. *Hastie* the parties contracted over the sale of a ship's cargo of corn which, unknown to them both, had already been damaged and sold. The court held that the contract was void for common mistake as both parties were mistaken as to some fundamental part of the contract, which was that the corn existed to be sold when it did not.

The courts have shown in their decisions a policy that a contract will be void for common mistake only when the mistake is about the substance of the contract or the actual existence of the subject-matter, as in the case of *Couturier* v. *Hastie.*

Mistake as to Quality

Although there may be a common mistake in other situations, the contract will not necessarily be void: for instance, when the parties are mistaken only about the *quality* of the subject-matter, rather than its existence. Thus, if A agrees to buy a horse from B which at the time of the contract had in fact died, the contract will be void. But if A had agreed to buy and B to sell a horse which they both thought was Arabian and later it was found to be Persian, then the contract is not void, as there has been a common mistake only about the horse's quality, and not its actual existence. This was the situation in *Leaf* v. *International Galleries* where the parties entered into a contract for the sale of a picture, both erroneously believing that it had been painted by Constable. The court held it was only a mistake as to the quality of the picture and not as to its substance, so the contract was not void.

2. Mutual Mistake

In common mistake at least there is an agreement between the parties, whereas in mutual mistake there is no true agreement at all because they have misunderstood each other.

For example, Mr A has two cameras, and he offers to sell a particular one to Mr B. However, Mr B accepts the offer thinking that it is Mr A's other camera he is buying. It can be seen that there is no genuine agreement since the acceptance does not correspond with the offer owing to a mistake by Mr B, of which both parties are unaware.

In *Raffles* v. *Wichelhaus* the defendants contracted to buy a cargo of cotton to arrive on board the steamship *Peerless* which was sailing from Bombay harbour. There were two ships named *Peerless* with similar cargo and both sailed from Bombay, but on different dates. The parties were each thinking of different vessels so the contract was void because of their mutual mistake.

Mistake Must be Reasonable

Because there has been a mutual mistake, it does not mean that the contract is automatically void. If this were so, many persons could escape their obligations under a contract merely by proving a misunderstanding and that the contract was not all that they expected.

Whether the contract will be void for mutual mistake is for the court to decide. The method they use is to decide whether a sensible person would also have made the same mistake the parties actually made. Therefore, if the plaintiff is unreasonable in making his mistake, he will be bound by the contract.

3. Unilateral Mistake

In unilateral mistake only one party is mistaken, but it differs from mutual mistake in that the other party knows that the mistake is being made.

The problem arises most frequently, but not exclusively, in connection with mistaken identity. For example, A intends to make a contract with B and with B only, but by mistake he makes the contract with C and C knows that A is making the mistake. In such cases the contract will be void for unilateral mistake because A only consented to the contract because he believed he was contracting with B.

The fact that one party knows the other is making a mistake means that cases of unilateral mistake usually involve an element of fraud which takes away the free consent. This can be seen in the case of *Ingram* v. *Little*. The plaintiff, Ingram, advertised her car for sale. A man falsely calling himself Hutchinson said he wished to buy it. The plaintiff refused unless he could prove he was Hutchinson and would not let him pay by cheque until she had proof of his identity. He gave her his business address which was checked in the telephone directory, and it was found that there was such a person with a business at that address. She then allowed him to have the car in return for a cheque that turned out to be a dud. Meanwhile, the 'rogue' had sold the car to an innocent purchaser called Little. When the car was traced to Little, the plaintiff brought an action to recover the car from him. The House of Lords held that the contract between Ingram and the rogue had been void for unilateral mistake, because she did not consent to make the contract with the rogue who had called to see her but only with a man called Hutchinson. Therefore, the effect of the void contract was that she had never parted with her ownership of the car to the rogue; and consequently the rogue had no title which he could pass on to Little.

So, Little had to return the car.

It can be seen by the situation in *Ingram* v. *Little* that the courts often have a difficult task when deciding who, out of two innocent persons, is to lose. Where the transaction involves a rogue who cannot be found, either the original owner or the innocent third party must suffer financial loss. For this reason, the courts have said that there is usually a presumption in these cases that the seller intends to make a contract with the person who is standing in front of him. Consequently, if the seller fails to take adequate precautions to make sure that he is not contracting with a rogue, it is only fair that he should lose his goods if he does sell them to a rogue, rather than the third party lose when he had no opportunity of preventing the fraud. If, however, the seller does all that is within his power to make sure the buyer is not a rogue, then it is only right that the contract should be void for unilateral mistake and that he should not lose his goods to the rogue, who cannot then pass title on to someone else (as in *Ingram* v. *Little*). The situation where the courts have decided that the contract is not void because the seller has failed to prove that he did not intend to deal with the person in front of him (i.e. the rogue) can be illustrated by two cases.

In *Phillips* v. *Brooks* a rogue went into the plaintiff's shop and selected some jewellery which the plaintiff said he could buy. The rogue then falsely stated that he was Sir George Bullough and wished to pay by cheque. The plaintiff, who had heard of such a person, allowed him to do so. The rogue gave him a dud cheque and took some of the jewels which he pawned at the defendant's shop. When the jewels were traced to the defendant the plaintiff brought an action to recover them. The court held that there was no unilateral mistake in this case, so the contract between the jeweller and the rogue was not void. As the contract was, therefore, valid, the rogue did gain ownership of the jewels and could pass ownership to Brooks who was entitled to keep the jewels. The reason why the contract was not void for unilateral mistake seems a very technical one: it was that the courts decided that the jeweller had consented to make a contract with the rogue who came into the shop and stood in front of him, before any question of identity arose. The identity of the rogue was only a matter of concern when payment by cheque was being considered by the parties.

In the case of *Lewis* v. *Averay*, the plaintiff advertised his car for sale. A rogue answered the advertisement and wished to buy the car. The rogue said he was Richard Green, a well-known film actor. The rogue wrote out a cheque, and when the plaintiff wished for proof of his identity he showed a special pass to Pinewood Studios with his photograph on it. Lewis then let him take the car in return for a cheque that turned out to be worthless. The rogue then sold the car to Averay who had no knowledge of the previous fraud. The court held that the contract was not void for unilateral mistake because the plaintiff had failed to prove that he had intended to contract only with Richard Green, the actor, rather than with the actual person who answered the advertisement. The mistake that Lewis made was only concerning the person's attributes when it came to payment by cheque. Therefore, Averay had bought good title in the car and could retain it.

II. Misrepresentation

The Nature of Misrepresentation

In many cases the actual agreement or contract made is only the outcome of many negotiations between the parties. Naturally, in these negotiations one party may be eager for the contract while the other party might be hesitant. Thus the eager party might become over-anxious and make statements, innocently or fraudulently, to induce the other to enter into the contract. Any statement which one party makes in the course of these negotiations which induces the other party to make the contract is known as a 'representation'. If such a statement is untrue it is a *misrepresentation* and the contract will be *voidable.*

We have seen, while dealing with mistake, that 'void' means that the agreement is a nullity and has no legal effect. A 'voidable' contract is one where a party who has been induced to enter into a contract by misrepresentation may choose either to end the contract or, if he considers it is still advantageous to him, he may carry on with the contract and claim damages for any loss the untrue statement has caused him.

The Requirements of Misrepresentation

A misrepresentation will affect the final contract only if it satisfies the following requirements:

(a) It Must be a Misrepresentation of FACT

The misrepresentation must be of a material fact; for instance, a statement that 'The horse is only three years old' is a statement of fact. The statement must not be a statement of *opinion*, or only an advertising puff; for instance, 'The horse is a better runner than most horses of its age' is a statement of opinion, and it would probably be an advertising puff to say 'You could not get a better horse than this anywhere in the country'. In *Bissett* v. *Wilkinson* the seller of land in New Zealand, which had not previously been used as a sheep farm, told a prospective buyer that in his mind the land would take two thousand sheep, when in fact it was only capable of carrying much less. It was held that this was a statement of opinion and not a representation of fact.

(b) It Must be Made BEFORE the Conclusion of the Contract

The statement must have been made *before* the contract was completed and must not be a term in the contract itself. In *Oscar Chess Ltd* v. *Williams* the defendant wished to sell his Morris car to the plaintiff. He told the plaintiff that the car was a 1948 Morris and produced the registration book that showed this. The plaintiff bought the car, but in fact the Morris was a 1938 model and unknown to either party at the time of the contract the registration book had been forged. The court held that the defendant's statement as to the date of the car was a representation and not a term in the contract, and as the misrepresentation had been made innocently the plaintiff could only claim damages.

(c) It Must Actually INDUCE the Party to Make the Contract

If the party to whom the representation was made ignores it, is unaware of it or does not rely on it, but relies instead, for instance, upon his own inquiries and judgment, he cannot bring an action as he was not *induced* to make the contract because of the false statement. In *Horsefall* v. *Thomas* a gun containing a defect was delivered to a buyer and after being fired for a few rounds fell to pieces. The buyer alleged that a defect in the breach had been concealed by a metal plug. The court held that this concealment of the defect was not a misrepresentation because the buyer had never examined the gun before buying it and therefore the concealment could not have had any effect on the prospective purchaser.

(d) The Statement Must have been FALSE

The statement must be false, in other words untrue, whether the maker knew it was false or had made it innocently.

If the person making the statement knew that it was untrue, the misrepresentation is *fraudulent.* In *Derry* v. *Peek* a company wished to run steam-powered trams in Plymouth and laid their plans before the Board of Trade and applied for permission from parliament. Parliament said that such trams could be used if authority was obtained from the Board of Trade. The directors of the company believed that this authorisation would be automatic, so they issued a prospectus saying they could run steam trams. Peek then bought some shares in the company. The Board of Trade then refused permission and the company was wound up. The House of Lords held that the company was not guilty of fraudulent misrepresentation because the directors had not knowingly made a false statement in the prospectus; in fact they honestly believed that permission to run the trams would be granted.

If the person who made the statement believed it to be true, the misrepresentation is *innocent.* There are two types of innocent misrepresentation. Firstly, where the statement is innocent but negligent. In other words, where a person makes a statement not knowing that it is untrue but which a reasonable man would have checked more carefully to make sure that it was not false. Secondly, where the statement is innocent and not negligent: for example, where the person makes the statement honestly and had reasonable grounds for believing it to be true.

This division of innocent misrepresentation into two types was made by the Misrepresentation Act, 1967, and it also states that any innocent misrepresentation is presumed to have been made negligently unless the person making it proves that he made it with reasonable honesty.

Remedies of the Misled Party

For fraudulent misrepresentation:

(*a*)   As the contract is voidable, the misled party is entitled to choose whether he wishes to continue with the contract or revoke it.

(*b*)   The misled party may claim damages for the loss he has suffered.

For innocent but negligent misrepresentation:

(*a*)   The Misrepresentation Act, 1967, treats negligent misrepresentation in the same way as fraudulent misrepresentation, but where the misled party was entitled to rescind the contract, in this case the court has a discretionary power to hold him to the contract and award him damages instead.

(*b*)   A right to claim damages.

For innocent and non-negligent misrepresentation:

(*a*)   The misled party may rescind the contract, but under the Misrepresentation Act, 1967, the court has a discretionary power to hold him to the contract and award him damages instead.

(*b*)   The misled party has no right to claim damages. If he is granted them by the court it will be at their discretion.

D. ILLEGAL CONTRACTS

Some contracts are illegal either because they are forbidden by statute or because the common law considers them contrary to public policy. A contract is contrary to public policy when it is in the public interest that it should not be enforced. The following are some examples of illegal contracts:

1. Agreements to Commit a Crime
If parties make an agreement that involves the commission of a crime, for instance murder, theft or defrauding the Inland Revenue, then the agreement is void as it is contrary to public policy.

2. Agreements to Impede the Administration of Justice
An agreement that is intended to suppress or prejudice justice in the courts of law, however slight, is illegal and void. One common example of this is the agreement between the parties to stifle a criminal prosecution, in other words to prevent or interfere with the ordinary course of justice.

3. Agreements of an Immoral Nature
Two types of agreement that are considered illegal are those which relate to sexual immorality or prejudice the sanctity of marriage.

Firstly, in the agreement concerning sexual immorality, it is obvious that the public policy will vary, which will in turn influence the decisions of the court. What was immoral to the Victorians, for instance, is not necessarily immoral today. In *Pearce* v. *Brooks* (1866) the plaintiff was a coach-builder and he hired out one of his vehicles to the defendant who was a prostitute. The vehicle was of a particularly alluring design and the plaintiff knew that the woman would be using the vehicle to go about her trade. The court held that he was unable to claim the hiring charges from the defendant as the hiring was contrary to public policy.

Secondly, agreements which prejudice the sanctity of marriage are also considered contrary to public policy and are illegal and void: for instance, such agreements as those between a husband and his paramour that they shall marry when the husband's wife has died.

4. Agreements Tending to Injure the Public Service
These include such agreements as the sale of public offices or agreements to procure a title of honour for reward. In *Parkinson* v. *College of Ambulances* the secretary of the defendant charity improperly told the plaintiff that if he made an appropriate donation to the charity, the fountain of honour could be diverted in his direction and he might even attain a knighthood out of it. For this reason the plaintiff made a donation in advance to the charity with a promise to pay more later. However, the knighthood was not forthcoming and the court held that the plaintiff could not claim the return of his money as the agreement was illegal.

5. Contracts in Restraint of Trade
A contract in restraint of trade is one which restricts a person, wholly

or partially, from carrying on his trade or business. All such contracts are, on the face of it, void unless they are made to protect some legitimate commercial interest.

(a) Restraints Made on the Purchase of a Business

The purchaser of a business concern will often wish to include a term in the contract which prevents the seller from opening another business which will damage the goodwill of the business he is buying. The courts will only allow such a restraint provided (i) it is reasonable between the parties, and (ii) the restraint is in the interests of the public.

(1) Reasonableness between the parties. In *Nordenfelt* v. *Maxim Nordenfelt Gun Co* the plaintiff was a manufacturer of machine-guns and ammunition. He sold his business to a company and in this contract agreed, firstly, that for twenty-five years he would not carry on his previous work in any part of the world, and secondly, that he would not compete with the company in any way. The court held that his first promise was reasonable between the parties and was not void, as even though the restraint was global the business connections of the company were world-wide. However, the second restraint was held to be unreasonable and void.

If a restraint is wider than is reasonably necessary to protect the party in whose interests it is imposed, in other words the purchaser of the business, the courts will refuse to enforce it.

(2) In the interest of the public. If the contract in restraint of trade is reasonable between the parties, it may still be void as being against the public interest: for instance, if the agreement creates a monopoly calculated to raise prices to an unreasonable extent.

(b) Restraints Intended to Prevent Competition

If the only reason why the restraint has been made is to prevent competition, the agreement will be illegal and void. The same will be the case if the agreement is purely to prevent the use of the personal skill and knowledge an employee has acquired during his work for the employer.

But if the restraint, although against competition, is necessary to protect the employer against any improper use by the employee of the knowledge he has acquired in the service of his employer, e.g. trade connections, trade secrets or confidential information, it will be allowed and enforced provided it is no wider than is reasonably necessary for that purpose.

Quite apart from any express terms of restraint in a contract between an employer and employee, some terms may be implied into the contract; for instance, an employee who copies the names and addresses of his employer's customers for use after he has left his employment can be restrained from using the list. Similarly, if he retains a secret process in his memory he can be restrained from using or disclosing it.

The extent of each restraint upon competition and the extent of protection depends on the nature of the employer's business and the business position of the employee.

In *Fitch* v. *Dewes* a solicitor at Tamworth employed a person who was firstly his articled clerk and then his managing clerk. In his contract of service the clerk agreed, if he left the solicitor's employment, that he would never practise as a solicitor within seven miles of Tamworth Town Hall. The court held that because during his service the clerk had become familiar with personal details of his employer's clients, he could be restrained from using that knowledge to the detriment of his employer. Therefore, the restraint was reasonable and valid. However, in the case of *Attwood* v. *Lamont* the restraint was held to be unreasonable. The plaintiff carried on business as a draper, tailor and general outfitter in Kidderminster. Lamont was an employee who in his contract of service agreed never, whether on his own account or for someone else, to carry on any business connected with his trade within ten miles of Kidderminster. When the plaintiff refused to make Lamont a partner, the latter left and set up a similar sort of trade outside the ten-mile limit. However, some customers from Kidderminster took their orders to him. Attwood asked for an injunction to prevent Lamont accepting these orders. The court held that the restraint upon Lamont was purely against competition and was void. Also, Lamont had only taken Attwood's customers because of his skill as a tailor and not necessarily because of trade connections that had been cultivated while with Attwood.

(c) Restraints which Regulate Trading Conditions

On occasions, traders agree between themselves to regulate their conditions of trading between each other or with the public. This is often for the purpose of maintaining high prices on certain goods.

(1) Restrictive trade practices. Restrictive trade agreements are agreements between the manufacturer and suppliers of certain goods to restrict the production, supply or distribution of the goods. The Restrictive Trade Practices Act, 1956, sets out certain classes of trading agreements which are said to be objectionable. The Act requires these restrictive trade agreements to be registered in a public register. The general rule is that a restrictive trading agreement is presumed to be of no effect and contrary to public interest unless the parties can justify the restriction before the Restrictive Trade Practices Court on such grounds as:

(i)   The restriction is reasonably necessary, having regard to the character of the goods, to protect the public against injury.

(ii) The removal of the restriction would be disadvantageous to the public as purchasers, consumers or users.

(iii) The removal of the restriction would have a serious adverse effect on the general level of unemployment.

(iv) The restriction does not directly or indirectly restrict or discourage competition to any material degree in any relevant trade or industry, and is not likely to do so.

(2) Resale price maintenance. The purpose of the Resale Prices Act, 1964, is to prevent manufacturers and other suppliers of goods from imposing conditions for the maintenance of minimum prices at which goods are to be sold. The Act also prohibits the suppliers and manufacturers from enforcing such prices by withholding supplies from dealers who do not observe their conditions.

Therefore, agreements for, or which relate to, resale price maintenance are void. However, suppliers are still able to recommend resale prices for their goods.

6. Race Relations Act, 1968

The Act makes it unlawful to discriminate against a person on the grounds of colour, race or ethnic or national origins in a number of situations, such as the supplying of goods or services, employment, accommodation, advertisements and notices.

The Act states that a contract shall not be void merely because it contravenes the Act; yet the contract may be revised by the court in proceedings brought by the Race Relations Board.

7. The Trade Descriptions Act, 1968

Although the Act provides criminal sanctions in the case of false trade descriptions, it states that a contract for the sale of goods shall not be void merely because the Act has been contravened. Naturally, the false description may amount to a misrepresentation that might induce a contract, in which case the ordinary civil remedies for misrepresentation are available.

E. THE DISCHARGE OF A CONTRACT

To discharge a contract means to end it. There are four ways in which this can be done.

1. Discharge by Performance

Naturally, if both parties have performed precisely what they had agreed to do under the contract, the contract will be discharged.

Performance Must be Entire

The rule is that performance of obligations under a contract must be complete and exact. For instance, in the case of a contract for the sale of goods the duty of the seller is to make delivery of the goods in exact accordance with the terms of the contract. Thus, if he delivers more goods than had been ordered, the buyer may reject the whole consignment and cannot be required to select the correct quantity out of the bulk that has been delivered. It is the same if less than what is required is delivered. For instance, A agreed to sell to B tinned fruits and to deliver them in cases each containing thirty tins. He tendered the correct number of cases, but about half the cases contained only twenty-four tins. It was held that the buyer was entitled to reject the whole consignment.

A party who has only partially performed his obligations cannot recover anything for the work that he has done. A ship owner who fails to reach the agreed port of destination receives nothing for the distance he has carried the goods, and a builder will receive no money for leaving a building only half completed. This is because no remedy is open to the partial or incomplete performer. This can often lead to injustices, because the person who has partially performed his obligation has done something for the benefit of the other party, yet is not entitled to any payment for what he has done. It can be seen that if this rule were adhered to rigidly by the courts it would lead to uncertainty and confusion in everyday commercial transactions. Therefore, the courts in certain situations have had to accept lower standards than exact and entire performance.

Exceptions to the Rule of Entire Performance

(1) Divisible contracts. There is a presumption that each party agrees to carry out his obligations in return for the other doing the same. In this case the contract is called 'entire', the promises are dependent upon each other, and if one party fails to carry out his promise the other can end the contract.

A divisible contract is one which is so framed that it permits one party to demand performance without giving performance himself. Here the promises and obligations under the contract are independent of each other. For instance, in a sale by credit, the seller's obligation to deliver the goods is independent of the buyer's obligation to pay the price. The price does not become payable until the end of the period of credit allowed.

Whether a contract is entire or divisible depends on its construction in the light of all the circumstances. Another example of the rule is that the tenant's promise to pay rent is independent of the landlord's promise to repair the premises.

(2) Prevention of performance by the other party. If one party to the contract prevents the other from completing his performance, the obstructed party may either recover damages for breach of contract or recover a reasonable sum for the work that he has done.

(3) When there has been substantial performance. When the party has failed to complete only an unimportant part of his obligation, it does not prevent him claiming for the agreed price, but he may be liable to a deduction based on the cost of making good whatever minor details he had not completed.

Tender of Performance
In some situations one party cannot complete his performance of the contract without the co-operation of the other party. In these cases, if he offers to perform his obligations, and the other party rejects the offer, he is entitled to discharge himself from further liability under the contract. The rule is that in some cases, therefore, to offer (i.e. tender) performance is equivalent to actual performance. For example, in a contract for the sale of goods, if the delivery of the goods is tendered by the seller but refused by the buyer, the seller is free from liability under the contract.

2. Discharge by Agreement
A contract may be discharged by agreement in any one of four ways:

(a) Waiver
This is where each party agrees to release the other party from his obligation under the contract. This agreement to release is in itself a binding contract, the consideration of each party being the forgoing of his rights under the contract.

(b) New Agreement
An existing contract may, at any time before performance by the parties, be discharged by both parties agreeing to substitute a new contract for the existing one.

(c) Accord and Satisfaction
This happens where one party can obtain release from his present obligations under the contract by giving or promising something to the other party: for example, if A owes B some money and B agrees to accept a car in satisfaction of the debt.

The accord is the new agreement for the discharge of the original contract, and the satisfaction is the new consideration.

(d) Provision for the Discharge in the Contract
The parties may make provision in their contract, either for suspending its performance (condition precedent) or for discharging the performance after it has begun operation (condition subsequent).

3. Discharge by Frustration
Sometimes during the operation of a contract an event may occur which destroys the basis of the whole contract. Provided this event is not due to the fault of either party, their agreement is said to be 'frustrated'. This means the contract has been terminated and each party is excused from further performance of his side of the agreement. For example, in *Taylor* v. *Caldwell* the defendant agreed to let his hall to the plaintiff for some music concerts. The hall was destroyed by fire even before the plaintiff had held the first concert. The plaintiff sued for damages because the defendant had broken his contract by not having the premises ready for him. The court held that the contract had been frustrated and this had relieved the defendant of his obligation to supply a hall.

The unexpected event must fundamentally change the circumstances of the agreement before the courts will decide that the contract is frustrated. The event must change the basis of the contract to such an extent that if the courts were to keep the parties to their agreement they would be enforcing an agreement that the parties had virtually never intended to make.

In *Krell* v. *Henry* the plaintiff owned a room overlooking the proposed route for the procession of Edward VII's coronation, and he had let the room to the defendant for viewing the procession. Owing to the King's illness the procession had to be cancelled, yet the plaintiff still demanded the agreed fee for the hire of the room. The court held that the whole reason for the hiring no longer existed, and to keep the parties to their agreement would not achieve the purpose for which the contract had been made. Therefore it was frustrated. However, the court came to a different decision in *Herne Bay Steamboat* v. *Hutton.* In this case the plaintiff agreed to hire a steamboat to the defendant for two days, so that the latter could take paying passengers to see a naval display on the occasion of Edward VII's coronation. The royal display was cancelled but the fleet was still assembled and the boat could have been used to view the fleet. The defendant did not use the boat and the plaintiff sued for the hiring fee. The court held that the contract was not discharged by frustration as the review of the fleet by the Sovereign was not the entire basis of the contract.

There are only a few cases where the discharge of a contract by frustration will be allowed. In particular, it will be possible where the contract has been frustrated owing to the following circumstances.

(a) Statutory or Legal Interference
For instance, where the parties make a contract over specific goods that are then requisitioned by the government before the contract has been put into operation.

(b) Destruction of the Essential Object of the Contract
In contracts where the performance depends on the existence of a person or object, it is obvious that if either ceases to exist the contract cannot be performed. In *Taylor* v. *Caldwell*, which has already been mentioned, this was the case, as it was also in *Robinson* v. *Davidson*, where a contract for a pianist to play in three concerts was held to be frustrated because he was ill.

(c) Fundamental Change in Circumstances
Parties should, in most situations, cater for a change in circumstances in their agreement, and so, if there is a mere unusual turn of events, their contract is not frustrated. Only if an event occurs which is outside the contemplation of the parties and for which neither party was responsible will the contract be frustrated.

The Effect of Frustration
Once it has been proved that a contract has been frustrated, it is automatically avoided. But there is still the problem of sorting out the financial position between the parties for all that they had done before the frustrating event. This is governed by the Law Reform (Frustrated Contracts) Act, 1943, which states:

(a)   All sums of money which had been paid to the other party before the frustrating event may be recovered. All sums which are still to be paid cease to be payable.

(b)   Where one party has, because of anything that has been done by the other party, obtained some valuable benefit, that other party may recover from him such sum as the court considers just.

There are certain classes of contract that are excluded from this Act.

4. Termination of Contract by Breach
Where one of the parties to a contract breaks his side of it entirely, the other party will be discharged from further performance, and will be

entitled to bring an action in respect of the damage he has suffered.

A breach of a contract always entitles the injured party to bring an action for damages. However, a breach will only entitle him to treat it as discharged when there is a breach of the entire contract or of some term which is so vital that it destroys the basis of the contract. The breach must be such as to show that the party in default has repudiated his obligations under the contract (see *Laws* v. *London Chronicle Ltd*, p. 212 below).

A discharge of the contract may also arise by one party renouncing his side of the contract even before the time for performance of the contract has been reached. This is called an *anticipatory breach*. In such a case the other party is not bound to wait until the actual time for performance has arrived, but may immediately treat the contract as discharged and sue for damages.

For example, if Mr A engaged Mr B as an employee to begin work on 1 January and in December he told Mr B that his services would not be required, Mr B would not have to wait until January before he sued.

F. REMEDIES FOR BREACH OF CONTRACT

Having considered the circumstances in which a contract may be discharged, we must now consider the main remedies that are open to the party injured by the termination.

The remedies for breach of contract, naturally, are obtained by bringing an action in the courts. However, an action will be barred unless it is brought within the period laid down in the Limitation Act, 1939, which for simple contracts is six years from the time the right of action arose.

1. Damages

Whenever there is a breach of contract by one party, the other has a right to damages. An action for damages is a common law remedy and consists of money compensation for the loss he has suffered. He is, as far as money can do it, to be placed in the same position as if the contract had been performed. In *B. Sunley & Co.* v. *Cunard White Star Ltd*, the defendants agreed to carry a machine belonging to the plaintiff to Guernsey. Because the defendants delayed, the machine was delivered a week late. The plaintiff was unable to show that he had any immediate use for the machine and could not prove any loss of profit. The court held that to compensate the plaintiff for the breach of contract he should be awarded £20 as one week's depreciation in value of the machine and £40 as interest on the capital they had lost.

The plaintiff will not necessarily get damages covering all the loss he has suffered, either because he should have mitigated the loss himself or because the damages he is claiming are too remote a consequence of the breach of contract.

Mitigating the Damages

When a breach of contract occurs, the party suffering from the breach must take reasonable steps to reduce the loss he is likely to suffer. He will not be able to recover damages which have resulted only from his failure to mitigate his loss. For example, if a person cancels a hotel booking, the hotel proprietor must try to find another booking.

Damage which is Too Remote

The consequences of a breach of contract may be far-reaching, and the law must draw the line somewhere and say that damages which arise beyond a certain point cannot be claimed by the plaintiff because they are too remote.

The rule regarding remoteness of damage in contracts is based on the decision in *Hadley* v. *Baxendale*. The plaintiff was a miller at Gloucester. The driving-shaft of the mill broke, so the plaintiff engaged the defendant, a carrier, to take it to the makers in London so that a new one could be made. The defendant delayed delivering the shaft, so the mill was idle for much longer than should have been necessary. The plaintiff sued in respect of the loss of profits during the period of the additional and unreasonable delay. The court decided that there were only two possible grounds on which the plaintiff could succeed. Firstly, that in the usual course of things the work of the mill would cease altogether for want of a shaft. This the court rejected because, to take only one reasonable possibility, the plaintiff might have had a spare shaft. Secondly, that the special circumstances were fully explained, so that the defendant was made aware of the possible loss that would result from any unreasonable delay. There had been no such explanation: the defendant knew only that he was carrying a broken mill shaft. Therefore, the court held that the plaintiff's claim must fail as the damage he had suffered was too remote, as it could not have been within the contemplation of the carrier.

Damages in contract will be too remote to be compensated unless they are such that the defendant, as a reasonable man, would have foreseen them as likely to result, either in the case of ordinary damage caused during the normal course of things, or in the case of special or abnormal damage because the special facts had been made known to him.

In *Victoria Laundry* v. *Newman Industries* the plaintiff, launderers and dyers, decided to expand their business. For this purpose, and in order to obtain certain dyeing contracts of a highly lucrative character, they required a larger boiler. The defendants, an engineering firm, contracted to sell and deliver to the plaintiff a certain boiler of the required capacity. This, however, was damaged in the course of removal and was not delivered until five months later. The defendants were aware of the nature of the plaintiff's business and that a boiler was required urgently. The plaintiff, in an action for breach of contract, claimed (a) damages for the loss of profit, assessed at £16 a week based on what the plaintiff would have earned with the new boiler, and (b) damages, assessed at £262 a week, for loss of the exceptional profits which they would have earned through the dyeing contracts. The court held that the defendants must have reasonably foreseen the loss of some business, therefore the plaintiff should be awarded compensation to cover the normal profits to be expected. However, the defendants did not know of the highly lucrative dyeing contracts so could not be liable for the special or abnormal amount of damage to this side of the business.

Types of Damages

(1) Nominal. Wherever a party breaks a contract the plaintiff is entitled to damages, but if the plaintiff cannot prove that he has suffered some loss, the defendant will have to pay only nominal damages. These damages are awarded when there has merely been an infringement of a legal right.

(2) Unliquidated and liquidated damages. Damages are unliquidated when they are not assessed by agreement between the parties, and the party claiming leaves it to the court to award the amount of damages it considers sufficient. In other words, in unliquidated damages the amount of compensation to be actually awarded is uncertain until the court has decided.

Liquidated damages are those damages that have been agreed upon by the parties as a term in the contract and it is agreed that they should become payable if the contract is broken. In this case, no more and no less than the agreed sum will be claimed. For example, in *Cellulose Acetate Silk Co* v. *Widnes Foundry* the defendants agreed to build a plant for the plaintiffs by a certain date, and also agreed to pay £20 for every week they took beyond that date. They were thirty weeks late and the plaintiffs, instead of claiming £600 in accordance with the agreement, claimed the actual loss they had suffered which was £5,850. The court held that they could only claim the amount at the fixed rate that had been agreed upon.

The sum that the parties agreed upon in the contract as liquidated damages must be a genuine pre-estimate of the value of the loss which they are likely to suffer. If this sum, however, is considered by the courts not to be a genuine pre-estimate but is more of a punishment in case the party does not complete his side of the contract, the sum is called a *penalty*. In other words, a penalty is a sum greatly in excess of the loss likely to be suffered.

The distinction between an agreement for a sum which is liquidated damages and a sum which is a penalty is important. This is because the courts will not honour a penalty and will only award the amount of loss actually suffered; whereas, as has been explained, an agreement for a liquidated sum will be enforced by the courts.

2. Specific Performance

A decree of specific performance will be issued when the court considers it important that a party should perform his obligations under the contract, rather than merely compensate the other party for his failure to perform.

It has been mentioned already that damages is a common law remedy for which the plaintiff has a right to claim. However, specific performance is an equitable remedy which is granted at the court's discretion only when it is considered fair and just.

Although this decree is discretionary, there are well-established rules under which specific performance will be granted.

(a)   It will not be granted where damages are an adequate remedy. In most cases monetary compensation will be sufficient. However, where the subject-matter is of some unique value, the court may find that monetary compensation is inadequate (see *Cohen* v. *Roche*, p. 198 below).

(b)   The court will not grant a decree where it would be difficult or impracticable to enforce it. In *Ryan* v. *Mutual Tontine* etc., a landlord promised to provide a resident porter at a block of flats but had failed to do so. The court held that specific performance would not be granted as to do so would involve continuous supervision to see whether the decree had been carried out.

(c)   Specific performance will not be granted in contracts of personal services, such as contracts of employment, partnership or agency. This is because it is contrary to the policy of the courts to force somebody to work for someone else.

3. Injunction

An injunction is an order of the court, and is a remedy more suited to the law of tort. In the context of torts this remedy has already been explained, but it is sometimes granted in actions arising out of a contract. For example, it can be used to prevent a threatened breach of contract.

Although the court will not usually grant specific performance of a contract of personal service, an injunction may be applied for by the plaintiff if the defendant, for example an employee, had made a clear negative promise in the contract that he will work for no one other than the plaintiff. In *Warner Bros.* v. *Nelson* the defendant, Bette Davis, a film actress, had contracted to work for the plaintiff for twelve months and not to work for rival concerns. She broke the contract and came to work in England. The court held that an injunction could be granted to restrain her from taking other stage and screen work, but she could take other employment unconnected with the plaintiff's business. This decision has often been criticised as being 'negative specific performance'.

G. CONTRACTS BY MINORS

Contracts Binding a Minor
A minor will be bound by any contract that he makes if (*a*) it is for 'necessaries', or (*b*) it is beneficial or of some educational value to him.

(a) Contract for 'Necessaries'
A minor who makes a contract for 'necessaries' will be bound by his agreement, but only to pay a *reasonable* price for them.

The Sale of Goods Act, 1893, states that 'necessaries' are goods suitable to the condition in life of the minor, and that are actually required by him at the time he makes the contract for these goods. Any number of goods may be regarded as necessaries: for example, food, books, a motor-cycle, a watch or any other goods important to the minor's way of life. The court may consider a motor-cycle to be a necessary to a minor who has a long way to travel to work, but in other circumstances it may be a luxury. Whether particular goods amount to necessaries will depend on the circumstances of each case. In *Nash* v. *Inman* the defendant was a minor and was an undergraduate at Cambridge. He ordered eleven fancy waistcoats from the plaintiff at a time when he was adequately supplied with clothes. The court held that the waistcoats were not necessaries and therefore the defendant was not bound by his contract to pay for them.

(b) Contracts Beneficial to the Minor
A minor will be bound by a contract which the court considers is for his benefit. Such contracts include contracts of apprenticeship or employment and contracts which are of some educational value to the minor. In *Roberts* v. *Gray* the defendant was a minor who had agreed to accompany the plaintiff, a professional billiard player, on a tour. The

minor changed his mind at the last minute and was reluctant to go. The court held that he was bound by his contract which was beneficial to him as he would receive some instruction in the game.

Voidable Contracts

Where a minor makes a contract of a continuing nature (i.e. one which imposes a continuous liability upon him), such as a lease or for the holding of shares in a company or a partnership contract, the contract cannot be enforced against him during his minority. In contracts of this nature the minor is free to put an end to them at any time before he reaches majority or within a reasonable time of his attaining eighteen years of age. If he does not avoid such contracts they will be binding on him.

In *Davies* v. *Beynon-Harris* a minor took a lease of a flat just before he reached majority. Three years after this he was sued for the rent. The court held that he was liable as the lease was binding on him because he had not avoided it within a reasonable time of reaching majority.

If a minor makes one of these contracts and then avoids it, he is liable to pay whatever was agreed upon up to the date of avoidance. He will not be able to recover any money paid under such a contract, unless he is able to show that he received no benefit whatsoever from the agreement. In *Holmes* v. *Blogg* a minor paid a sum of money to a lessor towards the lease of premises in which he and a partner proposed to carry on business. He occupied the premises for twelve weeks and then, after reaching majority, he dissolved the partnership, avoided the lease and vacated the premises. The court held that he could not recover the sum of money he had paid out because he had received twelve weeks' use of the premises.

Void Contracts

The Infants' Relief Act, 1874, section 1, states that the following contracts made with a minor are void:

(a) Contracts for the repayment of money lent.
(b) Contracts for the supply of goods that are not necessaries.
(c) Accounts stated—which is an admission that the person signing the account owes money.

In *Coutt & Co.* v. *Browne-Lecky*, B, a minor, had an overdraft with the bank. X and Y guaranteed it. The bank sued X and Y for payment. The court held that as the loan by the bank to B was void, X and Y could not be liable.

Even if the minor has fraudulently induced the other party to enter into the contract by representing that he is of full age, he cannot be sued whether in contract or in tort for fraud. This is because it would be an indirect way of enforcing a void contract. However, if a minor has fraudulently obtained goods, he may be ordered by the court to return all the goods that are still in his possession. He cannot be ordered to return money.

1. 　An offer must be distinguished from an invitation to treat. Explain the meaning of this statement with reference to decided cases.
2. In the weekly magazine 'Barter, Buy or Swop' P sees an advertisement by D who wishes to sell his car for £50. P writes a letter to Mr D saying 'I will buy your car, as advertised; see the enclosed cheque.' A few days later P receives a letter from D returning his cheque and saying he has sold the car to someone else. Advise P as to his chances in being able to claim the car.
3. Distinguish between (a) an acceptance (b) a counter-offer and (c) a request for further information.
4. D offers a reward for the return of his lost dog. P, on his way home, sees a dog with D's name and address on the collar. P returns the dog to D. Subsequently P learns of the reward and now wishes to claim it. Advise P.
5. P accepts an offer made by D, and subsequently finds that D has added further conditions to the agreement. Is P bound by these new terms?
6. In what ways may an offer terminate?
7. On 10 August D offers to sell P, a greengrocer, ten crates of tomatoes. When P accepts this offer on 11 September D has already sold them. Is D liable to P?
8. Consideration may be executory or executed, but it must not be past. Explain what this statement means.
9. What is meant by the expression, 'consideration must be of some value'? Illustrate your answer with reference to decided cases.
10. Miss P has been baby-sitting in D's house twice a week for the last year. Now D promises to buy her a record-player 'in consideration of her past services'. State, giving your reasons, whether this promise will be binding on D.
11. What is meant by the rule that the parties to a contract must have the intention to create a legal relationship?
12. L, M and N all have bed-sitters in a large house. Each Sunday they all take part in a newspaper competition. They have been doing so for over a year and they take it in turns to buy the newspaper and post their entry. They also take it in turns to put their names to the entry. They all agree that if one person's entry should be successful they will divide the winnings into three. At the bottom of each entry form these words appear, 'This competition is

binding in honour only'. What is the legal position in the following situations:

    (a) one week L wins and refuses to share the money with N and M.

    (b) one week they consider they are successful and then the newspaper refuses to pay them the money, saying that they had lost the application form.

13. 'An infant's contract for necessaries is a valid contract.' Explain what is meant by this statement.

14. Is D, a minor, liable for the following contracts?

    (a) For use in his employment as a messenger boy he buys a bicycle.

    (b) He buys six different pairs of shoes to match his different suits.

    (c) He breaks an agreement with P who promised to teach him to be a builder.

15. Section I of the Infants Relief Act 1874 provides that certain contracts made with minors shall be 'absolutely void'. Which types of contracts does this section refer to?

16. (a) P buys from D, an antique dealer, a chair which P believes to have been made by Hepplewhite. D does not realise that P thinks this. When P examines the chair at home he finds that it is an imitation. Can P claim his money back?

    (b) P buys from D, an art dealer, a painting which both P and D believe to be by a famous artist. Later P finds they were mistaken. Can he claim his money back?

    (c) P buys from D, a jeweller, a piece of jewellery believing it to consist of diamonds. D knows that P is making this mistake and that the 'stones' are glass. Can P claim his money back?

17. Distinguish between innocent and fraudulent misrepresentation.

18. P was considering buying D's car. He asked D how many miles it had done. D said that it had done about 25,000 miles. P then examined the car and forgot to look at the mileage. When P bought the car no reference was made to the mileage. Now P discovers that the car has travelled 90,000 miles. Advise P as to whether he could bring a successful action for his money back.

19. In what ways may a contract be terminated?

20. Explain the difference between (a) a contract illegal at common law and (b) a contract illegal by statute. Give examples of each.

21. What is the difference between (a) liquidated damages (b) unliquidated damages and (c) a penalty.

22. Explain the remedies that are available to a plaintiff if the defendant has broken their contract.

14. The Sale of Goods

Introduction

The doctrine of *caveat emptor* ('let the buyer beware') is descriptive of the nineteenth-century attitude of the courts towards contracts for the sale of goods. This attitude was to let the parties make whatever arrangements they pleased with the minimum amount of interference from the law. Thus, where a person was making a contract for the purchase of goods, he had to make sure that he bought the goods he wanted, in the condition he expected, and that they were fit to be used for the purpose for which he had bought them. If, for some reason, he bought goods that were not fit for his purpose, or they were not fit for any purpose, it was his own fault.

However, with the increase in commercial transactions at the end of the nineteenth century, the common law on the buying and selling of goods was codified in the Sale of Goods Act, 1893. Included within this Act are what can be considered as a number of statutory exceptions to the common law doctrine of *caveat emptor*. These exceptions are designed in general to protect the buyer against a seller who sells him defective goods or goods which he cannot use or does not want. The Act gives this protection by implying terms into the contracts between buyers and sellers of goods. For example, Mr A goes into an ironmongers and buys a chisel. On using it for the first time the blade splinters. This is a contract for the sale of goods, and the Act states that when goods are bought there is an implied term in the contract that they are of merchantable quality. This chisel is obviously not, so Mr A will be entitled to return the chisel and claim his money back.

After the 1893 Act the protection of persons who bought goods was championed by the Courts and judges who recognised the increasing need for consumer protection; thus until the 1970s consumer law has developed mainly through case law. The 1970s has once again seen legislation on the subject, for example The Supply of Goods (Implied Terms) Act, 1973, and the Unfair Contract Terms Act, 1977.

The actual contract by which the goods are bought is governed by the ordinary law of simple contract. Thus each sale will consist of an offer by one party, an acceptance by the other, and consideration.

Until the legislation of the 1970s it was possible for either party to exclude himself from liability for any breach of his side of the agreement. He could even exclude himself from any terms that had been implied into his contract under the Sale of Goods Act, 1893, mentioned in the next few pages. This opting out of contractual responsibilities often took the form of an exclusion or exemption clause inserted into the contract by one party, for example 'The seller will not be responsible for any defect in the goods howsoever caused. Nor will he be responsible for a breach of any term of the contract, whether condition or warranty, express or implied.'

Therefore, in our example above, if Mr A had bought the chisel from the ironmonger with such a term included in the sale, the courts of law would have little power to help him if he suffered as a result of a defect in the chisel.

Since the legislation of the 1970s consumer contracts such as those made by Mr A have received protection from indiscriminate and unreasonable use-of-exclusion clauses.

The Supply of Goods (Implied Terms) Act, 1973, stated that in the case of 'consumer sales' no party was permitted to exempt himself from liability for breach of any of the terms implied into the contract by the 1893 Act. The 1973 Act states that a consumer sale is one by a seller in the course of his business, where the goods are of a type ordinarily bought for private use or consumption and not bought by a person in the course of business. Sales by wholesaler to retailer, for example, are not 'consumer sales'. Where the sale is not a 'consumer' one, the 1893 Act's implied terms could still be excluded provided it was not unfair or unreasonable for the seller to rely on such an exclusion clause.

The Unfair Contract Terms Act, 1977, refers to many more situations than just sale of goods. It protects persons from unreasonable contractual exclusion clauses or terms, whether buying goods or contracting for services. It also protects consumers from injury to themselves or their property by the unreasonable negligence of businessmen or their employees.

A. THE ACTUAL CONTRACT FOR THE SALE OF GOODS

Definition of Sales of Goods Contract

As a contract for the sale of goods is based on the ordinary law of simple contracts, the sale may be made orally, in writing or by conduct. Such contracts happen in their millions every day, in such places as department stores, supermarkets, shops and restaurants.

A contract for the sale of goods is described in the Act as 'a contract whereby the seller transfers . . . the property in the goods to the buyer for a money consideration called the price'.

It is now necessary to explain the specific meanings that the Act has given to certain words in the definition.

(a) 'Goods'

The subject-matter of the contract is 'goods', a term which has been held to cover a propeller for a ship, a bath-bun, a catapult and a reaping machine. The range of articles that can be called goods is, naturally, so wide that it is easier to state first what the definition of goods does not include.

The definition does not include 'things in action'. These are things that have no value in themselves but only give the holder of them a right to something else. Thus, cheques, shares in a company and debts are not goods. Also, money itself is not goods. Furthermore, goods does not include land or any interest in land. So, for example, the sale of land or its lease or a mortgage will not be subject to the terms of the Sale of Goods Act.

'Goods' does, however, include all articles that are capable of being physically possessed, carried about or destroyed. The definition of goods mentioned in the Act includes not only goods already in existence, but goods that are yet to be acquired or manufactured by the seller after he has made the contract for their sale. In this case the goods are called 'future goods': for example, when a customer goes into a music shop and orders a type of piano which is not in stock but which the seller will have to order for him; or where a customer orders a new make of car from a motor dealer before the make has come off the production line.

(b) 'Property'

It must always be remembered that when dealing with a contract for the sale of goods, 'property' refers to the *right to own* the goods, and does not mean the goods themselves.

Therefore, when the definition says 'transfers the property in the goods', it refers to the ownership in the goods passing from the seller to the buyer.

Another point that it is vital to remember is that this 'property' in goods can be transferred from the seller to the buyer without the actual goods changing hands. In other words, the property or ownership in goods can move from one person to another without the goods changing possession. For example, Mr A sees a mowing machine in a shop and buys it. He asks for it to be delivered to his home the following day. In this situation there has been a complete contract for the sale of goods: Mr A has the property (i.e. ownership) in the mowing machine even though the shopkeeper remains in possession of the goods until the next day, when on its delivery Mr A will take possession.

Thus it can be seen that the passing of property in goods does not necessarily coincide with actual delivery of the goods to the buyer. We shall see below that this fact is important if the goods are damaged while still in the possession of the seller.

(c) 'Price'

The consideration given by the buyer in a contract for the sale of goods is money. This money is called the price. The consideration given by the seller is the goods.

If the contract is merely one person exchanging his goods for the goods of someone else it is not a sale, but a *barter*. Barters do not come within the Sale of Goods Act, 1893, because there has been no money consideration. However, it is a sale of goods within the meaning of the Act to exchange goods for goods plus money: for example, the trading-in of an old car plus money for a new car.

The Passing of the 'Risk'

'Risk' means the responsibility for accidental loss or damage. So, when the Act states that the 'risk' passes with the property in the goods, it means that the person who has the ownership of the goods will also have to bear the financial burden for accidental loss or any damage to the goods.

In most cases this rule applies even though the owner has not yet received delivery of the goods, which might still be in the possession of the seller. For example, Mr A buys a car from B Garage, to be delivered the following day, but that night the car is destroyed by some accident. In this case, as the property and the risk have passed to Mr A, he will have to bear the financial loss.

However, this rule does not apply if the financial loss has been caused by the fault of the person in possession of the goods. In such a case it is he who will have to bear the loss. Also, in many cases it is commercial practice for the parties to include a special clause in their contract stating which of them will have the 'risk' at the various stages of the transaction. For instance, with goods sent 'on approval' or 'on sale or return', the prospective seller usually inserts a clause stating that the 'would-be' buyer will be responsible for any damage done to the goods while in his possession, even if he decides not to buy them and therefore does not become the owner.

B. TERMS IMPLIED INTO THE CONTRACT

Conditions and Warranties

It has been said earlier that the 1893 Act lays down certain exceptions to the doctrine of *caveat emptor*. The Act does this by stating that, unless the parties have actually made express provision in their contract to the contrary, certain terms will be implied into each contract for the sale of goods.

These terms, as will be seen, are for the protection of the buyer, and if any of these terms are broken by the seller the buyer will either be able to claim damages from the seller or refuse to go through with his contract.

The terms that are implied into these contracts are of two types, depending on the importance of the right the statute protects. The important terms are called *conditions* and cover all the main aspects of the transaction. If a seller breaks an implied condition, the buyer is entitled to refuse to continue with the contract.

Terms of a lesser importance than those covered by conditions are known as *warranties*. If a seller breaks a warranty, the buyer can only claim damages for the loss it has caused him. Warranties are not sufficiently vital to the transaction for the buyer to reject the goods and refuse to continue with the contract. Some examples of warranties that are implied into a contract for the sale of goods by the Act are, firstly, that the buyer shall be able to enjoy quiet possession of the goods, and secondly, that no third person will have any rights over the goods which he buys.

The following are some of the important *conditions* that are implied by the Act into a contract for the sale of goods and which, if broken, entitle the purchaser to end the contract.

Goods Bought by Description or Sample

The purpose of these two conditions implied by the Act, under sections 13 and 15 respectively, is to protect a buyer in situations where he has not been able to examine the goods beforehand, either because he buys the goods by relying on a description (perhaps in an advertisement), or because he only saw a sample of what he was buying.

(a) Buying by Description

The Act states that there is an implied condition that if goods are bought by description they must comply with that description. A sale by description occurs where the buyer does not see the goods to examine them himself, but merely buys them by relying on the description that the seller has given him. If the buyer discovers when the goods are delivered that they do not fit the description he had been given, he may refuse to accept and pay for the goods.

In *Varley* v. *Whipp*, the defendant agreed to buy a reaping machine which he had never seen, but which had been described to him by the plaintiff, the seller, as being new the previous year and used only over a few acres. When the machine was delivered the defendant found it well used and antiquated, and he refused to pay for it. The court held that this was a sale of goods by description under section 13 of the 1893 Act, and as the machine did not correspond with the description the defendant was entitled to refuse payment.

(b) Buying by Sample

In some cases it is not practical for the buyer to check the whole of what he is buying at the time of the sale (for example, 6,000 sacks of wheat). In these cases the sale is usually made by the seller showing the buyer a sample of the goods. The Act states that when a sale of goods is made by sample there is an implied condition in the contract that the bulk of the goods corresponds with the sample in quality. Also, the Act states that the buyer shall have a reasonable opportunity of comparing the bulk with the sample that he has been shown.

In *Ruben* v. *Faire* the sellers agreed to supply the buyers with a quantity of special rubber in accordance with a small sample the buyers had been shown. The sample of the material was flat and soft, but the bulk delivered was crinkly and folded. The court held that this was a sale by sample under section 15 of the Act, and as this was a breach of condition the buyers could reject the goods, rather than merely claim damages.

Goods Bought which are not Fit for their Purpose

The Act, by section 14(3), imposes an implied condition on the seller that the goods he supplies be reasonably fit for the particular purpose for which the buyer bought them.

This section is to cover the situation where the buyer wishes to buy goods for a particular purpose and goes to a seller who deals in goods of the type he wants. Before buying the goods he tells the seller the particular purpose for which he needs them, and relies on the seller's skill and judgment to supply him with goods that will be fit for that purpose. For instance, Mr A wishes to buy a chemical to kill the weeds in his lawn. He goes to his local nurseries and asks Mr B if he can recommend a suitable weed-killer. Mr B recommends a certain type of spray which Mr A buys. If, when he uses the spray, he finds it kills his lawn but leaves his weeds flourishing, there will have been a breach of the implied condition under section 14(3) of the Act.

It is not necessary for the buyer dutifully to inform the seller of the purpose for which he wants the goods if the goods he asks for have an obvious purpose. For instance, the buyer can assume that the seller knows why he wants to buy food or a fountain-pen. This principle has been applied in the following cases: where a solicitor bought a bath-bun it was assumed he wanted it for eating and that a stone in it made it unfit for this purpose (*Chapronière* v. *Mason*); where it was assumed that the seller knew the purpose for buying a hot-water bottle and when it burst it was obviously unfit for that purpose (*Priest* v. *Last*).

However, the buyer cannot expect the seller to use his skill and judgment correctly in supplying goods if he does not give him all the relevant information. For instance, in *Griffiths* v. *Peter Conway Ltd* a lady bought a tweed coat without informing the seller that she had an unusually sensitive skin. She contracted dermatitis from wearing the coat and claimed that it was not fit for wearing. The court held that her claim must fail as the evidence showed that the coat would not have caused trouble to normal skin and she had not made known her particular purpose, which was that she needed a coat for a sensitive skin.

The reliance on the seller's skill and judgment can also be inferred from the transaction. For instance, when a buyer goes into a shop he is entitled to assume that the seller has used his skill and judgment in selecting his stock. This point was mentioned in the case of *Grant* v. *Australian Knitting Mills* where a person bought a pair of woollen underpants from a men's outfitters and contracted dermatitis as a result of wearing them because they contained an excess of sulphur. The court held that the seller was liable to pay him damages because the purpose for buying a pair of underpants was self-evident, and by going into a shop of this nature he was impliedly relying on their skill and judgment.

Section 14(3) is designed to cater for the buyer stating the purpose for which he wants the goods and relying on the seller to supply them; it does not cover the situation where the buyer asks for goods by their trade name. For example, if a buyer asked a hardware store for glue that would stick china, the case is within section 14(3). Yet if the buyer merely asked the seller for the glue by its trade name 'Stickfast', he could not complain under this section if he found this glue would not stick crockery but only paper. (Furthermore, if the glue would not stick anything at all, the goods would be useless and not of merchantable quality. This situation is covered by section 14(2) of the Sale of Goods Act, 1893, which is the next topic.)

Goods Bought which are not of Merchantable Quality
Nowadays, in an increasing number of transactions the purchaser does not tell the seller the purpose for which he is buying the goods, nor

does he rely on the seller's skill and judgment, but he will ask for the goods only by their brand or trade name. In such situations there is an implied condition under section 14(2) of the Act that these goods are of 'merchantable quality'.

In *Wilson* v. *Rickett* a lady ordered some 'Coalite' and the goods supplied contained a detonator. Naturally, when the goods were used for her fire there was an explosion. It was held that the sale was one under section 14(2) as the goods had been bought by their trade name, and as they were not of merchantable quality the defendant was liable.

Goods are unmerchantable if they are not reasonably capable of the ordinary use for which they are meant. It can be seen, therefore, that there is a distinction between this and 'unfit for their purpose' in section 14(3), which means incapable of the particular purpose for which the buyer bought them. But nevertheless the distinction is a fine one, because the goods might still be quite capable of their ordinary use, and therefore be of merchantable quality even though they were not fit for the buyer's particular use.

However, in many cases the situation may amount to a breach of sections 14(3) and 14(2). For instance, in *Godley* v. *Perry* the defendant, who sold toys, sold a plastic catapult to a boy of six. When the child used the catapult it broke and blinded him in one eye. The court held that the defendant was liable under section 14(3) because a catapult was fit for only one purpose and this one was certainly not fit for that, and also the seller was liable under section 14(2) because the article was defective and of unmerchantable quality.

It has been said that goods will be unmerchantable if they are not reasonably capable of ordinary use. However, in some cases the goods that are sold will not be immediately of merchantable quality and ready for ordinary use. They might require the buyer to put them into a merchantable state, either by following instructions that come with the goods or by carrying out some reasonable and obvious process on the goods. Therefore, in many cases the seller is allowed to assume that the buyer will carry out some reasonable process before expecting the goods to be of merchantable quality. In *Heil* v. *Hedges* a lady became ill as a result of eating pork chops containing tapeworms. She did not cook the chops properly. If she had cooked them the worms would have died. Her action for damages failed because the chops were delivered in such a state that they would have been merchantable had they been cooked, and it is reasonable for a seller to expect them to be cooked properly.

C. SALE OF GOODS WHERE THE SELLER IS NOT THE OWNER

So far we have dealt with situations where the seller has property (i.e. ownership) in the goods which he sells. However, what of the situation where the seller does not own the goods, but nevertheless passes them on to another person who pays money for them in the belief that he is becoming the owner?

For example, if Mr A 'sells' to Mr B goods belonging to Mr C, who should be entitled to the goods? Mr B or Mr C? Mr B has paid for the property in them, innocently believing that they were Mr A's to sell, so Mr B believes he has a right to them. Yet Mr C is the original owner of the goods and had no wish to sell them, and therefore considers that he is entitled to his goods.

The general rule of law in this situation is always referred to by the Latin phrase *nemo dat quod non habet*, which means literally that a person cannot transfer a better title than he has in the goods himself. Therefore, by this rule, a person who does not own goods cannot sell the property in them to the buyer. This general rule is designed to protect an individual's right to the ownership of his goods. So, if in the above example Mr A had stolen the goods from Mr C, the law is quite rightly protecting Mr C's ownership by stating that Mr A cannot pass on ownership to Mr B.

However, on some occasions the law considers it more important to protect the buyer than to safeguard the seller's ownership. Therefore, in a few situations the law states that a buyer can receive ownership in goods from a seller who is not the owner. These exceptions to the rule *nemo dat quod non habet*, which are laid down in the Sale of Goods Act, are designed to assist and give an element of certainty to buyers in commercial transactions.

The following are some of the exceptions to the rule *nemo dat quod non habet*, where the seller who is not the owner may nevertheless transfer the property in the goods to the buyer.

1. Legal Order to Sell
A person who is not the owner of goods may sell them if he is entitled to do so by a court order or by a power given to him by a statute. For example, the Disposal of Uncollected Goods Act, 1952, states that if Mr C deposits goods with Mr A for Mr A to repair them, and then Mr C fails to collect them and pay for the repairs, Mr A is entitled to sell the goods to Mr B.

2. Where Seller is Represented as Having a Right to Sell
If the true owner of the goods stands by and allows an innocent buyer to purchase these goods from another person, who professes that he

himself has the right to sell the goods, the true owner cannot later deny the buyer's ownership of the goods. It is said that the true owner is 'estopped' from denying the seller's right to sell; that is, once the true owner has represented in some way to the buyer that the seller has authority to sell, the owner cannot go back on his representation.

In *Pickard* v. *Sears*, Mr C permitted some of his goods to be wrongfully kept by A, and allowed B to think that A had the legal right to sell them. A sold the goods to B. The court held that as C had represented A as having the right to pass property in the goods, C was estopped from denying this right and B became the rightful owner when he bought them.

3. Sales by Mercantile Agents
The owner of goods is bound by the acts of a mercantile agent. A mercantile agent is a professional selling agent or person who, in the ordinary course of his business, has, among other rights, authority to sell or buy goods.

If the mercantile agent has possession of the owner's goods, or the documents of title to the goods, with the owner's consent, then the owner is bound by any sale of his goods that the mercantile agent makes in the course of his business, whether or not the seller actually authorised the sale.

4. Sale in Market Overt
When goods are sold in open market, according to the custom of that market, the buyer obtains good title to the goods provided he buys them innocently. For example, if goods are stolen and sold in open market to a buyer who is unaware that the goods had been stolen, the buyer will acquire the property in the goods.

The market must be legally constituted either by statute, charter, or merely by long use. For instance, it is a well-established custom that a sale in the public part of any shop in the City of London is considered a sale in market overt.

5. Sale by a Person with a Voidable Title
We have seen in the case of unilateral mistake, in Chapter 13 above, that such contracts are *void* through lack of consent. For example, in *Ingram* v. *Little* the owner only intended to sell her car to a person called Hutchinson; she did not intend to sell it to a 'rogue', therefore the contract was void. It will also be remembered that as the contract was void the 'rogue' took no property in the goods and therefore could not pass on property to Little.

However, it was seen in the cases of *Phillips* v. *Brooks* and *Lewis* v. *Averay* that these two contracts were not void for unilateral mistake, because the court held that the sellers intended to make a contract with the person standing in front of them, even if this was induced by fraud. In these cases, where the seller has consented to the contract although induced by fraud, the contract is called *voidable*. When a contract is voidable it is taken as being valid until the seller has avoided it; that is, until he has given notice that he intends not to be bound by his agreement. Therefore, until the seller avoids the contract, the 'rogue' has a good title in the goods he has obtained and is able to pass on a good title to a purchaser who knows nothing of his fraud. This is what happened in *Phillips* v. *Brooks* and *Lewis* v. *Averay* and why the purchasers were entitled to keep the goods. In both cases it was a sale of goods by a person with a voidable title which had not been avoided by the owner before the innocent party bought them.

If, however, the seller who parted with goods under a voidable contract avoids the contract before the 'rogue' sells the goods, the property in the goods will not be passed on to the innocent purchaser. This happened in *Car & Universal Finance Co Ltd* v. *Caldwell*. A 'rogue' obtained a car with a dud cheque. On discovering the fraud the seller immediately informed the police and the Automobile Association. Subsequent to this, the 'rogue' sold the car to another 'rogue' who then sold it to an innocent purchaser. The court held that as the owner had done all that he could to avoid his contract, the innocent purchaser did not acquire the property in the car.

D. REMEDIES OF THE SELLER AND BUYER

Basically, the parties to a contract for the sale of goods have the remedies of the ordinary law of contract. However, some of these must be mentioned in greater detail, together with some special rights which have been set out in the 1893 Act.

1. Remedies of the Seller
(a) Against the Buyer Personally
The seller has two rights of action against the buyer personally. Firstly, if the property in the goods has passed to the buyer and the buyer has not paid, the seller may bring an action for the price of the goods.

Secondly, where the buyer neglects or refuses to accept and pay for the goods, the seller may bring an action against him for damages for non-acceptance of the goods. If the property has passed to the buyer, the seller may sue either for the price or for damages for non-acceptance; but if the property in the goods is still with the seller, naturally he cannot sue for the price but only for the buyer's failure to accept the goods.

(b) Against the Goods

In some cases a remedy against the buyer personally for the price, or compensation for loss, will be inadequate: for instance, if the buyer has no money or is bankrupt. So the Act has, in some situations, given the seller rights against the goods themselves. These rights are based on the fact that although there has been a contract for the sale of goods, and therefore the property has passed to the buyer, in some cases the seller will still have possession of the goods because he has not yet delivered them to the buyer.

If the seller, before the goods have passed into the possession of the buyer, hears that the buyer has no money to pay for them, he has the following rights. These are known as the rights of the unpaid seller against the goods.

(1) A lien. This right exists where the property in goods has passed to the buyer but the seller is still in possession of them. A lien is the seller's right to retain possession of the goods until the buyer has paid for them.

(2) Stoppage in transitu. Once the seller has lost possession of the goods, for instance by handing them to a carrier for delivery to a buyer, he loses his right to exercise a lien over the goods.

If, however, the buyer becomes insolvent while the goods are still in transit, or the seller does not hear of his insolvency until this time, the unpaid seller has a right of 'stoppage *in transitu*'. By exercising this right the seller can recover possession of the goods from the carrier.

The seller can exercise his right of stoppage either by physically repossessing the goods or by giving notice to the carrier that he is to hold the goods for him and not for the buyer.

This right can only be exercised during transit and ends when the goods come under the buyer's control or possession.

(3) Right of resale. The exercise of the right of lien or stoppage *in transitu* does not, in itself, bring the contract between the buyer and seller to an end. Therefore, if the seller, after exercising one of these rights, sells the goods to a third party, he will be liable in damages to the original buyer.

The unpaid seller will, however, be able to resell the goods if he gives notice of his intention to resell to the buyer, and the buyer does not pay the price within a reasonable time. It can be seen that this right of resale by the seller is a further exception to the rule *nemo dat quod non habet.*

2. Remedies of the Buyer

(a) Breach of Conditions and Warranties

We have already discussed the difference between a condition and a warranty. In the case of a breach of condition, such as merchantable quality, the buyer is entitled to reject the goods and sue for recovery of the price, if he has paid it. If the seller has merely broken a warranty, the buyer may claim damages, but he is not entitled to end the contract.

(b) Failure to Deliver

Just as the seller can claim damages if the buyer wrongfully refuses to accept, so the buyer can claim damages if the seller wrongfully fails to deliver the goods. Even if the goods are merely late in being delivered owing to the fault of the seller, the buyer may still claim damages if, for instance, he has lost a customer who was waiting for the goods. In this case, the buyer could claim the difference between the value of the goods when they should have been delivered and their value at the time of actual delivery.

(c) Buyer's Right to Specific Performance

This remedy has been discussed under the remedies in contract. It must be remembered that this remedy is at the discretion of the court and the buyer cannot claim it as of right. The court will not issue a decree of specific performance when the goods are an ordinary article of commerce which has no special interest or value to the buyer and where damages would fully compensate him.

In *Cohen* v. *Roche* a decree of specific performance was refused to a buyer of 'a set of genuine Hepplewhite chairs' for the reason that they 'possessed no special features at all. They were ordinary Hepplewhite furniture.' On the other hand, specific performance has been granted to a buyer of a ship because damages would not have been an adequate remedy.

E. CONSUMER CREDIT AGREEMENTS

1. Hire Purchase

A hire-purchase agreement is where the owner of goods parts with his possession of the goods to the hirer in return for the hirer making periodical payments for this hiring. The hirer has the option to purchase the goods at the end of the hire agreement. Thus ownership does not pass to the hirer until the end of the whole transaction.

Before the hire agreement is made the owner must, in most circumstances, state the cash price of the goods in writing. The actual agreement must contain the following:

(a) a statement of the cash price, the hire-purchase price and the amounts and dates for payment of the instalments;

(b)   a list of goods;
(c)   a notice setting out the rights of the hirer to terminate the agreement; and
(d)   a notice explaining the restrictions on the owner's right to recover possession of the goods.

2. Credit Sale

This is an agreement for the sale of goods where the price is payable by five or more instalments. A credit sale comes within the Sale of Goods Act, 1893. Therefore, the ownership of goods passes to the buyer as soon as the contract is made.

3. Consumer Credit Act, 1974

Scope of the Act

It establishes a comprehensive set of rules designed to regulate all transactions where credit not exceeding £5000 is given to individuals. It is a general Act which will eventually replace all other statutes which at present still regulate different types of credit agreements, for example the Moneylenders Acts and the Hire Purchase Acts. Thus it intends to bring uniformity to this area of law and much of the rules will be created by statutory instrument.

Licensing of Lenders

All who carry on a regulated consumer-credit or consumer-hire business are required to have a licence which is administered by the Director General of Fair Trading. Licensed holders will include banks, money-lenders, hire purchase companies, conditional and credit sale institutions, credit-card companies, retailers providing subscription or credit-account facilities and mail-order firms.

The Agreement

Before a regulated agreement can be made the lender must disclose in the correct manner certain information to the borrower or hirer, such as written information on the cash price and the credit charge. The actual agreement must:

(a)   be in writing, signed by the debtor;
(b)   contain the prescribed information in the correct form – this will include the rights and duties of the debtor and his remedies under the Act and notice of right of cancellation in the case of a 'cancellable' agreement.

The debtor must always receive a copy of the form he signs, at the time of signing. If the form is not immediately completed by the creditor, the debtor must also receive a copy of the final form within seven days of completion.

Default

Notice of default must be given to the debtor before the creditor can terminate a regulated agreement or enforce any rights he may have. The notice contains details of the breach and the action proposed by the creditor. Failure to heed the notice may mean the creditor has the following rights:

(a)   to end the agreement,
(b)   to require earlier payment,
(c)   to consider any right of the debtor terminated,
(d)   to recover the property.

Termination

The debtor under a regulated hire-purchase or conditional sale agreement may terminate the agreement if he has paid:

(a)   all sums due,
(b)   one-half of the price, or less with the court's approval, and
(c)   any necessary compensation, if the debtor has not taken reasonable care of the property.

Explain with reference to the Sale of Goods Act, 1893, the legal position of P in the following situations:

1.   P buys a lawn mower from D and it is agreed that D shall deliver it to P's house the following week. Over the weekend there is a fire at D's shop and the lawn mower is destroyed. Can P claim his money back?
2.   P buys a pair of socks from D, a men's outfitter. He wears the socks for one day and then suffers from a skin complaint. P's doctor says this is because P has unusually sensitive feet. Can P claim from D?
3.   P sees a weedkiller machine on display at an agricultural exhibition. He examines it and finds it is just what he needs down on his farm. P returns home and then orders one of these machines. When it arrives he finds it is substantially different from the one he had seen before.
4.   P goes to market to buy four sacks of a certain kind of potato. D offers to sell P the type of potato he is looking for and shows him a sample of what is in the sacks. P buys four sacks and when he examines them at home he finds that one sack contains a different type of potato.

5. D, a motor dealer, sells P a car for which P pays by cheque. At the bottom of the contract there is the following clause, 'We shall not be responsible for a breach of any condition or warranty, express or implied'. When the car is delivered to P he finds that it is in such bad condition that it cannot be driven. P stops the cheque to D and D demands his money.

6. P goes into an ironmongers and asks for Evertite Glue. When he uses it he finds that not only will it not stick his broken crockery, the reason for which he bought it, but it has no sticking power whatsoever.

(1) Where contracts for the sale of goods are concerned there are exceptions to the rule *nemo dat quod non habet*. Explain what this rule means and give four exceptions.

(2) What remedies has the seller of goods against (a) the buyer personally and (b) against the goods themselves?

Explain what is meant by the following:
(1) A contract for the sale of goods
(2) the passing of 'risk'
(3) 'property' in goods
(4) merchantable quality
(5) right of stoppage in transit
(6) conditions and warranties
(7) market overt
(8) sale by person with a voidable title.

15. Agency

A. THE NATURE OF AGENCY

There are many situations where an individual may wish to make a contract but will either not be in the right place, or will not have the skill or time, to do it himself; in which case the law allows him to appoint somebody to make the contract on his behalf.

The person who wishes a contract to be made for him is called the *principal*, and the person he appoints to make it on his behalf is called the *agent*. The person with whom the agent makes the contract on behalf of the principal is called the *third party*.

Contracts involving agency are based on the usual rules relating to simple contracts, but their structure is more complex because of the number of persons involved and the fact that there are two contracts to take into account.

The contract we shall first be concerned with is the one which creates the relationship of principal and agent between the two persons. This agreement is complete where one party, the principal, agrees that the other party, the agent, shall act on his behalf and the agent agrees to do this. For example, Mr P says to Mr A: 'Will you find a buyer for my house? If you are successful I will pay you commission.' If Mr A agrees, the relationship of principal and agent will have been established by this simple contract.

The purpose of this agency agreement is for the agent to bring his principal into contractual relations with the third party. In the above example the third party will be the purchaser of Mr P's house. Thus, the second contract that must be considered is the contract which the agent makes on behalf of his principal with the third party. In this contract it is important to remember that the parties are the principal and the third party. The agent is no more than the person who brings them together: he is created only for the purpose of bringing his principal into a contract with the third party, and as soon as he has done this his duties are over and he 'drops out' without incurring any rights or liabilities under this second contract. Therefore, in the above example, the first contract was to form the agency relationship between Mr P and Mr A in order for Mr A to find a third party; and the second contract will be the sale of the house between Mr P and the third party.

B. THE CREATION OF AN AGENT

The following are the ways in which an agent may be created:

1. Express or Implied Contract
A principal may expressly appoint his agent either orally or in writing.

As with other contracts, an agency contract may also be impliedly created between the parties, without anything having been expressly agreed upon. This will often occur where a person is employed by another in a certain capacity or to do certain work, and in carrying out his work it will be implied that the person shall be able to act as an agent in matters connected with his work. For instance, it has been held that a matron who was employed under an express contract with a hospital had implied authority to buy food on behalf of the hospital, although this right was not expressly mentioned in her contract.

2. Estoppel and Representation
The agency relationship may be created where one person has represented in some way to another person that somebody has authority to act or make contracts on his behalf even though, in fact, he has no such authority. For example, in *Lloyd* v. *Grace Smith & Co* a company of solicitors employed a managing clerk. They gave him an office and allowed him to deal with clients. Without the authority of the solicitors the clerk persuaded a client to transfer her property over to him. Although this was fraudulent and outside his authority, the solicitors were liable to the client as they had represented to the client that the clerk had authority to carry out such transactions as their agent.

Therefore, if a person represents, or permits it to be represented, that a person has authority to act as an agent on his behalf, he will be estopped from denying this authority. This means that he will be bound by any agreement made for him with a third party in the same way as he would have been had he expressly given that person authority to act as an agent.

In such cases the principal must have represented in some way that the person is an agent, even though in fact he is not. Also, the third party must have relied on the representation by making a contract with the person whom he believes to be a properly authorised agent.

In *Panorama Developments* v. *Fidelis Furnishing* the company secretary to the defendant company used his position in the company to hire cars from the plaintiffs. The plaintiffs thought that the cars were for company use when actually they were for the company secretary's personal pleasure. The court held that the defendants were liable to pay for the cost of the hirings even though they had not authorised the secretary to make such contracts because they had represented him as having authority to sign contracts connected with the administrative side of the company's business, such as hiring cars.

3. Necessity

An agent who has possession or safe custody of his principal's goods may, in some circumstances, be forced to act outside his express duties in order to protect the interests or goods of the principal. On such occasions the law says that the agent has authority to bind his principal by any act honestly done on the principal's behalf under the pressure of a real commercial necessity.

The elements that must exist before the person can be considered an agent of *necessity* are:

(*a*)   There is an actual and definite commercial necessity. For example, in *Great Northern Railway* v. *Swaffield* a horse was sent by train and on its arrival at the station there was no one to collect it. The railway company, who were only agents for the purpose of transporting the horse, paid for the stabling of the horse for the night and for its food. The plaintiffs claimed these expenses from the owner of the horse and it was held that they had been acting on behalf of the owner as an agent of necessity. The owner of the horse was therefore bound to pay the bill.

In *Munroe* v. *Willmott* the defendants, as they had been unable to contact the owner of a car parked in their yard which had become a nuisance, sold the plaintiff's car. It was held that they were not entitled to do so because the situation was not one of real commercial necessity.

(*b*)   It must be impossible for the agent to obtain the principal's instructions or advice before acting. In *Springer* v. *Great Western Railway* the principal sent a load of tomatoes from Jersey to London. The ship delivered them to Weymouth three days late, and owing to a railway strike the tomatoes were in such a bad condition that, before they became unmerchantable, the railway company decided to sell them locally. Before doing this they did not contact the principal to ask his advice. The court held that the railway company were liable to pay the principal damages. Even though there was probably a commercial emergency they were not agents of necessity, as they could have asked the principal's advice before they took such measures.

4. Ratification

In some situations an agent may contract with a third party saying that he is making the contract on behalf of a principal and that he has his authority, when in fact he has no authority whatsoever. In such cases the principal will not be bound by the agent's transactions. However, the principal may, when he hears of the contract, wish to be bound by the contract. In this case he may approve and confirm it. In such situations the principal is said to *ratify* the contract which the agent made on his behalf.

The effect of the principal's ratification of the contract is to make the contract binding on him as if the agent had been authorised to make the contract in the first place. In other words, the contract is said to exist, not from the time the principal ratified it, but from the time the agent originally made the agreement with the third party.

However, a principal can only ratify such a contract made without his prior authority if certain conditions are satisfied. The three main conditions are:

(*a*)   When the agent made the contract with the third party he must have said he was acting as an agent for a certain principal. If he does not mention that he is an agent, the principal cannot ratify the contract.

(*b*)   The person who is named as the principal must be in existence at the time the agent made the contract. In *Kelner* v. *Baxter* the plaintiff, a wine-merchant, agreed to sell wine to a person who said he was acting on behalf of a company which in fact had not yet been formed. The court held that the company could not ratify the agent's contract as it had not been in existence at the time the contract was made.

(*c*)   The principal must, at the time of ratification, have full knowledge of all the material facts concerning the contract made on his behalf. If he has not, he cannot ratify because he will be consenting to things he knows nothing about.

C. RIGHTS AND DUTIES BETWEEN AGENT AND PRINCIPAL

As agency is primarily a contractual relationship, most of the rights and duties will arise from the agreement made between the principal and the agent. The parties may expressly make any agreement they wish, but in the absence of any express agreement the law will imply into an agency relationship the following duties.

Agent's Duties

(1) The agent must perform the contract he has agreed to perform. In doing this he must exercise the cares and skills that the principal expects of him. For example, if the agent is employed to sell, it is his duty not only to sell but also to obtain the best available price.

(2) The agent must pay over to the principal all money he receives on behalf of the principal. Furthermore, he must keep proper accounts of the transactions which he must produce for inspection if asked for by the principal.

(3) The agent must not let his own interests conflict with those of the principal. For instance, he must not act as a principal himself against his own principal. In *Armstrong* v. *Jackson* the principal employed a stockbroker to buy some shares for him. Instead of buying the shares on the open market, the agent sold the principal his own shares. The court held that the principal need not go through with the contract.

(4) The agent must not make any profit beyond the commission or other remuneration he is receiving from his principal. This does not prevent him from taking the opportunity of earning money, provided he does not do so at the principal's expense or by using the principal's goods. If the agent does make a secret profit or takes bribes from the third party, the principal has a right to dismiss the agent without notice and without paying him his remuneration. The principal also has the right to recover the secret profit and refuse to go through with the contract with the third party.

(5) The agent must not delegate his work to someone else. The general rule is that the agent must perform his duties personally. This is because the relationship between the principal and the agent is a personal one.

However, the agent will be allowed to delegate his authority either when it is expressly permitted in his contract or where it can be implied into the agreement: for example, where it is usual for the agent to employ clerks or assistants to assist him with his work.

In *De Bussche* v. *Alt* the principal appointed his agent to sell a ship at a certain price in China. As the agent could not find a buyer at that price in China, he obtained the principal's consent to appoint a sub-agent in Japan to sell the ship. The court held that this was not a breach of the agent's duties.

(6) The agent must always act in good faith. This is a very general duty which includes most of the particular duties already mentioned. A good illustration of this duty is the rule that an agent must not disclose confidential information or documents entrusted to him by his principal. Also, an agent is not allowed to use, for his own personal benefit, information that he has acquired in the course of his

employment as an agent: for example, when the agent has access to lists of customers as he did in *Robb* v. *Green*. In this case the employer obtained an injunction against his employee to prevent him using such lists after he had left the employment.

Principal's Duties

(1) The principal must pay the agent his commission or any other remuneration that has been agreed upon. The amount of the commission and the terms of its payment depend entirely on the terms of the contract creating the agency relationship.

Furthermore, the principal is under a duty not to prevent or hinder the agent from carrying out his side of the agreement or from earning his remuneration.

(2) The principal must indemnify the agent for all liabilities lawfully incurred in carrying out his business.

D. THE POSITION OF THE THIRD PARTY

So far we have been dealing with personal contracts between the principal and the agent. It will be remembered that the reason for employing an agent is to bring the principal into contractual relations with a third party. The effect of this major contract between principal and third party will depend on how the agent presents himself to the third party.

1. Where the Agent Contracts as Agent for a Named Principal

This is the usual position under which the agent will act. He will approach the third party on behalf of his principal and tell the third party he is acting for a certain named principal. In this situation the agent's sole duty is to bring them into a contractual relationship. He does not become a party to the contract himself; therefore he does not incur any rights, nor is he subject to any of the liabilities under the contract. When the agent has brought the two parties together he 'drops out'.

2. Where the Agent does not Mention he is Contracting for a Principal

In this case the agent does not disclose to the third party the existence or identity of the principal, even though he has the principal's authority to act. Therefore, the third party does not know that the person with whom he is dealing is somebody's agent. As far as he is concerned the agent is a principal. In such cases, when the third party hears that there is an undisclosed principal, he has the option of holding either the principal or the agent liable on the contract. Yet he cannot sue both, so if he elects to hold the agent liable he cannot then change his mind and sue the principal.

Conversely, the undisclosed principal is permitted to intervene and claim from the third party when he hears of the contract. However, the principal will not be able to intervene if the contract between the third party and the agent is incompatible with a contract of agency: for instance, if the contract is one of a personal nature or the third party would not have contracted with the agent if he had known he was acting as an agent. In *Said* v. *Butt* the principal wanted a ticket for the theatre. As he knew the management would not sell him a ticket, he sent an agent to purchase one in the agent's own name. When the principal used the ticket to gain admission to the theatre he was turned away. He sued the third party for breach of contract. It was held that no contract had been made with the principal because the manager would not have contracted had he known that the agent was an agent who was acting for that particular principal.

3. Where the Agent Acts for the Principal but without Authority
In this situation the agent states to the third party that he has authority to act on behalf of his principal when he has not. The principal will not be liable for the contract unless he ratifies it or the principal is estopped from denying the agent's authority because he has previously represented to the third party that the agent has authority.

E. TERMINATION OF AGENCY

The agency relationship may be terminated either by an act of the parties themselves or by the operation of law.

1. By Act of the Parties
Firstly, the contract of agency can be terminated by mutual agreement: either by both parties agreeing not to continue with the contract, or when the relationship comes to an end after the agreed period of time, or when all their business is completed.

Secondly, as a general rule, the authority of the agent can be revoked at any time by the principal. If the principal's revocation also amounts to a breach of the agency contract, he will be liable to pay the agent damages for the commission or remuneration the agent has lost.

In some situations it is not enough merely for the principal and agent to end the relationship. Any third party likely to make a contract with the agent must be informed of the termination, otherwise the principal may be estopped from denying liability for the contracts.

2. By Operation of Law
A contract of agency will end if the object of the agency becomes illegal: for example, if the principal becomes an enemy alien or the goods over which the contract is made become illegal to buy or sell.

Secondly, as the contract of agency is a personal one, the death of either party will terminate the relationship.

Thirdly, although the insanity of the principal terminates the relationship between principal and agent, the principal will probably still be bound by contracts made with third parties who did not know of this disability.

F. EXAMPLES OF SPECIAL AGENTS

Factors
A factor is a mercantile agent who buys and sells goods for a principal in the ordinary course of his business. He will usually have possession of his principal's goods for the purpose of sale. If, however, he sells the goods without the principal's consent, the third party will still obtain good title to the goods (see the exceptions to the rule *nemo dat quod non habet*).

Brokers
A broker is an agent employed to make commercial contracts between his principal and the third party for a commission, a practice usually called brokerage. Unlike factors, brokers do not usually have possession of goods for sale on behalf of the principal; therefore a third party will not get good title as a result of an unauthorised sale.

Auctioneers
An auctioneer is agent for the seller of goods at a public auction or open sale. Although he is primarily the agent of the seller, on accepting a bid he will become agent for the buyer.

Del credere Agents
An agent for the sale of goods sometimes acts under a commission of *del credere*. This means that for a higher remuneration he promises to become responsible to his principal for the solvency of the buyer he finds. In other words, he guarantees the payment of the price for the goods he has sold.

1. Explain how the concept of agency by ratification is applied and state its requirements.
2. What is meant by a contract of agency?

3. What is an agent? Illustrate your answers with different types of agent.
4. Who is an agent of necessity? Give the ways in which such an agency relationship can arise.
5. Enumerate the duties owed by an agent to his principal.
6. You are the manager of a department store. What is your legal position if you discover that A, a buyer in the department store, received a present of £30 from C, a supplier of goods to the store, and that A has ordered goods worth £1000 from C? The goods are of the same quality and price as goods obtainable from other suppliers to the department store.
7. In what ways may agency relationships be created? How can they be ended?

Explain what is meant by the following:
(1) agency by estoppel
(2) *del credere* agent
(3) undisclosed principal
(4) principal's duties towards his agent.

16. Employer and Employee

A. THE CONTRACT OF EMPLOYMENT

Nature of the Contract

The legal relationship between an employer and an employee is created by a contract. This contract is usually known as a contract 'of services' or 'of employment'. The basis of the contract is that the employee undertakes to work for the employer and in consideration he is paid for the work by the employer. The Industrial Relations Act, 1971, defined a contract of employment as a contract of service or of apprenticeship, whether it is express or implied, and if express whether oral or in writing.

A contract of employment is based on the structure of an ordinary simple contract. Therefore, the contract consists of an offer, acceptance and consideration, and both parties must intend to be legally bound by the agreement. However, a contract of employment does differ in some ways from the ordinary contract.

Lack of Freedom in the Agreement

In an ordinary simple contract there is a relative freedom to make a contract on the terms that the parties wish. However, in a contract of employment there is less contractual freedom or room for bargaining. In an employment contract the offer is frequently made by the employer to a prospective employee on a 'take it or leave it' basis and the average employee has little opportunity to bargain or alter its terms. He has the choice of accepting the entire terms of this standard-form contract offered to him by the employer or rejecting it and finding alternative employment.

Furthermore, some of the terms included in the contract may be the choice neither of the employer nor of the employee. Frequently, the terms that are included for a particular type of employment have been laid down beforehand by a collective agreement which both employers and employees are bound to recognise. For example, by an order made by the Dock Workers' Scheme, the dockers' rates of pay and their conditions of service must be in accordance with the national or local agreements for the time being in force.

Formality in the Contract

A second difference between an ordinary simple contract and a contract of employment lies in the formality with which some of the terms must be made known. Although a contract of employment may be made in the same way as any simple contract, there are certain terms in the contract that have to be put into writing.

The Contracts of Employment Act, 1963, states that certain terms must be given in the form of 'written particulars'. These must be given by the employer to the employee within thirteen weeks of his starting work. The 'written particulars' must specify such terms as the employee's date of beginning work, the length of holidays, arrangements for pay during sickness or injury, pensions, and periods for giving notice to end the contract. The reason for requiring these particulars to be in writing is to draw certain important terms to the attention of employees. The Act says that, provided the terms are in some way made accessible to the employee, the employer may dispense with having the particulars in writing: for instance, if copies of the terms are so freely available that the employee will have an opportunity of reading them in the course of his employment.

Employers must now include further terms in the 'written particulars'. These are more precise details about holidays, information about the employee's rights in relation to trade union membership and activities, to whom the employee should apply if he has a grievance about his employment, how the application should be made, and the procedure for dealing with the grievance.

Contract 'of Service'

It has already been mentioned that a contract of employment is a contract 'of service'. This type of contract must be carefully distinguished from a contract 'for services'. In both cases there is a contract for one person to do work for another for payment, but it is only a contract of service that creates the employer—employee relationship together with all the rights and duties that go with it, such as the entitlement to industrial injuries benefit.

In a contract 'for services' the relationship usually exists where an individual pays an independent contractor to do certain work for him. Although this work is done for the individual's benefit and at his request, he has less control over an independent contractor than he would have over an employee. For example, he has no power to tell the contractor *how* to do his job or what method to use. Also, in most cases the individual will not be liable vicariously for the torts the contractor may commit while he is carrying out his work.

The courts always seem to have difficulty in deciding whether a contract to do work is a contract of service or a contract for services. They have therefore adopted various tests to discover in what circumstances the relationship of employer—employee exists. None of the tests is invariably followed; they act as guidelines and a judge may use any one of them depending on the circumstances of the case before him.

The 'Control' Test

The basis of this test is that a contract of service can be discovered by the degree of control one person exercises over the work of another. The relationship of employer—employee is said to exist if the employer can say not only *what* has to be done by the employee, but also *how* it is to be done by dictating the *means* that the employee is to use in doing the work. For example, Mr A engages Mr B, an interior decorator, to paint his house. If Mr A tells Mr B what has to be done, what paint to use and the colour schemes he desires, then the contract is probably one of services. However, if Mr B is allowed an entirely free hand to use whatever materials he wishes and to create the colour schemes he feels suitable, then there is probably a contract for services.

The 'control' test is easier to use in cases which involve unskilled work. In such cases the employer can obviously tell the employee *how* to do his work more easily than he can tell skilled technicians. Therefore, in the case of scientists, technicians, craftsmen, doctors and the like, the 'control' test is not really adequate. Also, this test is not very effective when dealing with large-scale industrial concerns or vast companies. because it is difficult to discover exactly which person within the organisation exercises the control.

The 'Integral' or 'Organisation' Test

In *Stevenson, Jordan & Harrison* v. *Macdonald & Evans,* Lord Denning said: 'Under a contract of service a man is employed as part of the business and his work is done as an integral part of the business; whereas under a contract for services his work, although done for the business, is not integrated into it but only accessory to it.'

This test takes into account the degree of integration into the organisation, whether it be a factory, hospital or large company. Those who are sufficiently integrated into the enterprise are employees wherever the control of that person may lie.

In *Whittaker* v. *Ministry of Pensions and National Insurance* it was held that a trapeze artist who had suffered a broken wrist as a result of a fall during her performance was entitled to industrial injuries benefit as an employed person. She was under a written contract which, apart from her act, included miscellaneous duties to be carried out for the troupe as a whole. The court said the artist 'had no real independence and had to carry out her contractual duties as an integral part of the business of the company during her engagement'.

The 'Multiple' Test

In *Ready Mixed Concrete* v. *Ministry of Pensions and National Insurance* it was stated that a contract of service exists if:

(a)   The employee agrees that in consideration for payment he will provide his own work and skill in the performance of some service for his employer.

(b)   The employee agrees that in the performance of that service he will be subject to the other's control in a sufficient degree to make that other the employer.

(c)   The remaining terms of the employee's contract are consistent with it being a contract of service, such as the power to be dismissed, the type of place where he works, the hours he works and the plant and equipment he uses.

In this case the court held that owner-drivers of lorries, who were paid by the manufacturers of concrete to deliver concrete, were under a contract for services and were independent contractors. They were not employees under a contract of service because condition (c) was not satisfied. The contract was not consistent with a contract of service. It was a contract for carriage of goods where the drivers were paid according to load and mileage and were permitted to have substitute drivers.

B. DUTIES ARISING FROM THE EMPLOYER–EMPLOYEE RELATIONSHIP

Naturally, an employer and an employee will be bound by all that is expressly mentioned in their contract; but in many situations the actual contract of service only covers the minimum number of terms. For instance, the contract may only state the work that is to be done and how much is to be paid for doing it, together with what is required in the way of 'written particulars'. When the contract of service does not expressly set out the duties between the parties, the courts will imply certain obligations between them.

Some Duties of the Employer

(a) To Pay Wages

If no express provision is made as to the remuneration the employee is to receive for his work, the court will fix a reasonable sum. Apart from this common law obligation that the employer should pay for work done, there are various statutory obligations that are connected with the wages of employees. For example, the employer is required to deduct the appropriate amount of income tax from the employee's wages and pay it to the Inland Revenue. Also, the employer is responsible for payment of his own and his employee's contribution to national insurance. The employee's contribution is deducted from his wages at source.

(b) To Ensure a Safe Place of Work

An employer is under a duty to provide a reasonably safe place of work for his employees. For example, in *Bradford* v. *Robinson Rentals Ltd* the employer had sent a fifty-seven-year-old employee on a long wintry journey in an unheated van. The court held that the employer was liable to pay compensation for the frostbite the employee suffered in consequence. Not only will this duty of ensuring a safe place of work be implied by the courts into a contract of service, but the employer is also under a statutory duty to provide such conditions. The Factories Act, 1961, contains a list of requirements the employer must observe in order to secure the health and safety of factory workers. Also, the Offices, Shops and Railway Premises Act, 1963, set up similar standards to be adhered to by the employer of office and shop staff.

(c) To Provide Safe Equipment

A court may imply a term into a contract that the employer should provide safe tools for his employee's work, and that he should maintain them in a good state of repair. The Employers' Liability (Defective Equipment) Act, 1969, states that an employer will be liable for defects in any equipment which he knows about, should know about, or which could have been discovered with regular inspection.

Some Duties of the Employee

(a) To Obey

The employee must obey all lawful and reasonable orders of his employer which relate to his contract of service. In *Pepper* v. *Webb* the head-gardener, who had been asked by his employer to plant flowers before they died, refused to do so and was insolent. The court held that his wilful disobedience of this lawful and reasonable order, his uncaring attitude towards the grounds and greenhouse in addition to his insolence, justified his dismissal without notice.

However, not every act of disobedience will justify the dismissal of the employee. In *Laws* v. *London Chronicle Ltd* the plaintiff, an advertising agent, was present in the managing director's office when her immediate superior had quarrelled with the managing director. Although the managing director had ordered her to stay, she had left the room with her immediate superior. The court held that the disobedience was a breach of her contract, but it did not entitle her employer to dismiss her because the disobedience was not so serious as to show that she was repudiating her contract or any of its basic terms.

(b) To Use Care and Skill

The employee must use all the reasonable care and skill that is expected of him while he is carrying out his work. In *Lister* v. *Romford Ice & Cold Storage*, Lister was a lorry driver employed by Romford Ice, and while he was reversing his vehicle he negligently ran into and injured another employee, who happened to be his father. The father was entitled to damages against the company on the basis that the company were vicariously liable for Lister's negligence in carrying out his work. However, the court held that as Lister had not exercised reasonable care and skill in carrying out his work, the company were entitled to recover from him the amount of damages they had been obliged to pay to his father. This case also illustrates a further duty, that the employee has to indemnify his employer against any loss the latter suffered due to the former's breach of duty.

(c) To be Loyal and Faithful

An employee owes a duty of loyalty and fidelity to his employer. This means he must carry out his work in the best interests of his employer and must not let his personal interests conflict with this work. For example, in *Hivac Ltd* v. *Park Royal Scientific Instruments* five employees of the plaintiff company had spent their Sundays assembling hearing-aids for a rival company without their employer's permission. The court held that the employees were in breach of an implied term in their contracts of service, which was that they should not undertake any outside work that could harm the interests of their employer.

It is also part of this duty of fidelity that an employee must not disclose confidential information that he has gained during the course of his employment, and must not entice clients away from the employer. This duty has been mentioned in greater detail under contracts in restraint of trade.

C. TERMINATION OF THE CONTRACT OF EMPLOYMENT

If an individual is employed for a specific length of time or for a particular purpose, his contract of service will terminate at the end of the agreed time or on the completion of his work. If there are no express terms in the contract of service stating when the employment shall end, the court may imply a length of time for which it is considered the contract was intended to last.

The other most usual ways by which a contract of employment will terminate are, firstly, when either party gives the other *notice* that he intends to end the employer–employee relationship, and secondly, when the relationship is ended by the summary *dismissal* of the employee.

Notice

Often a contract of service will end by one of the parties giving notice to the other that he intends to terminate the contract. The common law rules regarding notice are that, where no specific length of time is mentioned for which notice is required to be given, the contract can be terminated after giving a reasonable length of time as notice. In deciding what is reasonable notice the court has to take into account such circumstances as the length of time the contract has been in existence, the nature of the work done, the method of payment, and what is customary notice in that type of work.

The common law rules regarding length of notice have virtually been superseded by the Contracts of Employment Act, 1963, and now by the Contracts of Employment Act, 1972. This recent legislation lays down a new set of minimum periods of notice. The length of notice to which an employer and an employee shall be entitled is calculated on the number of weeks for which the contract has been in existence. If the contract has been in existence thirteen weeks, either side must give at least one week's notice before ending the employment; two weeks' notice must be given after two years of employment, four weeks after five years, six weeks after ten years and eight weeks after fifteen years' service. However, as these are only the statutory minima for the length of notice, a greater length of time may be agreed upon between the parties.

Dismissal

If an employee is in breach of a major term of his contract of service, the employer may either dismiss him with notice or dismiss him summarily–in other words, instantly without notice.

Summary notice may be justified when an employee's misconduct endangers his fellow-employees or the public. Also, the employee may be instantly dismissed if he has been dishonest or repeatedly warned about his carelessness. However, in each case the summary dismissal will depend upon what is reasonable in the circumstances.

Unfair Dismissal

The Trade Union and Labour Relations Act, 1974, gives employees, with a few exceptions, protection against unfair dismissal. The Act states that it is unfair industrial practice for an employee to be dismissed without good reason. When the employer has dismissed an employee, the former is required to show the reason for the dismissal.

The dismissal will be considered fair if it is reasonable in the circumstances, having regard to the employee's capability, qualifications, conduct or some other substantial reason, such as dishonesty or participation in irregular industrial action.

The Act says that the dismissal will be unfair if it is because an employee is exercising, or seeking to exercise, either his right to belong to a registered trade union or his right not to belong.

Furthermore, it is considered fair dismissal in the case of redundancy, unless the employee is selected for dismissal in contravention of some customary arrangement or agreed procedure for redundancy. Where an employee is fairly dismissed because of redundancy and through no fault of his own, he may, in certain circumstances laid down in the Redundancy Payments Act, 1965, be entitled to redundancy payment by his employer. The amount of this payment varies according to the length of time he has been in employment.

Complaints of Unfair Dismissal

When an employee considers he has been unfairly dismissed, he may make a complaint to an industrial tribunal. If the tribunal finds that the employee has been unfairly dismissed, it may either recommend to the employer that the employee should be re-engaged on reasonable terms, or it may, where the advice as to re-engagement is not accepted by the employer or the employee, award the employee compensation to be paid by the employer.

The amount of compensation that will be awarded by the tribunal will depend on what is just and equitable in the circumstances, having regard to the loss which has been suffered by the employee and the expenses he has reasonably incurred. Where the tribunal has recommended re-engagement and the recommendation has been unreasonably refused by the employer, the compensation will be increased by any amount the tribunal considers reasonable. If it is the employee who has unreasonably refused re-engagement, his amount of compensation will be reduced.

D. SICKNESS AND UNEMPLOYMENT

National Insurance Benefits

It has been laid down by statute that it is compulsory for every individual, over school-leaving age and under a pensionable age, to insure against sickness and unemployment. The majority of the present law is contained in the Social Security Act, 1975.

This necessity for insurance against such misfortunes does not refer only to persons who are employed or under a contract of service. The obligation refers to persons who are self-employed and even applies to those who are not employed at all. However, there are some persons who are exempt from payment, such as married women who have the option of contributing.

The contributor to the national insurance scheme has the advantage of being able to claim benefits if he is unable to work through sickness or has become unemployed. He is entitled to claim these benefits if he has:

(a)   paid twenty-six or more contributions since his entry into the insurance scheme; and

(b)   paid fifty or more contributions in respect of the last contribution year before the benefit year in which he is claiming.

An individual is not able to claim the benefit for the first three days of sickness or unemployment, but if he has paid at least one hundred and fifty-six contributions, he will be able to claim benefit for as long as he remains sick or unemployed. Howeer, any person who has paid fewer than one hundred and fifty-six contributions will be limited to three hundred and twelve days' benefit, after which time he will have to re-qualify by paying a further thirteen contributions.

Disqualifications from Unemployment Benefit
An individual will be unsucessful with his claim for unemployment benefit if:

(a)   he lost his employment through his own misconduct;
(b)   he refuses approved training;
(c)   he left his previous employment voluntarily, without just cause;
(d)   he refuses to carry out reasonable recommendations of the employment exchange, which are aimed at helping him find suitable employment;
(e)   he refuses, without good cause, suitable employment.

Disqualifications from Sickness Benefit
An individual will be unsuccessful with his claim for sickness benefit if:

(a)   he has become incapable of work through his own misconduct; or
(b)   he refuses, unreasonably, to submit to medical examination or treatment; or

(c)   he fails to observe any other rules that have been laid down
concerning claims.

E. INDUSTRIAL ACCIDENTS AND DISEASES

Industrial Injuries Benefit

If an employee suffers injury at work he may be able to sue his
employer for compensation, for instance under the tort of negligence.
However, whether the injury is due to the employer's fault or not, the
employee may claim the amount he has suffered as a result of his
injuries from the State under the national insurance scheme. If an
employee claims industrial injuries benefit and also successfully sues his
employer, one half of any national insurance benefit he receives must
be deducted from any damages awarded as a result of the court action
against the employer.

The Social Security Act, 1975, provides a comprehensive and compulsory insurance scheme for persons who are employed or self-
employed in order to assist those injured persons who suffer from
industrial accidents or diseases. This scheme is run by the State and the
monetary compensation for injury is based on a fixed scale paid by the
Department of Health and Social Security from the Industrial Injuries
Fund. The finances of the Fund are obtained from the contributions of
employers, employees and apprentices and by a grant from the State.
The contributions are deducted from the wages of employees as part of
and in the same way as the general national insurance scheme.

Industrial Accidents

In order for an insured employee to claim industrial injury benefit, he
must show that he has suffered personal injury caused by an accident
arising out of and in the course of his employment.

'Accident'

An 'accident' is an unexpected, unlooked-for mishap. It is an event or
occurrence happening at a particular time, and not something which
takes place gradually over a period of time. For example, in *Ministry of
Social Security* v. *Amalgamated Engineering Union* an employee, while
lifting a heavy flagstone, felt a pain in his chest which was later
diagnosed as a hernia. The House of Lords confirmed that such an event
was an accident.

Accidents have been held by the courts or tribunals to include: an
ulcer caused by wearing protective boots, issued for work, that were the
wrong size; fibrositis caused in one morning by a draught through a

broken lorry window; the murder of a schoolmaster by the pupils whom he had threatened to punish; and the death by broncho-pneumonia of a fireman working in water.

'Arising out of and in the Course of' his Employment

An employee is working in the course of his employment when he is doing something that is required of him by his contract of service. It has been held that certain matters reasonably incidental to the carrying out of his contract of service are counted as being done within the employee's course of employment: for instance, accidents occurring during authorised meal or coffee breaks. In one case a woman employee while at work bought a slice of toast to eat during her break. She was injured by a piece of glass in it and it was decided that the injury arose in the course of and out of her employment.

It is not enough that the employee is merely in the course of his employment when the accident and injury occurs. The accident and injury must also arise out of, or be causally connected with, his employment. If this rule were not so, an employee would be able to claim for an injury that happened to him at work which might have had nothing to do with his work: for instance, where an employee faints and injures her head at work because of her pregnancy. However, the Act lays down that an accident arising 'in the course of' employment is presumed to have arisen 'out of' it, unless the contrary is proved.

Industrial Diseases

An accident, in order to qualify for benefit, must have been an occurrence or event. However, an industrial disease may have been the result of a process which had continued from day to day and gradually, over a period of years, had produced the incapacity for which the employee claims compensation.

Detailed regulations lay down the types of industrial disease and the occupations in which they are particularly likely to occur. An insured employee will be able to claim industrial injuries benefit if he suffers from any of these diseases which arise out of his particular type of employment.

The employee, before he is entitled to benefit, must satisfy three conditions. Firstly, he must show that he is suffering from a prescribed disease. Secondly, he must have been in one of the occupations related to the disease from which he is suffering: for example, 'glanders' contracted through working with equine animals or their carcases, or 'anthrax' contracted through sheep or cattle. Thirdly, he must show that the disease is attributable to the work he has been doing.

Types of Insurance Benefits

The three types of benefit that may be awarded under the Act are:

(a) Injury Benefit

For the time that an employee is incapable of working as a result of an industrial injury or disease, he may be entitled to injury benefit at a weekly rate for a period of up to one hundred and fifty-six days.

(b) Disablement Benefit

This benefit varies according to the assessment of physical or mental disability. Unlike injury benefit, it may be paid irrespective of any loss of earning capacity. So, a person who has not stayed away from work at all may still receive a disablement benefit.

The employee must be at least 1 per cent disabled before his claim will be successful. The assessment is carried out by a medical board who will measure the extent of his disablement. For example, loss of both hands is 100 per cent and loss of four fingers on one hand is 50 per cent disablement.

If the disablement is assessed at over 20 per cent, the benefit will be paid as a pension. Any disability assessed at under 20 per cent will be compensated by payment of a lump sum. The disablement pension may be increased on account of the person's unemployability or in cases where he has special hardship, such as the need for constant medical attention.

(c) Death Benefit

When the employee dies as a result of an industrial accident or disease, this benefit is usually payable to the widow, widower or certain other dependants.

F. VICARIOUS LIABILITY

There are certain relationships where the law states that one person will be held responsible for the wrong committed by another. Thus, a principal may be liable for the wrongs committed by his agent, a partner may be liable for the torts of another partner, and in the relationship we are concerned with here, an employer may be liable for the torts of his employee.

Vicarious liability of an employer for the wrongs of an employee depends primarily upon the existence of a contract of service or, as it is often described, there must be a *master* and *servant* relationship. Some of the tests that are used to discover whether this relationship exists have been discussed earlier in this chapter. If the courts find that the worker is not an employee or servant but an independent contractor whose methods and modes of work are not controlled by the person who pays him, it would be unjust to make that person paying the independent contractor vicariously liable for his wrongs. In *Padbury* v. *Holliday & Greenwood Ltd* independent contractors were working on a window and one of them had negligently placed his iron tool on the window-sill. The tool fell and injured the plaintiff. The court held that the defendants who were paying the independent contractors were not liable for the wrong.

A person will only be responsible for the wrongs of an independent contractor when he has authorised or ratified the contractor's wrong or where the person making the payment has himself broken some duty that he owed. In *Paine* v. *Colne Valley Electricity* an independent contractor supplied an electrical gadget to the defendants who were the employers of Paine, a workman. While working inside the apparatus Paine was killed. His widow claimed damages and the court held that she would succeed as the employers had themselves been in breach of their duty to provide a safe place for their employees to work.

Wrong Must be Committed during the Course of Employment

In order for the employer to be vicariously liable for the torts of the employee, the wrong must have arisen during the course of the employee's employment. For example, in *Beard* v. *London General Omnibus Co* a bus conductor, because of the absence of the driver, drove a bus. While doing this the conductor negligently injured the plaintiff. The court held that the defendants were not liable to the plaintiff, as the conductor was not acting within the course or scope of his employment. He was doing an act which he was not employed to do.

Provided the wrong is done in the course of the employee's employment, the employer will be liable even if the employee does what he is authorised to do but in the wrong way. In *Bayley* v. *Manchester Railway* one of the defendant's porters mistakenly believed that the plaintiff was on the wrong train. As the train was moving off he violently pulled the plaintiff out of the carriage, which resulted in him being injured by falling on to the platform. The court held that the defendants were liable as the porter had acted within the scope and course of his employment, since it was his duty to ensure that passengers caught the right train, even though he was carrying out his work in the wrong manner.

Also, in *Limpus* v. *London General Omnibus Co* a driver of one of the defendant's vehicles had been instructed that 'he must not race with or obstruct' another bus. The court held that the defendants were liable for their driver's wrongful conduct as it took place within the course of his employment, even though it was unauthorised.

However, an employer will not be vicariously liable for a wrongful act of his employee which is completely unconnected with the contract of service. For example, in *Warren* v. *Henlys Ltd* a pump attendant employed at the defendant's garage mistakenly thought that the plaintiff, a customer, was driving away without paying for some petrol. The employee used abusive language to the plaintiff who then threatened to report his conduct to his employer. The employee then 'gave him one on the chin to get on with' and the plaintiff brought an action for damages. The court held that the defendants were not liable, as an act of personal vengeance was not within the course of his employment.

The Employee who is on a 'Frolic of his Own'

An employer is not liable for the torts of his employee who has deviated so far from the course of his employment that he is said to be on a 'frolic of his own'. In other words, if the employee steps outside his employment to do some act for himself, unconnected with the employer's business, the employer will not be liable. In *Storey* v. *Ashton* the defendant sent two of his employees, a driver and a clerk, on an errand. On the return journey the driver went out of his way to do some of the clerk's private business and while off route, on a frolic of their own, he negligently ran into and injured the plaintiff. The court held that the defendant employers were not liable as their employees were, at the time of the accident, outside the course of their employment.

G. HEALTH AND SAFETY AT WORK

So far I have mentioned various branches of the civil law that can apply to the health and/or the safety of persons at work, for example in the tort of negligence, where an employer or employee may owe a duty to others who are around him in the work situation, and furthermore in the terms that the common law may imply into a contract of employment concerning safe equipment, premises, and so forth. Those duties, whether tort or contract, are imposed by the civil law, a breach of which will lead to the injured party seeking compensation.

However, my intention here is to introduce the Health and Safety at Work Act, 1974, which lays down a comprehensive range of criminal duties, the breach of which may lead to the prosecution of the offender, irrespective of any thoughts the injured party may have of seeking compensation.

It was intended that the 1974 Act would progressively replace most of the then existing legislation on health and safety with a simple and more integral and universal system of rules. The Act is intended to represent the State's greater concern on the topic by introducing a new system of regulations and approved codes of practice designed to improve existing standards of health, safety and welfare. Statutes such as the Factories Act, 1961, and the Office, Shops and Railway Premises Act, 1963, are to be replaced. The 1974 Act talks in general, overall, terms about the wide topic of health and safety in work situations and it leaves the details for any particular industry or work to be laid down by specific regulations made under the Act.

The Act lays down general duties to be complied with by employers, employees, controllers of premises and designers, manufacturers, importers and suppliers of articles for use at work. Some of these general duties are:

(a) An employer's duty to ensure, so far as reasonably practicable, the health, safety and welfare at work of all his employees.
(b) An employer's and self-employed person's duty to conduct his undertaking in such a way that every person outside the work situation shall not be exposed to risk.
(c) An employee's duty while at work to take reasonable care for the health and safety of himself and others who may be affected by his conduct at work and co-operate with his employer to enable the latter to carry out his duties.
(d) A duty of a designer, manufacturer, importer or supplier of an article for use at work to ensure, as far as reasonable, that this article is safe.

Whatever steps are considered reasonably practicable to carry out these general duties will, naturally, vary in each case. The responsibility of enforcing this legislation is with the Health and Safety Executive carried out through their Inspectors.

1. When will one person be liable for the wrongs committed by another person?
2. James, the chauffeur, has driven his master, Nicholas, to Dover ferry. Nicholas orders James to return to London immediately. James, thinking he has plenty of spare time, drives to visit his mother and sister in Deal before returning to London. Whilst in Deal, James through his own negligence is involved in a car crash. Is Nicholas liable for the action of James?
3. Explain the general duties set out in the Health and Safety at Work Act.
4. Explain some of the differences between a servant and an independent contractor in relation to an employer.

5. Clare works on the production line of a factory. The instrument she has to use snaps and a splinter enters her eye. An expert says that the accident was due to a fault in the manufacturing of the instrument. Advise Clare as to her claim for compensation.

6. What are the duties that a servant owes to his master?

7. Describe some of the various tests that the law has used to discover whether the relationship of employer and employee exists in a particular situation.

8. As an employee in a business of your choosing, you have been given the task of writing a short report. The report is to set out for fellow employees, in everyday, simple language, the duties arising from health and safety legislation towards employers, employees, customers and others.

9. Discuss the Occupier Liability Act, 1957, and the Health and Safety at Work Act, 1974, with regard to a shopkeeper's liability to his customers.

10. Outline the role of the Inspectorate in relation to health and safety.

Explain the meaning of the following:
(1) 'written particulars'
(2) a contract 'of service'
(3) a contract 'for services'
(4) an industrial accident
(5) vicarious liability
(6) on a 'frolic of his own'.

17. Business Units

The sole trader, the partnership and the limited company are examples of business units, and each of these forms is recognised in a different way by the law.

A. THE SOLE TRADER

The sole trader is a person who carries on his business activities on his own account and, in the main, the law treats the individual and his trade as inseparable. In other words, the individual is his business and vice versa; the business activity has no legal personality separate from the individual who carries it out. Thus the sole trader is personally liable for all the contracts he makes in connection with his business and also for all the torts that he might commit in the course of carrying out his business. Therefore, the sole trader has 'unlimited liability' in all his business activities and will be personally responsible, even to the full extent of his private wealth, for such things as debts that he might incur while carrying out his business. Furthermore, on his death the business is treated as part of his estate and may have to die with him in order that death duties can be paid.

The Registration of Business Names Act, 1916, requires the sole trader to register the name of his business if it is anything other than the true name of the proprietor. Moreover, the law has stated that before certain classes of business can be carried out they must be licensed, for such reasons as public health or safety.

B. PARTNERSHIPS

Definition

It has already been mentioned that a partnership is an unincorporated association; that is, it has no corporate legal personality separate from the individuals who have formed the partnership. However, from some aspects of its work the law has recognised the partnership as a business unit.

The Partnership Act, 1890, defines a partnership as 'The relation which subsists between persons carrying on business in common with a view to profit'.

The general rule is that a partnership cannot consist of more than twenty persons, but this limitation does not include partnerships formed by professional persons such as solicitors and accountants. In the case of a banking partnership the number used to be restricted to ten partners; but since the Companies Act, 1967, they may now have up to twenty partners, provided each partner has been authorised by the Board of Trade.

A partnership differs from a corporation and must also be distinguished from other types of unincorporated associations such as the local ping-pong club or social club. A partnership is primarily a business unit and has to be formed with a view to profit, whereas the others are formed for a variety of reasons.

Creation of a Partnership

It will be remembered that a corporation must be created in one of three ways: by Royal Charter, by a particular statute, or under the formalities that have been laid down by a general statute (such as the Companies Act, 1948). However, a partnership is unincorporated and its formation is mainly based on the ordinary law of simple contract. That is, a partnership is created by an agreement between the persons who intend to become partners. This agreement may be in writing, oral, or even implied from the conduct of the persons involved. Furthermore, a partnership may be created by means of a deed, which takes the form of an agreement under seal which is signed by the persons who have agreed to become partners.

Articles of Partnership

As a general rule, the partnership is created by a written contract which is known as the 'articles of partnership'. Each partner is bound by the articles in the same way as they would all be bound by any contract. This document, which will be signed by all the partners, contains all the rules under which the partners intend to carry on their business. The articles usually include clauses dealing with the nature of the business activity which they intend to operate, its capital and property, and the capital of each partner. It is also usual to state the way in which the profits and losses will be shared among them, and provision is usually made for the retirement and death of any partner.

If any provision concerning the working of the partnership is not dealt with in their articles, the standard provisions laid down in the Partnership Act, 1890, will apply.

The Partnership Name

Persons who have formed a partnership are collectively called a 'firm'. However, it must be remembered that, unlike a limited company, the firm has no separate legal identity, and this word is merely a convenient way of referring to the body of partners who make up the firm. Although it is possible to bring an action against all the partners in the firm's name, it is still in effect an action against each partner individually.

Furthermore, a partnership is entitled to call itself 'a company'; thus it may add to the firm's name the abbreviation '& Co.', but it cannot use the words 'Limited' or 'Ltd'.

A partnership, unlike limited companies, is not subject to registration, unless it is a limited partnership or it comes within the rules of the Registration of Business Names Act, 1916. This Act makes registration compulsory for every firm having a name which does not disclose the true surname of every partner. For instance, if Mr A, Mr B and Mr C formed a partnership to sell potted plants, they may call themselves A, B, C & Co. Yet if they wished to call their firm 'Grorite' it would require registration under the 1916 Act, and the full name of each partner would still have to be printed on every catalogue or business letter sent out by the firm.

Rights and Duties between Partners

The articles of partnership which have been signed by all the partners will usually regulate the relations between the partners. However, in the absence of an express agreement between the partners setting out their rights and duties, the following rules laid down by the Partnership Act, 1890, will apply :

1. All partners are entitled to share equally in the capital and profits of the business, and must contribute equally towards the losses, whether of capital or otherwise, sustained by the firm.
2. A partner is not entitled, before the ascertainment of profits, to interest on the capital subscribed by him.
3. Every partner may take part in the management of the partnership business.
4. No partner shall be entitled to remuneration for acting in the partnership business.
5. No person may be introduced as a partner without the consent of all existing partners.
6. No majority of the partners can expel any partner unless a power to do so has been conferred by express agreement between the partners.
7. Partners are bound to produce true accounts and full information of all things affecting the partnership to any partner.
8. Every partner must account to the firm for any benefit he has

made without the consent of the other partners, from any transaction concerning the partnership, or from any use by him of the partnership property, name or business connections.

9. If a partner, without consent of the other partners, carries on any business of the same nature as and competing with that of the firm, he must account for and pay over to the firm all profits made by him.

10. The firm must indemnify every partner in respect of payments made and personal liabilities incurred by him (*a*) in the ordinary and proper conduct of the business of the firm, or (*b*) in or about anything necessarily done for the preservation of the business or property of the firm.

Liability of 'the Firm' to Third Parties
(a) For Contracts

Basically, the legal relationship of partners to persons who deal with them is according to the ordinary law of contract and agency. Each partner is a business agent for the firm and, in this capacity, he may bind himself and his co-partners by any contract apparently connected with the firm's ordinary business. For instance, the courts have held that every partner has implied authority to bind the firm by contract for such things as:

(i)   the sale of goods of the firm;
(ii)   the purchase of goods necessary for the firm;
(iii) engaging of servants for the business.

However, if the partner who makes the contract has in fact no authority to act for the firm in the particular contract, and the third party with whom he is dealing either knows he has no authority or does not believe him to be a partner, then the co-partners will not be bound by the contract that he made. Yet if the third party has no knowledge of the partner's lack of authority and could not be expected to know, then the firm will be liable.

Nature of contractual liability. In general, partners are *jointly* liable for the contracts that have been made on behalf of the firm.

Joint liability means that the third party can bring only one action against the partners. Therefore, where a third party has sued one or a number of partners, and the court has given him judgment, he cannot bring a further action against the remaining partners if the judgment on the first action is unsatisfied.

As the partners are only jointly liable, it is advisable for the third party to join all the partners as co-defendants in the same action. In *Kendall* v. *Hamilton* the plaintiff lent a sum of money to Mr X, Mr Y and Hamilton, the defendant, who were partners. The plaintiff was compelled to sue for repayment and sued X and Y jointly, but failed to obtain satisfaction. The plaintiff then attempted to sue the defendant for repayment of the loan, but the court held that he could not do this as he had exhausted his one right of redress and no further action in the matter could be brought.

(b) For Torts
In the same way as a principal is liable for the torts or wrongs committed by his agents in the course of their employment, so are co-partners liable for the torts committed by a partner of the firm.

The firm will only be liable if the tort was committed either in the ordinary course of the firm's business or with the authority of all the partners. In *Hamlyn* v. *Houston & Co* a partner bribed the clerk of a rival business to betray his master's secrets, and in an action for damages against the firm it was held that all the partners were liable because it was the business of the partner to obtain information about competitors and he was only doing in an unlawful way something which it was part of his business to do legitimately.

Nature of tortious liability. The partners are *jointly and severally* liable for the firm's torts. This means that a third party may sue all the partners together (jointly), or may sue each partner individually one after the other until he receives satisfaction for the wrong. For instance, if X, Y and Z are partners, the third party may either sue all three partners jointly for the tort which was committed by X, or he may sue X alone and then, if he fails to gain satisfaction from him, the third party can still sue Y and then Z.

Liability of New and Retiring Partners
(a) Incoming Partner
The general rule is that, unless some agreement has been made to the contrary, a new partner will not be liable in respect of the firm's debts that were incurred before he became a partner. He will naturally be liable for all debts that have arisen since his becoming a partner.

(b) Retiring Partner
A retiring partner can only be made liable for the debts that were incurred before his retirement, unless any agreement has been made to the contrary. If, however, the partnership is to continue in business after his retirement, then the retiring partner will be liable in respect of any debt incurred after his retirement if notice of his retirement has not been given to third parties dealing with the firm. Notice of retirement is given by an advertisement in the *London Gazette* or by letter or circular to persons who have had previous dealings with the firm.

Dissolution of a Partnership

The partnership relationship is brought to an end by the dissolution of the firm as a business unit. This may be brought about in one of three ways.

(a) Dissolution by Agreement

As a general rule, the articles of partnership will give the reasons for which the partnership may be dissolved. For instance, the articles may state that the relationship will end at a specific time, or on the completion of the work it was set up to achieve, or by mutual consent of all the partners.

(b) Dissolution without a Court Order

In the absence of any agreement between the partners to the contrary, the Partnership Act, 1890, states that a partnership will automatically be dissolved by operation of the law, irrespective of any court order, in the following cases: if any one partner gives notice to his co-partners of his intention to terminate the partnership; on the death or bankruptcy of any partner; or if any event occurs which makes the continuation of their business illegal.

(c) Dissolution by Court Order

The Partnership Act states that in certain cases any partner may apply to the court for an order to dissolve the partnership. The application for such an order may become necessary where there is disagreement between the partners as to whether or not the firm should be dissolved. The court may order the dissolution of a partnership in any of the following cases:

1. When a partner, by reason of mental disorder, is incapable of managing his property and affairs.
2. When a partner, other than the partner suing, has been found guilty of such conduct as, in the opinion of the court, will prejudicially affect the carrying-on of the business.
3. When a partner, other than the partner suing, wilfully or persistently breaks the partnership agreement, or otherwise so conducts himself in matters relating to the partnership business that it is not reasonably practicable for the other partner or partners to carry on working with him.
4. When the business of the partnership can only be carried on at a loss.
5. Whenever circumstances have arisen which, in the opinion of the court, make it *just* and *equitable* that the partnership should be dissolved. In *Re Yenidje Tobacco Co Ltd*, Mr W and Mr R had

carried on separate businesses manufacturing cigarettes and tobacco. They agreed to combine their business to form a private company. W and R held all the shares and each became a director with equal voting rights and power to manage the business. After a time they became hostile to each other, disagreed in all matters concerning the business, and the relationship was so fraught with arguments that communication between the two had to be through the company secretary. Yet the company continued to make large profits. W made an application to the court to have the company wound up on account of the deadlock between the two of them. The court held that, although this was a private company, W and R were in reality a partnership and it was just and equitable that the business should be dissolved.

The Effect of Dissolution

(a) Bankruptcy of One Partner

It has already been mentioned that, in the absence of any agreement to the contrary, the bankruptcy of one partner will cause the dissolution of the firm without the need for a court order. In such a dissolution all the partnership property will be applied to pay off any of the firm's debts and the surplus will be shared between the partners; that portion of the surplus which is due to the bankrupt partner will go to his trustee in bankruptcy.

If, at the time of the dissolution, the firm's assets are not sufficient to pay their debts, all the remaining solvent partners will have to make good the debts out of their private assets because they are all jointly liable for the debts of the firm. However, if the remaining solvent partners have had to do this, they may claim the amount of the assets they had to put into the firm from the bankrupt partner after all the firm's creditors have been paid in full.

(b) Bankruptcy of the Firm

If the firm itself is bankrupt, it means that all the partners are also bankrupt. In such a situation it is important to remember that not only will the firm itself have debts for which the partnership estate will be used to pay them off and for which the partners will be liable jointly, but each partner may have his own private debts for which he alone will be liable and which will be settled out of his own private estate.

From the point of view of the firm, there will be the firm's debts (or, in other words, all the partners' joint debts on behalf of·the firm) that have to be settled, and it is the firm's estate (in other words the partners' joint estate) which will firstly be used to pay off these debts.

If the firm's estate is more than sufficient to satisfy the firm's debts, the surplus of the estate will be divided among the partners. However, if the firm's estate is not sufficient to meet its debts, then each partner is liable from his own private estate and any surplus he may have had from paying off his private creditors.

(c) Settling of Accounts
The rules for the settling of the accounts of the firm on its dissolution are usually set out in the articles of partnership. If no such provision is made in the articles, then the rules laid down by the 1890 Act apply as follows:

1. Losses, including losses and deficiencies of capital, shall be paid first out of profits, next out of capital and lastly, if necessary, by the partners individually in the proportion in which they were entitled to share profits.
2. The assets of the firm, including the sums, if any, contributed by the partners to make up losses or deficiencies of capital, shall be applied in the following order:

(i)   Firstly, in paying the debts and liabilities of the firm to persons who are not partners.

(ii) Secondly, in paying to each partner rateably what is due from the firm to him for advances as distinguished from capital.

(iii) Thirdly, in paying to each partner rateably what is due from the firm to him in respect of capital.

(iv) Fourthly, the residue, if any, shall be divided among the partners in the proportion in which profits are shared.

Limited Partnerships
The Limited Partnership Act, 1907, permits a partnership to be formed where some of its members enjoy only limited liability, provided there is always at least one partner in the firm who remains completely liable (i.e. unlimited liability) for all the partnership debts.

By becoming a limited partner, a person may use his money or property for the promotion or furtherance of a business activity provided he does not take part in the running of the business or the management of the firm. He will be liable only to the extent of the capital he has contributed.

As soon as a firm has one or more limited partners, it must register with the registrar of joint-stock companies.

C. LIMITED COMPANIES

Types of Company
A company is an association of persons incorporated under the

Companies Acts of 1948 and 1967. These companies may be:

(a) Unlimited
In this case a member may be liable for all the debts incurred by the company.

(b) Limited by Guarantee
Here the liability of a member is limited to the amount which he has undertaken to contribute only in the event of the company being terminated.

(c) Limited by Shares
These companies are often known as joint-stock companies. Their capital is divided into a number of shares and the liability of each member is limited to the sum of money he has promised to pay for his shares.

Companies Limited by Shares
This is the most usual form of company and, like the other types of company, is divided into two kinds.

Firstly, a limited company may be registered as a *private* company. In this case the number of its members is restricted to fifty, transactions concerning its shares are usually restricted to its members, and it is forbidden to issue a prospectus. In other words, there is no invitation to the public to apply for its shares.

Secondly, a limited company may register as a *public* company, in which case there is no restriction on the number of members or on the issuing of a prospectus or the transfer of its shares. Furthermore, a public company must have at least seven members and two directors, whereas a private company need have only two members and one director.

Formation of a Company
Registration
A company is formed by its promoters delivering to the Registrar of Companies all the documents and information that are required for registration laid down by the Companies Act, 1948. These include:

1. A *memorandum* of association.
2. The *articles* of association.
3. A list of persons who have consented to be *directors.*
4. A *statutory declaration* of compliance with the above require-ments.
5. A statement of the *nominal share capital.*

The Registrar will examine the documents to see whether all the statutory requirements have been complied with. When the company has been registered, the Registrar will issue a Certificate of Incorporation.

The Effect of Registration
Once the company has been registered, it will become a corporate legal entity separate and distinct from the individuals who have formed it and those who are its members. This means that the company may actually own property rather than it being owned by all the members; furthermore, the company's debts are its own responsibility and not that of its members.

Commencement of Business
A private company is able to commence business and start making contracts in its own name as soon as the Certificate of Incorporation has been issued. However, a public company with a share capital which has issued a prospectus inviting the public to subscribe to shares cannot usually commence business until the minimum amount of its shares has been allotted to subscribers. When this has been achieved, the Registrar will issue a Trading Certificate and the company will be able to commence business.

Memorandum of Association
The memorandum of association is the registered company's charter which sets out the powers with which it can carry on business. Its purpose is to set out information for shareholders, creditors and any person dealing with the company that will show them the extent of the company's activities. It is the document which regulates the company's external affairs, while the articles of association regulate the internal affairs of the company. The memorandum of every company must state:

(a) The Name
The general rule is that each company may have whatever name it chooses. However, the Board of Trade may refuse registration if the name is considered to be undesirable; for instance, if it is too like the name of an existing company, or if the name is misleading or suggests some connection with the Queen, members of the Royal Family or the government.

The word 'Limited' must be the last word of the name. This is to clarify that the company is a corporate body and not a partnership. Some companies whose objects are to promote art, science, religion or charity may be granted a Board of Trade licence to omit 'Limited' from their name.

(b) The Registered Office

As each company is a legal person yet without a physical presence, it must have a registered office where it can be found and to which all communications can be addressed. The memorandum must state whether the office is to be in England or in Scotland, as the place of the registered office determines the nationality and domicile of the company.

At the registered office there are kept various registers which the company is required to maintain by the Companies Acts of 1948 and 1967: for example, the Register of Members, the Register of Directors and Secretaries, and the registers concerned with the allocation of shares.

(c) The Objects

As the company is an artificial person, it must not only be created in a formal way, it must also be created for a specific purpose. The purpose for which it is created and the type of work it is allowed to carry on are known as the *objects* of the company.

The requirement that the objects of the company should be set down in the memorandum serves two purposes: firstly, it protects the shareholders who will be able to see from the memorandum the purpose for which their money is being used. Secondly, the objects clause of the memorandum acts as a protection for persons doing business with the company; this is because they are able to see from the memorandum the purpose for which their money is being used. Secondly, the objects clause of the memorandum acts as a protection for persons doing business with the company; this is because they are able to see the type of business that the company is authorised to carry out. Those persons doing business with the company, even if they are not actually aware of the company's objects, are presumed to know what the objects of the company are. This is because the memorandum is open to public inspection and could have been inspected. Therefore, if they make a contract which they should have known is outside the objects *(ultra vires)* of the company, they cannot enfore it. If, for example, they have supplied goods to the company or have lent money to the company for purposes that are outside the company's objects, the general rule is that they cannot recover them. In *Re Jon Beauforte* a company, by its objects, had the power to carry on business as costumiers and gown-makers, but it branched out into the business of making veneered panels. Without knowing this new enterprise was *ultra vires* the objects clause in the memorandum, builders and other outsiders did work for the company in its new project and none of them was entitled to recover their money as creditors of the company.

The European Communities Act, 1972, has made some inroad into the principle of the objects clause. It provides that a person dealing with a company in good faith may assume that a transaction entered into by the directors of a company is within the capacity of that company.

(d) Limitations of Liability
In the case of a limited company the memorandum must state that the liability of the members is limited.

(e) The Share Capital
In the case of a limited company the memorandum must set out the maximum amount of capital which the company is authorised to issue. However, a company need not issue capital to the full amount unless it needs or wishes to do so. This capital which the company is authorised to raise by the issue of shares is called the *nominal* or *authorised* capital.

The memorandum must also state that it has divided the capital into shares of a certain fixed amount. The stated amount of each share is the share's nominal value. For example, a limited company may have an authorised or nominal capital of £10,000 which has been divided into 10,000 shares of £1 each nominal value.

The nominal value of each share must not be confused with the actual price a person might have to pay for the share. A share which was originally issued by the company for £1 may have increased in value so that the market price for buying may be ten times the nominal value. Similarly, the value of a share may decrease. The nominal value always remains the same, and has little significance to persons wishing to invest in the company's shares. The market value is the important price for purchasers, and this depends on whether investors consider that the future prospects of the company are good or bad.

When shares are issued they need not necessarily be paid for in full. Sometimes the company does not need to use the whole amount represented by the share capital at the time of issuing the shares. Consequently, £1 shares may need only 50p paid on them; the balance will remain payable 'on call' by the shareholder when the company requires the funds.

The liability of the shareholder is limited to paying the nominal value (or outstanding amount payable 'on call') of his shares. He cannot be required to contribute any more to the company. In other words, once the shareholder has purchased fully paid shares, he is under no obligation to assist in paying the debts of the company.

The shares may be divided into classes, but it is usual to mention this in the articles of association rather than in the memorandum. The two main types of shares are *preference* and *ordinary* shares. The former entitle the holder to be paid a dividend at a fixed rate per cent before any other dividend is paid out. In the latter the holders are entitled to the distribution of a dividend out of the remaining profit. The rate of this dividend on ordinary shares is decided each year according to what the company can afford.

Articles of Association
The articles are rules which regulate the internal affairs of the company. These rules are contractually binding on the company itself and on all its members individually.

The Companies Act, 1948, states that the articles of a limited company may be registered along with the memorandum when the company is being formed. In the case of unlimited companies or companies limited by guarantee, the articles must be registered.

The articles set out in detail the rules that are needed for the actual management of the company. For instance, it will normally state the classes into which the shares are to be divided, it will lay down the method of allotting shares to members, and it will state the rights of the shareholders. The articles will also set out the powers of the company to borrow money by the issue of *debentures*. A debenture is basically a promise to repay the money which the company has borrowed for the purpose of its enterprise. It is usual, in return for the money lent, for the company to give security to the creditor or debenture holder by a mortgage or charge on the assets of the company, so that, in the event of the company being wound up, they have a first claim to receive payment. The articles will also set out the position of the *directors* within the company, the rules regarding the holding of *meetings* and the procedure for *voting*, the necessity for keeping *accounts* and the auditing of accounts, and the rules regarding the *winding-up* or termination of the company.

Termination of a Company
(a) Compulsory Liquidation
The compulsory liquidation or winding-up of a company is by an order of the court, and may be directed for such reasons as:

1. It is just and equitable to terminate the company (see *Re Yenidje Tobacco Co Ltd*).
2. The company has fewer than the required number of members.
3. The presentation of a petition by a creditor and by the court declaring that the company has not sufficient assets to meet its debts.

4. When a special resolution has been passed by the company that it cannot pay its debts and is therefore unable to carry on business.

(b) Voluntary Liquidation
If the directors of the company have passed the necessary resolution to wind up the company and have filed a statutory declaration that they are of the opinion that the company will pay all its debts in full within twelve months, then the liquidation is known as a members' voluntary winding-up.

If no such statutory declaration has been filed, the liquidation is called a creditors' voluntary winding-up.

1. Enumerate the duties that one partner owes to other partners.
2. In what situations has a partner implied authority to bind the firm by his contracts?
3. What is the liability of (a) an incoming partner (b) a retiring partner, for the debts of the firm?
4. In what ways may a partnership be (a) created and (b) ended?
5. In what situations may a court order the dissolution of a partnership?
6. What formalities must be complied with by promoters wishing to register a company?
7. What is the purpose of the memorandum of association of a company and what does it consist of?
8. In what ways may a company be terminated?
9. Distinguish between an unincorporated association and an incorporated association.

Write short notes on the importance of the following:
(a) the Partnership Act, 1890
(b) Registration of Business Names Act 1916
(c) Limited Partnership Act 1907
(d) the Companies Acts 1948 and 1967

Explain the meaning of the following:
(1) a partnership
(2) articles of partnership
(3) the 'firm'
(4) joint liability of partners
(5) several liability of partners
(6) unlimited company
(7) public and private companies
(8) the 'objects' clause in a memorandum
(9) share capital
(10) the *ultra vires* rule.

Table of Cases

Table of Statutes

Index